DATE DUE			

Recent Titles in
Contributions in Afro-American and African Studies
Series Advisers: John W. Blassingame and Henry Louis Gates., Jr.

AMALGAMATION!

Race, Sex, and Rhetoric in the Nineteenth-Century American Novel

JAMES KINNEY

Contributions in Afro-American and African Studies,
Number 90

Greenwood Press
Westport, Connecticut • London, England

Library of Congress Cataloging in Publication Data
Kinney, James, 1942-
    Amalgamation! : Race, sex, and rhetoric in the
nineteenth-century American novel.

    (Contributions in Afro-American and African studies,
ISSN 0069-9624 ; no. 90)
    Bibliography: p.
    Includes index.
    1. American fiction—19th century—History and
criticism. 2. Miscegenation in literature. 3. Race
relations in literature. 4. Sex in literature.
5. Afro-Americans in literature. 6. Slavery and slaves
in literature. I. Title. II. Series.
    PS374.M53K56 1985   813'.009'355   84-28984
    ISBN 0-313-24275-5 (lib. bdg.)
Copyright © 1985 by James Kinney

Library of Congress Catalog Card Number: 84-28984
ISBN: 0-313-24275-5
ISBN (paperback): 0-313-25064-2
ISSN: 0069-9624

First published in 1985

Greenwood Press
A division of Congressional Information Service, Inc.
88 Post Road West
Westport, Connecticut 06881

Printed in the United States of America

10 9 8 7 6 5 4 3 2 1

Copyright Acknowledgments

Passages reprinted from *Race Relations in Virginia and Miscegenation in the
South, 1776-1860*, by James Hugo Johnston, University of Massachusetts Press,
1970, copyright © 1970 by the University of Massachusetts Press, are used by
permission of the publisher.

Material on Thomas Dixon is taken from "'The Rhetoric of Racism: Thomas
Dixon and 'The Damned Black Beast,' '" by James Kinney, *American Literary
Realism 1870-1910* 15 (1982): 145-54. Copyright © 1983, Department of En-
glish, University of Texas at Arlington.

813. 009355
    K62a
  143497
mar.1988

To
Honora Batson Kinney
in memory of
James Coyle Kinney
and to
Jerome A. Kelly, O.F.M.

Contents

Series Foreword

The paucity of creative and scholarly works available for library and classroom use remains a crucial barrier to the adequate study of African and Afro-American arts and letters. Despite a floor of hastily conceived and rashly executed monograph and bibliographical series that ostensibly meant to address this quandary, students, scholars, and librarians agree that African and Afro-American materials continue to be either inadequate as research tools or, more often, simply unavailable at all.

Despite the intention of well-meaning publishers and eager Afro-Americanists, the 1880 lament of the black critic, Richard T. Greener, retains its poignancy as an account of knowledge of black arts and letters: "It would be interesting, were it not painful, to observe how little even educated Americans, judging from articles in current literature, know of the capacity, disposition, achievements, services, or sacrifices of the Negro in general and the Negro-American in particular." The American academy has only a limited notion of the manner in which black writers and scholars have structured their responses to the complex fate of institutionalized racial and economic discrimination. Nor does the academy have a sufficient idea of the peculiar manner in which black texts respond to considerations raised in other, related, texts, which responses themselves constitute an aspect of intellectual history. What's more, there exists no systematic publishing venture that has addressed this problem intelligently, by commissioning major Africanists and

Afro-Americanists to prepare sophisticated studies on the vast and challenging subject of the black arts and letters.

To sharpen the definition of African and Afro-American Studies and to present a more coherent view of the continuum of black thought and action, a new departure is necessary. This series is designed to fill this need. Often inter-disciplinary and cross-cultural, it seeks to address not only the complexities of the cultural and aesthetic confrontation of black cultures with non-black ones, but also the nature and function of African and Afro-American arts and letters themselves.

James Kinney's *Amalgamation!: Race, Sex, and Rhetoric in the Nineteenth-Century American Novel* is the definitive study of miscegenation in American literature. With a stunningly detailed familiarity with sixty American novels, Kinney traces the textual evolution of "amalgamation"—"the process of combining mercury with another metal to create a uniform alloy"— as a centrally repeated trope, indeed as an obsessive presence, in popular American novels.

Kinney introduces or "frames" his explication of the figure of amalgamation with a well-researched and thoughtfully rendered historical introduction that traces the astounding extent to which interracial sexual relations flourished in colonial and antebellum America between white women and black men, and black women and white men. Equally startling is his conclusion that the violent *ad hoc* responses to miscegenation did not commence *en masse* until the 1830s, when the economics of slavery led to its systematic justification on innate irreconcilable "racial" differences. Kinney uses this superb historical context as the frame through which to read these texts of genetic assimilation. His concern here is with miscegenation as the political signifier and as a structure of *mediation* in romances and allegories that mimic mythology's function of "reconciling" fundamentally opposed social forces through the "trick" of structural reconciliation. Kinney explicates each of the novels analyzed in his book by discussing miscegenation as an abstract concept and as manifested in character development, plot structure, and rhetorical strategy. Guilt, retribution, and alienation are the three recurring themes of this fiction, and Kinney draws upon these to show the "mythic" aspirations of these fictions. Even more so, however, Kinney shows with impressive control how amalgamation is a master trope for concrete, historical, social and political issues that plagued American society when these texts were written and informed the shape of these novels. His is an ideal study of the complex but direct relation between a text and the political context that it mirrors, extends, refutes, and comments upon. *Amalgamation!* is a model demonstration of the relation between literature and society and how a sensitive scholar accounts for this relation without diminishing or reducing the integrity of either.

John W. Blassingame, Sr.
Henry Louis Gates, Jr.

Acknowledgments

Much in this book comes from work I have been doing over the past fifteen years in noncanonical nineteenth-century American fiction. I began at the University of Tennessee, Knoxville, and among many friends and colleagues there, I would like to thank F. DeWolfe Miller, Frank Robinson, Leroy Graff, Chancellor Jack E. Reese, and the late Richard Beale Davis. During my stay at the University of Massachusetts, Amherst, Walker Gibson helped me learn to read with an eye to rhetoric, for which I am indebted to him. I also owe much thanks to Gordon Kelly of the University of Maryland for his advice and encouragement, and to the anonymous manuscript reader secured by Greenwood Press whose thoughtful and detailed comments made it possible for me to improve the final version.

Among many debts owed colleagues at Virginia Commonwealth University, special thanks go to Dorothy Scura, Chair of the English Department, who both read the manuscript and provided many kinds of support, and to Mark Booth, Associate Chair, who shouldered my administrative duties at crucial times. I also want to thank Daryl Dance for her interest and suggestions. The College of Humanities and Sciences provided staff support, and my thanks go to Gene Dunaway of the Dean's Office for his professional typescript preparation on an IBM Displaywriter. At Greenwood Press, I thank James Sabin, Susan Costanzo, and Lynn Alden Kendall. I am, of course, indebted to series editors John Blassingame and Henry Louis Gates, Jr.

Finally, during 1976–77, the National Endowment for the Humanities supported my research, and a 1984 Faculty-Grant-in-Aid from Virginia Commonwealth University made it possible for me to complete the manuscript. To my wife, Judith, and my daughter, Deirdre, I owe the kind of debt that cannot easily named.

AMALGAMATION!

1
Introduction

One cold November night in 1824, the patrollers were out in
Virginia's Louisa County, searching slave cabins for some missing leather. On the John Richardson plantation, shortly after
midnight, they entered the cabin of a mulatto slave named
Edmund. Instead of stolen leather, they found Dorothea, the
young white wife of an elderly planter in the area.[1] The story
of Edmund and Dorothea is but one of many. During nearly
250 years of slavery in America, black and white men and
women lived together and loved together, shared joys and sor-
rows together, and together produced a race of mulatto children. With slavery's end, miscegenation declined until the brutal
segregation of the 1890s made such relationships practically
impossible. By 1915, a generation had come of age—black and
white—who knew only that miscegenation was forbidden. As
our heritage of this taboo, confusion, guilt and anger still shroud
interracial sex in America.

THE COLONIAL ERA

In 1609, the Whitechapel preacher who blessed the voyage
of Virginia-bound English planters inveighed against intercourse with New World heathens. But John Rolfe saved the
Jamestown colony from Indian attacks by marrying Pocahan-
tas, who later sailed to England with him and there bore his
son Thomas. As a colonial leader, Rolfe accomplished much
during the first ten years after landing in Virginia, and by

1619 he had made tobacco the main export of the colony. That year twenty African slaves were introduced to cultivate the crop. The first mulattoes in the English colonies were born shortly thereafter, in some cases the sons and daughters of white slave-traders in Africa and seamen on the Middle Passage. Despite records of early and continual attempts by colonial leaders to ban miscegenation both within and outside of marriage, by the time the English colonies became the United States, more than 60,000 people of mixed black and white ancestry lived in the new country.[2]

Many frontier whites in the colonial era had extensive sexual contacts with Indians, but, unlike Rolfe, few had permanent relationships. Many runaway blacks, however, joined Indian tribes, often intermarrying and achieving some degree of brotherhood. The Seminoles, for example, mingled freely with black fugitives, making Florida a haven for escaped slaves from the Spanish days until the end of the Seminole Wars in the 1840s. In fact, the many attempts by white slaveholders to retrieve fugitives and to seize the half-Indian children of runaway slave mothers were a major cause of the Seminole Wars that ended only when Chief Abraham, a black man, negotiated the Treaty of Fort Dade, allowing black Seminoles to go west with the others in defiance of the slaveholders' claims.[3]

In the sexual affairs of blacks and whites during the colonial years, miscegenation was most common among black slaves and white indentured servants. The planter ruling class lumped the two laboring classes together so that, for example, white servant girls worked side by side with black men in the planters' houses. Servants and slaves were often quartered together, creating situations that led to natural results. Runaway bills frequently listed white servants and black slaves as fleeing together. Nor did the convict women shipped to the colonies, where most became prostitutes, discriminate against black men. Throughout the colonial period, each new group of servants and convicts arrived lacking the strong colonial background in racial prejudice. Poor and friendless in a new world, with no reason to love their masters, these lower-class whites sought friendship and took comfort where they could.

While miscegenation occurred easily among laboring-class

colonials, those of aristocratic background—the governors and controllers of colonial society—tried to stop the practice, particularly in the form of intermarriage. As early as 1630, we find evidence of their opposition in a Jamestown order that Hugh Davis, a white man, "be soundly whipped before an assemblage of Negroes and others for abusing himself to the dishonor of God and the shame of Christians by defiling his body in lying with a Negro, which fault he is to acknowledge next Sabboth day" (p. 166). A number of causes led to the planters' attitude, including an undeveloped form of racism. Their word choices—"abusing," "dishonor," "shame," "defiling,"—indicate clear feelings that color set the slaves apart, outside the normal human realm.[4]

In 1662, Virginia enacted the first statute prohibiting intermarriage, and by 1725 six other colonies had followed suit. Because the most common liaison was between a white man and a black woman, these laws broke with the patristic tradition of British common law and relegated any child to the status of the mother. This change insured that the offspring of black women slaves remained slaves, thus preventing the loss of profitable slave labor that would occur if intermarriage were permitted and the mulatto offspring set free. Of course the mulatto children of white women were free, but were commonly bound to long terms of indentured servitude. In addition to racism and the economic concern for the potential loss of slave labor, these laws also intended to prevent too close an alliance between slaves and servants that might unite the laboring classes against the ruling class, in economic demands at least, if not in open revolution.

As time passed, more stringent laws and revisions of earlier ones were introduced. In 1691 Virginia strengthened penalties against intermarriage in a new law weighted even more heavily against free white women bearing mulatto children. A stiff fine had to be paid within thirty days or the woman would be indentured for five years and her child for thirty. In 1705, the law added a heavy fine—10,000 pounds of tobacco—for any minister who married a racially-mixed couple. Maryland changed its law in 1717 to make a slave out of any free black who married a white woman. North Carolina, South Carolina,

Pennsylvania, and Massachusetts also punished miscegenation by whippings, fines, and forced servitude. Colonial legislators obviously felt an increasing threat from the widespread and growing practice of miscegenation throughout the seventeenth and eighteenth centuries.

The antimiscegenation laws the planters passed little affected their own lives, because with very few exceptions colonial aristocrats married only within their own class. An interesting curiosity is Elizabeth Adams, the granddaughter of John Fenwick, Lord Proprietor of New Jersey. When she married a black servant, her grandfather cut her out of his will:

Item, I do except against Elizabeth Adams of having any ye leaste part of my estate, unless the Lord open her eyes to see her abominable transgression against him, me [,] her good father, by giving her true repentance, and forsaking ye Black ye hath been ye ruin of her, and becoming penetent [sic] of her sins (pp. 181–82).

While colonial leaders seldom desired to marry blacks, these men frequently had liaisons with female slaves. We recall the familiar argument over Thomas Jefferson's relationship with Sally Hemmings. Regardless of whether Jefferson or another male in that family fathered her redhaired children, some member of the plantation aristocracy was involved. Indeed, the practice of a widower's entering a relationship with his late wife's mulatto maid—as Jefferson's father-in-law John Wayles did with Sally's mother—was so common that it encouraged the story about the widower Jefferson's involvement with Sally.[5] Given, under slavery, the ready access of dominant white men to dependent black women, and some lawmakers' self-interest in such relationships, colonial leaders declined to legislate against them. In the end, their nearly two-century struggle to contain miscegenation amounted to this—they prohibited legal intermarriage, punished illicit unions between black men and white women, but tolerated those between white men and black women as long as the mulatto children followed the condition of their slave mothers. In 1944, nearly three hundred years after the first antimiscegenation statutes, Gunnar Myrdal found approximately the same attitude:

The astonishing fact is the great indifference of most white Americans toward real but illicit miscegenation.... The illicit relations freely allowed or only frowned upon are, however, restricted to those between white men and Negro women. A white woman's relation with a Negro man is met by the full fury of anti-amalgamation sanctions.[6]

But, as Lerone Bennett observes, despite the legal, religious, and social pressures and harsh punishments, "nothing worked" to prevent widespread miscegenation during the colonial period.[7] Extensive court records from the period reveal constant violations—we find petitions from white women seeking release from servitude imposed for bearing a mulatto child, from mulatto children asking for their release from servitude, records of fines levied against ministers for marrying mixed couples, and petitions for divorce based on grounds of interracial adultery. Clearly the extent of miscegenation that existed outside the legal records was even greater, meaning that the many cases recorded were only a small part of those occurring.

Joel Williamson proposes a three-part demographic model to explain the conditions necessary to produce a substantial mulatto population: "opportunity, inclination, and time.... The fundamental requirement for producing a large number of mulatto children is a large number of women of childbearing capacity of one race and relatively few men of the other race."[8] The conditions in Virginia and the rest of the upper South during 1690–1720, including the fade-out of white indentured servants and a vast increase in black slaves, set up the circumstances to breed "the first great wave of free mulattoes. These mulatto children began to flow into the relatively loose molds established by the relatively few mulattoes of the seventeenth century, overran them, and flooded the countryside...."[9] By 1757, for example, Peter Fontaine of Westover, Virginia, complained in a letter to his brother that "the country swarms with mulatto bastards."[10] A century later, in 1864, when emancipated slaves presented themselves to federal officials to be legally married, one records office in Vicksburg, Mississippi, noted that 37 percent of the more than nine thousand lower South slaves registered there were of mixed ancestry traceable to white grandparents and great-grandparents in the eighteenth century.[11]

THE REVOLUTION TO THE CIVIL WAR

Nor did miscegenation wane with the Revolution and the coming of the nineteenth century. When liberal Pennsylvania repealed its antiamalgamation laws in the revolutionary fervor of the 1770s, a traveler in Philadelphia observed a few years later that there were "hundreds" of white women married to black men and "thousands of black children by them at present."[12] After the Revolution, many slaves were freed in the spirit of the time. The increased number of free mulattoes led to additional problems, particularly the need to define who was a free white citizen and who was not. In 1785, for example, Virginia defined as black anyone with a black parent or grandparent. Anyone with less than one-fourth black ancestry was legally white. These distinctions were more important in the upper South because many more mulattoes lived there than in the lower South. In the lower South only a few mulattoes were free, but these free persons of color became slaveholding planters themselves in such places as Charleston and New Orleans.

Williamson also distinguishes between the "old slave South" (those areas settled before 1730) and the "new slave South." While the old slave states, especially in the upper South, contained many free mulattoes, in the new slave states almost all mulattoes were slaves. This circumstance developed because the importing of African slaves ended in 1807 and the domestic slave trade burgeoned after the 1820s. Tens of thousands of slaves were sold out of the older portions of the upper South such as Virginia and Kentucky. By the 1850s the new boom areas of slavery were Texas and Arkansas. As slavery on the frontier became more profitable, the economics of the system drew in the old and upper South mulattoes, "a supply of human material not previously exploited."[13]

Between the Revolutionary and the Civil Wars, marked changes took place in the slave codes and laws intended to prevent racial mixing, called "amalgamation" after the process of combining mercury with another metal to create a uniform alloy. In the South, especially after the Slave Act of 1807 increased the need to breed domestic slaves, and after 1830 when extensive use of the cotton gin, Nat Turner's Rebellion, and other factors increased proslavery pressures, the laws became more restrictive. Before that time, white fathers had commonly freed their mulatto children, especially in such cases as youthful indiscretion when, as adolescents, they had acted out their new-found sexuality in the slave quarters and in more mature years felt some moral obligation toward their unfortunate offspring. In other cases, the children were the products of long-term, stable relationships with mulatto mistresses.[14]

Typical of the legal petitions filed to manumit children is the one by Virginian William Kendall in 1813, stating that "your petitioner believes himself to be the father of the said mulatto boy by a woman at that time the property of himself, and as his parent he feels great concern for his future welfare and liberty. It is with great concern and uneasiness that he looks forward to the possibility of his being a slave to any other person" (p. 219). In other cases, stable long-term relationships existed and were often revealed in wills that provided freedom and support for mistress and mulatto children—occasionally to the extent of bequeathing them an entire estate, as did Thomas Wright's 1816 testament:

I, Thomas Wright ... give and bequeath to Sylvia, a woman of color, formerly my slave but since emancipated and with whom I have had children, the sole and exclusive use of my house ... also all the household furniture therein ... also all the monies of which I die possessed; secondly I give and bequeath to my natural son, Robert Wright, by the said Sylvia who I have duly emancipated all that tract of land on which I now live ... containing by estimation three hundred and seventy acres (p. 221).

Still other planters divided their estates between their two families as did Philip Henshaw in 1825:

I give and bequeath to my daughter (for such I believe her to be) Floreal Floretta (a girl I bought of Robert Robb, she was born of a yellow woman whom I bought of the said Robb), her freedom, I also bequeath to her one-half of my estate of every description whatsoever (p. 221).

More commonly, the deceased had simply freed and made provision for support, as had this planter in his 1818 will, often without admitting the miscegenetic relationship:

I desire that Lucy, a mulatto girl daughter to Sophia may be set free— I lend to the said child one thousand dollars to be laid out in bank stock, and the profits therefrom to be paid annually to her by my executors for her support so long as she lives, and at her death I give the same to be divided among her children (p. 225).

But in the court petitions and wills from 1783–1863 examined by James Hugo Johnston, we see clearly that after 1830 laws regarding slavery became increasingly harsh. Petitions for manumission were turned down, wills were broken, and legacies turned over to white relatives. Stratagems for manumission became complex, with slave-owning fathers taking their mistresses and children to free states such as Ohio, in order to manumit them there after the laws of their own state had made it legally impossible to do so at home. Wills now directed that children should be sent to England or settled in Ohio after their father's death. Bennett provides examples of prominent blacks who were taken from slavery by such stratagems.[15] Robert Purvis, a black abolitionist, had been sent North by his father, a Charleston merchant, who educated him at Amherst College. Another example, James Augustine Healy, the first black Roman Catholic bishop in America, had been born in Georgia in 1830, but had been sent to a Quaker school on Long Island and then on to Holy Cross. He was named Bishop of Portland, Maine, in February 1875. His father also aided James' siblings, one of whom became a Jesuit priest and president of Georgetown University.

Despite such safeguards, many mulatto children after 1850 were seized as slave property rather than graced as heirs. These dramatic cases led to the enduring "tragic mulatto" stereotype of abolitionist fiction—the slave owner's beautiful daughter, raised as white, who is seized and cast into slavery upon his death.

During this same period, when the demands of the domestic slave trade to meet the needs of the frontier made mulattoes too valuable to free, many previously freed mulattoes became afraid of what might happen and fled the South for free states; Charles Waddell Chesnutt's parents, for example, left Cumberland County, North Carolina, in 1856 for Cleveland, Ohio, where he was born.[16]

Striking evidence of the shifting situation between 1830 and Emancipation comes from Louisiana where, even among the upper classes, miscegenation had been common because of the shortage of white women. Under the French Napoleonic code, children took the status of their father, and thus most mulattoes were free. Under the Americans, however, Louisiana courts decided in 1832 to enslave the children of slave mothers. In addition, numerous court cases from the 1840s show increased restrictions on legacies to mulattoes, generally limiting inheritance to one-fourth or less of an estate. Finally, in 1857, Louisiana prohibited the emancipation of mulatto children, despite protest from French and Spanish creoles.

Throughout the period before Emancipation, many white fathers had freed and provided for their mulatto children, going to greater and greater lengths as the legal system increased the pressure to condemn such children to slavery. The 1850 census lists a total of 159,095 mulattoes as "free Negroes," clear evidence that many fathers had saved their children from life in the quarters. But the census also shows that a far larger number of mulattoes—246,656—were abandoned by their fathers or trapped by the system into bondage.[17]

The most romanticized form of stable miscegenation under slavery was the system of organized concubinage in cities such as New Orleans and Charleston. Relatively speaking, of course, it involved very few participants and was largely a luxury of the idle rich, those who could afford the expense of a "fancy girl" purchased in New Orleans or Frankfort, Kentucky, the main markets for this particular trade. The young women sold at the New Orleans market, at times, commanded a price of $5,000, compared to half that amount, for example, for a skilled craftsman such as a blacksmith.[18] But in New Orleans, the *placer* system provided an alternative or adjunct to marriage for young men with money to spend. The attractive placées, decently educated and trained in domestic arts, could be scouted by interested men at Quadroon Balls, held regularly at the Salle d'Orleans, later converted to a convent for black nuns.[19]

Not all miscegenation under slavery took the form of stable or even caring relationships. While some of the upper-class white men established such relationships, many of them—and of lower-class white men as well—engaged in much more promiscuous activity, that reached a "crescendo" of miscegenation around 1850.[20] As Bennett says, "The Old South abounded in wholesale amalgamation—in casual rapes and concubinage, in polygamy and polyandry, in prostitution and interracial incest."[21]

This exploitation of black women resulted in problems other than mixed children. According to Herbert Gutman, sexual mores among black slaves were typical of "premodern" attitudes that allowed for premarital intercourse and pregnancy without shame or disgrace, but which prized marital fidelity and condemned adultery. Because of the sexual activity of unmarried black women, whites viewed all black women as sexually loose. While slave marriages were seldom recognized, Gutman argues throughout *The Black Family* that male and female slaves lived in long-term and relatively stable relationships, although very often the total family would be broken up by the sale of children. Or one long-term marriage would be broken by sale but would be replaced by another. Violations by whites of these marriages among a slave population that treasured marital fidelity created many problems. Black women, especially married ones, frequently resisted their owners' advances, and attempted both folk birth control and abortion methods (especially cotton root) to prevent themselves from having his children.[22] Another stratagem adopted by slaves was to to marry off the plantation so that they would not have to see a spouse physically abused or sexually assaulted.[23]

Nor was it unknown for black men to kill whites for violating their wives. In fact, black men frequently protected their women even at the risk of death. In one case, a black man stopped the attempted rape of his wife by an overseer. For interfering, he was given one hundred lashes; his ear was nailed to the whip-

ping post and then cut off.[24] In another case, a slave being tried
for the murder of his overseer asked to have his wife testify
that the man had raped her, but the court denied the request
on the grounds that the fact was irrelevant. Another slave,
Ben, attempted to poison the white man who had taken his
wife, but she ate the poisoned food by accident and died. In his
grief, Ben stole a shotgun and killed the man too. In an 1830
trial, in New Kent County, Virginia, slaves Peggy and her lover
Patrick were condemned to hang for the murder of their master.
A witness for the slaves testified that

the deceased to whom Peggy belonged . . . generally kept her confined,
by keeping her chained to a block, and locked up in his meat house;
that he believed the reason why the deceased had treated Peggy in
this way was because Peggy would not consent to intercourse with
him, and that he had heard the deceased say that if Peggy did not
agree to his request in that way, he would beat her almost to death,
that he would barely leave the life in her, and would send her to New
Orleans. The witness said that Peggy said the reason she would not
yield to his request was because the deceased was her father, and that
she could not do a thing of that sort with her father. The witness
heard the deceased say to Peggy that if she did not consent, he would
make him, the witness, and Patrick hold her, to enable him to effect
his object (pp. 305–307).

In addition to rape, murder, and incest, the exploitation of
black women by white men caused other problems. Miscegenation not only damaged slave marriages, it caused the breakup
of white marriages as well. Johnston cites many divorce petitions brought to the Virginia General Assembly (only the legislature could end a marriage by passing a bill of divorce in
each case) that named slave women as the reason the white
woman sought the separation. In 1814, a wife petitioned because her "husband was criminally, unlawfully, and carnally
intimate with, and kept her the said Milly, from the time your
petitioner first married him until she was from necessity com-
pelled to leave him." The husband confessed to "repeated carnal
knowledge of the said [N]egro woman Milly and moreover acknowledged that he perpetrated that diabolical act against
which every generous and virtuous principle of the human soul

revolts, he took her in his own wife's bed and ... the said [N]egro woman Milly has since been delivered up of a mulatto child" (p. 239).

Another wife's petition states that her husband had "taken up with one of his female slaves ... [and] for three months without interruption, night after night, slept with the said slave. Your petitioner states that without complaint, she submitted in silence to her husband's infidelity, and attempted to reclaim him by caresses and obedience, but in vain" (p. 241). Other petitions record the tales of one woman who learned "the dreadful heart-rending truth that she possessed no place in his heart; that another had usurped her empire over him, and that other (shameless truth) his own slave" (p. 243), and of another wife whose husband had sent his mulatto mistress and children away before the wedding but returned them afterward "with much interest and shew [sic] of affection. He now acknowledged the children openly" (pp. 244–45).

Johnston cites many more such petitions, and also reminds us that it was a time "when divorces were few and when religion, custom, and law made divorce hard to procure,"[25] suggesting that for every petition filed, many more women simply lived out their lives in marriages riven by miscegenetic jealousy. There is an ubiquitous quotation from Mary Boykin Chesnut, of Charleston:

God forgive us, but ours is a monstrous system, a wrong and iniquity. Like the patriarchs of old, our men live all in one house with their wives and their concubines; and the mulatto children one sees in every family partly resemble the white children. Any lady is ready to tell you who is the father of all the mulatto children in everybody's household but her own. Those, she seems to think, drop from the clouds.[26]

Often enough that jealousy manifested itself in physical abuse or sale of the slave mother and mulatto children.[27] Such an abusive situation formed the plot of the first novel by a black American, William Wells Brown's *Clotelle: or, the President's Daughter* (1853).

By the early 1700s, after indentured servitude declined and slavery increased, miscegenation occurred most commonly between white men and black slave women, producing all the problems discussed above. But the prevailing view that no respectable white woman would have anything to do with a black man, that any who did would be driven from society and the black man lynched, seems based on conditions in the South from about 1850 on, rather than the 230 years of slavery prior to that period.[28] As we have seen, relationships between black men and white servant women were common, producing a great wave of free mulattoes in the Upper South before 1730. And Eugene Genovese insists that "despite the legend white women of all classes had black lovers and sometimes husbands in all parts of the South."[29] The violent hostility toward miscegenation did not begin until after 1830 when slavery became an economic necessity, and those benefitting from it began to justify slavery on racial grounds.

Because of the heavy legal penalties imposed on white women, however, the ploy of crying rape when caught with a black man began early. The white woman who bore a mulatto child had much more to fear than the white man who fathered one. To avoid being indentured, some white women accused their black lovers of rape. A remarkable fact about these and other rape cases, however, is that they were handled within the judicial system, rather than by lynch mobs as would have been the case after the war. Virginia court records reveal at least sixty rape convictions of black men between 1789 and 1833. The rape of black women by men of either race did not exist under law; therefore in all rape cases the victim had to be a white woman. The large number of cases certainly puts the lie to postwar claims common in the South that the black rape of white women had never existed under slavery. Even more contrary to our traditional ideas, in twenty-seven of the sixty convictions, whites testified on behalf of the accused black, declaring that it was not a case of rape because the white woman consented to the act.

Typical of these petitions for clemency is one filed in 1803 on behalf of "Carter a [N]egro man slave belonging to William Boyd and charged with rape on the body of Catherine Brinal.... It appeared that the said Catherine Brinal was a woman of the worst fame, that ... she (being a white woman) has three mulatto children, which by her own confession were begotten by different [N]egro men" (p. 260). The twenty-six other petitions for clemency present equal testimony that voluntary relationships between black men and white women were common. Indeed, a North Carolinian writing in 1886 remembers that before the war "hardly a neighborhood was free from low white women who married or cohabited with free [N]egroes." Nor were such affairs limited to lower-class women. A Kentucky minister's 1836 letter says, "were it necessary, I could refer you to several instances of slaves, [sic] actually seducing the daughters of their masters. Such seductions sometimes happened in the most respectable families."[30] And we should not forget Dorothea in Edmund's cabin.

Other evidence exists of cohabitation and marriage between white women and black men before the Civil War. The 1830 Census required all "free Negro" families to be listed by family head and the number of free persons of color in each family. Examining these records, Johnston found that "in repeated instances and in all of the states ... the sum falls one person short of persons included in the family. The explanation seems to be that the additional female was the white wife of the Negro head of family." In one Virginia county, the census taker went beyond what was required to list "and white wife" next to the black family head. In that one county alone, nine families were headed by a free black man with a white wife. In an 1844 state enumeration of "free Negroes and mulattoes," one district census taker placed the notation "white mother" after the names of numerous mulatto children in his county. In addition, various official correspondence refers to cases involving white women with black men; in at least three cases the white woman fled with or attempted to steal a black male slave.[31]

A clear record of the extent to which white women crossed the color line, and class lines as well, can be found in the same records of divorce petitions that revealed the marital transgressions of white men. Johnston recounts sixteen typical cases from court records in Virginia in which white men filed divorce petitions because of their wives' infidelities with black men. An 1802 petition reads in part:

Your petitioner lived with the said Elizabeth, with all the affection and tenderness that could possibly exist between husband and wife, for about four months, when to the great astonishment and inexpressible mortification of your petitioner, the said Elizabeth was delivered of a mulatto child, and is now so bold as to say it was begotten by a [N]egro man slave in the neighborhood (pp. 250–51).

In most of the petitions, the wife's miscegenetic adultery is revealed when she bears a mulatto child, but this happenstance was not always the case. One wronged husband writes of his love and affection for his wife that led him to admonish her "repeatedly of the wickedness of such a course, and of the infamy and disgrace which must result from it.... But alas! All this produced a contrary effect and your petitioner having at two different times detected her and the partner of her crime (a certain James Watts, a man of colour) in bed together. [The petitioner] resolved to leave her" (pp. 252–53). Another husband discovered his wife's infidelity as follows:

But your petitioner not being willing to lend too favorable an ear to reports prevalent in the neighborhood, determined to see for himself; and it is now with painful recollection that he states, that on his return home, at a late hour of the night, on entering his house he found the said Elizabeth, undressed and in bed with a certain Aldrige Evans, a man of color (p. 254).

And a gentleman from Fairfax county explained that

In 1827 he lawfully intermarried with one Rebecca _____, who in about three weeks thereafter, without the least cause known to your petitioner, eloped from his bed and board, and has never since returned; and that during all that time she has lived in open adultery with a free man of color, named Wilfred Mortimer. That since her elopement, she has had a bastard child (p. 256).

The story of Edmund and Dorothea also comes to us through legislative records. Taken from Edmund's cabin that cold November night, Dorothea escaped from the patrollers but not from all consequences. Her husband's divorce petition cited that incident among others, including the discovery of Edmund in bed with Dorothea at her house one morning when visitors dropped by "a little after daybreak." Witnesses testified that her reason for "quitting" her husband Lewis and "taking up with" Edmund was that "the slave was much younger and a more likely man." In his petition to the Virginia General Assembly for a bill of divorce, Lewis stated that

... in spite of the remonstrations and persuasions of your petitioner, she has lived for the last six or seven years and still continues to live in open adultery with a [N]egro man, a slave, the property of one of your petitioner's neighbors. That the said slave is known by your petitioner and many respectable persons to be on such terms of intimacy with her that there is no room to doubt that an illicit intercourse is regularly kept up between them. That your petitioner believes and such is the belief of all living in the neighborhood, as your petitioner will shew [sic] that the said [N]egro man has had by her two children, one of whom is now alive, and is living evidence of her guilty and dishonorable course of conduct.... Your petitioner further states that he has never either before or after his wife left his house and his bed, treated her with cruelty or inhumanity, but has permitted her to remain peaceably in a house upon his own lands (pp. 254–55).

These recorded instances suggest much wider occurrence of sex between black men and white women. They reveal only the indiscretions of married women, and even among this limited group mostly those who were exposed by a telltale mulatto child. In refuting Robert Fogel and Stanley Engerman's flawed statistical argument about miscegenation under slavery, Susan Brownmiller reminds us that relatively few acts of intercourse result in pregnancy.[32] And, as with the divorce petitions filed by white wives, for every husband who approached the legislature to dissolve his marriage, many more must have suffered in silence. Indeed, a striking fact about these petitions is that the injured husbands sought legal relief as opposed to venting the homicidal fury that would have prevailed in such circumstances after the Civil War.

Although intermarriage and other liaisons between white women and black men were more common in the prewar South than we have generally believed, by far the greatest incidence of miscegenation took place between white men and black female slaves. This form of amalgamation was the only one not specifically forbidden by law, and Genovese traces the white ancestry of as many as three-fourths of all Afro-Americans today to the slave plantations where black women were subject to "a cross between rape and seduction."[33] In a typical case, when questioned why she had born a white overseer's child, one slave woman replied to her mistress, "when he made me follow him into the bush, what use to tell him no? He have the strength to make me."[34]

AFTER THE WAR

In the years immediately following the Emancipation Proclamation and the end of the Civil War, freedmen were still tightly restrained by the black codes.[35] It was not until the rise of the radical congress and passage of the 13th, 14th, and 15th Amendments that laws against intermarriage were revoked across the South: Louisiana and Mississippi in 1870, South Carolina in 1872, Arkansas in 1874. But the era of legal intermarriage was brief, ending when Reconstruction did in 1877, after the 1876 compromise election of Rutherford B. Hayes. During the half-dozen or so years when intermarriage was legal, at least some Southerners, black and white, thought that the new order was here to stay and married accordingly. There was in fact, a brief flurry of mixed marriage between white women and black men, brought about by the skewed sex ratios of white women to white men after the war. There existed a distinct shortage of eligible white men, leading a significant number of poorer white women in need of a provider to marry black men. The economic conditions surrounding these unions generally led to community acceptance.[36] When the white Democrats later regained power after Reconstruction, they reinstituted the laws against intermarriage. In South Carolina in 1879, one of the strongest arguments for banning intermarriage was that so many white women were married to and living with black men. As many as "twenty-five or thirty," the York County representative said, "in his township alone."[37] The new antimiscegenation laws remained on the books of

Southern states until desegregation and the Civil Rights movement of the 1950s and 1960s. One such law was still in place in Louisiana as recently as 1983.

Indeed, in the years following slavery, as had been true in the North before the war, freedom did not mean freedom from abuse related to miscegenation.[38] Throughout the years before Emancipation, the North had developed increasingly negative attitudes toward black people, despite growing support for the end of slavery. Before the war, most Northern states denied voting and other civil rights to blacks as well as forbade intermarriage. For example, by 1840, 93 percent of free blacks in the North lived in states that denied them the vote, and at the end of the war only Massachusetts allowed blacks their basic rights. The strong sentiments in the North against slavery were paralleled by equally strong sentiments against miscegenation and for segregation, preferably by colonization of blacks in Africa once they were free.[39]

Following the war, Union soldiers from this racist background, as well as unreconstructed Confederates, continued the rape and other sexual abuse of black women in the South.[40] The "old rule" that permitted white male sexual license still held sway, and black women were commonly subject to insults and pawing as they walked the streets. In one incident in June 1865, a black man named Ned Scott tried to protect his wife from being mauled by white Union soldiers on Main Street in Richmond, Virginia. For his efforts, Scott was first badly beaten on the spot, then jailed where he was systematically tortured. Other graphic evidence of sexual abuse came during the race riot by Memphis whites in 1866. Court records of the bloodshed reveal the brutal rape and sodomy of helpless black women.[41] Nor did concubinage end with Emancipation. For example, both the Mississippi and Arkansas constitutional conventions were held in 1868 and heard arguments against legal concubinage and in favor of legal intermarriage. Both conventions, however, refused to ban concubinage but adopted amendments making intermarriage illegal. Throughout the South, other state legislatures consistently made intermarriage illegal while refusing to ban concubinage.

One thing that did change after the war was the white male

attitude toward black males. Before the war, white men speculated little on the sexual behavior of black males and saved their scorn for black women because they needed to excuse their abuse of them. According to Genovese, "the violence-provoking theory of the super potency of that black super-penis . . . did not become an obsession until after emancipation, when it served the purposes of racial segregationists."[42] George Frederickson argues that depicting black males as rapacious beasts justified the lynchings that occurred more and more frequently after Reconstruction. On the one hand, whites projected their guilt over the increasingly horrible torture and mutilation during these lynchings onto the victims—that is, blacks must be terrible beasts to deserve such terrible punishment. On the other hand, according to Frederickson, lynchings had to be justified somehow because they were an important tool of social and political control. Lynchings solved the dilemma posed by increased segregation—how to keep blacks completely separate yet totally under white control.[43] The late nineteenth-century stereotype of the mulatto or black rapist is also an outgrowth of what W. J. Cash labeled "the Southern rape complex," in which the idealized white woman was identified with the South itself, so that the rape of any white woman is symbolic of the "rape" of the South during Reconstruction.[44]

But the greatest impetus for the increasingly negative view of blacks and total hostility to miscegenation came from the growth of "scientific" racism during the nineteenth century.[45] The formal concept of racial inferiority, backed by "scientific" study and theory, evolved to meet the need for justifying slavery based on race alone. By the 1890s, the doctrine had turned viciously competitive, with the two races portrayed as slugging it out in a Darwinian battle for survival. Eventually, the late nineteenth-century sense of chaos and disintegration brought on by urbanization and industrialization gave way to a more optimistic sense of increased control through reform, with movement away from social Darwinism toward cooperation and compromise. After World War I, the new cultural anthropology and modern behaviorism moved the scientific community away from genetic racism.

MULATTO IDENTITY

Throughout the history of miscegenation in America, the question of mulatto identity has loomed large. In his chapter on "The Problem of Racial Identity," Johnston says that there was no attempt to define "mulatto" until after the Revolution, when lawmakers were attempting to transform English common law into appropriate codes for America. The actions taken then indicate that because of widespread miscegenation the question of racial identity had become, and would remain, important.

Beginning with Virginia in 1785, Kentucky, North Carolina, Tennessee, Georgia, Florida, Alabama, and Mississippi all generally defined a "mulatto," or "free [N]egro," or "person of color" as one having no more than one-fourth black ancestry, that is, one black grandparent. In no case did the law say that a person having an eighth or less black ancestry should be considered anything but white, because lawmakers felt that such a rule would be both impossible to enforce and embarrassing for some white families. In many recorded cases, courts were asked to determine the race of an individual. If a person were currently accepted as white, the burden of proving otherwise fell to any claimant to the contrary; if accepted as black, it was the petitioner's obligation to prove otherwise. The final determination was made by a jury who simply inspected the individual in question, although testimony was sometimes solicited from witnesses known for their ability to distinguish blacks from whites. Numerous decisions were in favor of light-skinned mulattoes who wished to be legally classified as white, making it clear that the prewar community consistently opposed using a slight bit of "Negro blood" to determine status.

Most decisions, reflecting simple observation and common sense, were made by appearance and a history of having lived and behaved as white. The opinion rendered by Justice Harper in an 1857 South Carolina case reflects this liberal attitude:

The condition of the individual is not determined solely by distinct and visible mixture of [N]egro blood, but by reputation, by his reception in society, and his having commonly exercised the privileges of

a white man.... It may be well and proper, that a man of worth,
honesty, industry, and respectability, should have the rank of a white
man, while a vagabond of the same degree of blood should be confined
to the inferior caste (p. 201).

Johnston cites the story of William Hayden as evidence of
the sentiment against enslaving apparent whites. Hayden had
been seized in Virginia because he refused to associate with
whites and let it be known that despite his white appearance,
he was a mulatto. When authorities attempted to sell him,
however, the court records show that buyers in Brentsville,
Fredericksburg, and Richmond "refused to make any bid for
him, all alleging that his color was too light and that he could
by reason thereof, too easily escape from slavery and pass as
a white man" (pp. 213–14). In short, despite abolitionists' beloved stories of white-appearing "tragic octoroons" being re-
manded to slavery, in reality both the laws and the courts
operated against an otherwise "white" person's being classified
as a mulatto because of as little as one-eighth of "Negro blood."
The legal standards did not change until after the war and
Reconstruction. Late in the nineteenth century, bolstered by
"scientific" racism, states attempted to set the standard that
"one drop of Negro blood" meant classification as black, particularly for the purpose of preventing intermarriage.

These realities do not mean, however, that no mulatto children suffered the sudden reversal of fortune typical of the "tragic
octoroon." By late in the antebellum period, particularly after
1850, when slave laws had been tightened and manumission
generally prohibited, court records reveal that sometimes mulatto children whom a white father sought to free were, in fact,
seized as property after his death. In one case cited by Johnston,
Mississippi planter James Brown took his mulatto sons to Cincinnati in 1849 in order to free them. After doing so he returned
with the boys to Mississippi. When Brown died in 1858, the
state courts decided that rather than being heirs, the two boys
were still slaves and property of the estate (p. 230).

Between 1857 and 1860, a number of such cases involved
women and children willed their freedom and a share of an
estate at a time when emancipation was no longer legal. As a

result, these women and children were considered valuable property and ordered sold for the benefit of the legal heirs (p. 235). The point here is simply that while there were cases of mulatto offspring who were seized as the property of an estate after the owner's death, the literal octoroon—one having an eighth or less "Negro blood"—was less likely to be in that tragic situation than the mulatto having more and discernible black ancestry. Perhaps the term "tragic mulatto" is thus more appropriate than the often used "tragic octoroon." Again, these cases date from the 1850s when significant changes took place in attitudes toward both slavery and race, producing conditions that were not typical of the long history of Southern slavery before then.

In *New People: Miscegenation and Mulattoes in the United States*, Joel Williamson provides an up-to-date history of mulattoness in this country.[46] Williamson argues that the Industrial Revolution, by turning the South into a one-crop cotton kingdom, made black and mulatto slaves essential to industry in 1850. By 1915, however, blacks had been systematically excluded from industrial employment. In 1850, the white elite in the South was linked to the black mass and excluded the white mass. By 1915 the Southern white elite was aligned with the white mass and both excluded blacks in every way possible. Between 1850 and 1915, blacks, and especially mulattoes, attempted to enter the white world; after 1915, blacks and mulattoes built their own world of "brown America."

During the 1850s when cotton was king and the booming frontier slave states needed all the labor they could get, slavery became "whiter ... visibly so and with amazing rapidity"— mulatto slavery increased 66.9 percent during this decade.[47] This period saw disruption of families and "tragic mulatto" incidents at their height, as Virginia and Kentucky plantations bred and sold thousands of slaves—especially mulattoes—to meet the demands of the interstate market.

By 1850, the South had committed itself to the defense of slavery on the racial grounds that blacks were subhuman and fit for nothing else, that God had created them to be slaves. Mulattoes, of course, posed a serious problem because they blurred the distinction between races.[48] When the increasing whiteness of slavery could no longer be ignored, it was dealt with by introducing the "one-drop rule." A great transformation in race relations began about 1850 and extended to 1915, with the "central fact" about the development of race relations during this period being "the evolution of the one-drop rule."[49] Because of the increasing danger to them in the last years before the war, many free mulattoes (as noted earlier) fled slave states for the North. During Reconstruction, these mulattoes, and even more so their children, returned South as missionaries, teachers, relief and rescue workers. These free-born mulattoes, together with their peers from Charleston and New Orleans, had a strong history of education and other advantages over the newly freed black mass, leading to a period of leadership by members of a "mulatto elite"—including missionaries and educators such as Francis L. Cardozo and William J. McKinlay from Charleston, Margaret and Thaddeus Sasportas from Philadelphia, Hezekiah H. Hunter and Benjamin A. Boseman from New York, and Benjamin F. Randolph, who was born in Kentucky, raised in Ohio, and educated at Oberlin. After the war, Randolph served in South Carolina as Freedman's Bureau teacher, minister, and politician until he was assassinated while campaigning for the Republican Party in 1868.[50] Such historical figures provide striking parallels for the selfless mulatto characters, young idealists dedicated to the cause of blacks in the South, who people the novels of late nineteenth-century black authors such as Frances E. W. Harper and J. McHenry Jones.

Following Reconstruction, the white South insisted on absolute demarcation between the two—black and white—cultures. This dichotomy replaced the prewar one of slave and free. Because of this attitude and the rapid spread of legalized segregation, the mulatto elite that had previously linked itself to white culture and society now moved to join forces with the black mass. Despite the brief increase in marriages between white women and black men just after the war, because of segregation and a new, massive social resistance to miscegenation, the practice fell off sharply. Williamson quotes Caroline Bond Day's study (1918–22) that documented a tremendous drop in miscegenation between blacks and whites after 1865

representing "a fundamental change in the history of miscegenation in America."[51] After Reconstruction, the flurry of antimiscegenation laws and the detailed Jim Crow rules destroyed
the opportunity for social contact between blacks and whites,
but this segregation greatly increased marriages between blacks
and mulattoes.

Given an absolute division between black and white, "passing" became an important issue by the turn of the century. The
worse segregation became, the greater the benefit to one who
chose to pass. Johnston argues, however, that even given strong
inducement, "the vast majority of 'white Negroes' made no
effort to desert the mulatto group.... Such persons were bound
by the strong ties of friendship, relationship, affection, and
family tradition to the despised and persecuted group, and in
most cases they remained with those who loved them and they
suffered with them. In this problem of racial identity, social
forces proved stronger than economic inducements and far more
effective in preserving racial integrity than legal acts."[52] The
threat posed by passing, however, created a white Southern
obsession with racial purity, manifested in excruciating concern for family genealogies and in keeping white women away
from black men through the complex web of segregation rules.
The accepted attitude held that only by introducing mulatto
children through a white mother would the purity of the race
be threatened; racial purity would not be "polluted" by whites'
fathering mulatto children who would follow their mother's
status and be "black."[53]

In 1915, 90 percent of all blacks still lived in the rural South,
blacks and mulattoes were isolated from the white world, and
their combined gene pool was twenty percent white. From this
point on, no statistically significant miscegenation took place
between blacks and whites; the white genes were diffused
through the intermarriage of blacks and mulattoes that created
the "new people" of brown America.[54] By this date, the young
blacks and whites coming of age had lived all their lives in a
society that preached the one-drop rule. Both blacks and whites
accepted this rule and were both strongly opposed to miscegenation. The dream of the assimilationists that blacks would
marry lighter and lighter until they disappeared into the white

world was over. Indeed, acceptance of the one-drop rule was so universal that the 1920 Census was the last to count mulattoes; after that all mulattoes were classified as "Negroes," officially creating a simplified biracial America.

Williamson sees the Harlem Renaissance as a reversal of role for cultured mulattoes. Previously they had carried white culture to the black mass. During the Renaissance, however, mulattoes picked up black culture with its African and agricultural roots from the mass and combined it with the white culture they already knew, producing a new "brown" culture for the "new people." In the end, he suggests that the civil rights movement (1950–65) tried to follow the line from Reconstruction that sought integration and assimilation. Black separatism (1965–75), however, followed the line from Marcus Garvey and the Harlem Renaissance in returning to black roots, and in valuing darkness of color. Williamson concludes that "the great fact about miscegenation today is that it is minimal."

THE NOVELS

In the oldest of critical cliches, literature is about life, and much American literature is about race as a fact of life in this country. Much of this racial literature touches upon the ultimate form of racial contact, sexual union, and the fruits of such union, the children who are the inheritors of both races. Generally speaking, mainstream literary critics have studied miscegenation only in modern American fiction. Until the late 1960s brought a new focus on black literature, miscegenation was assumed to be too strong for Victorian sensibilities, too powerful to have been written about until the breakthrough work of Faulkner and later writers.[55] But more than sixty novels, dating from World War I back to the earliest days of the genre in America, treat miscegenation substantially.

What follows is the literary history of miscegenation as it is embodied in selected American novels from this period. In addition, an attempt has been made throughout to provide a sense of the social and political context in which these books were written. Within each novel, and within the unfolding textual context they provide for each other, I look at miscegenation as present in two ways: both as an abstract concept, or theme, and as concrete manifestation of craft in character development, arrangement of plot, and rhetorical effect.

As a theme, miscegenation has often been used to symbolize conceptual structures such as racial clash or harmony, black and white value systems, human divisions or human ability to overcome obstacles, good and evil, and alienation and the search for identity. As early as 1924, Francis Pendleton Gaines suggested a thematic study of miscegenation in American literature, identifying the two dominant themes as power and helplessness (the bestial lust of a white master for a defenseless female slave) and the tragic status of being trapped between two worlds (the fate of the unhappy slave of mixed blood).[56] Two years later, he added another major theme, suggesting miscegenation as the New World counterpart to the European tragedy of true love thwarted by the impassable barriers of class.[57] In 1969, Helena Smith looked at works by Cable, Clemens, Glasgow, and Faulkner to argue that the question of where the mulatto belongs—in which race can he or she find identity—is the central theme in the literature of miscegenation.[58] A half century after Gaines, in line with the universalizing tendency of most criticism during the intervening years, William Bedford Clark saw in miscegenation "its immense literary potential ... to transcend regional concerns and take on universal implications." He found in miscegenation a "mythic" quality and identified its symbolic use as an archetypal pattern of guilt and retribution, and, in the mulatto's search for identity, as a symbol for alienation.[59] Not long afterwards, Judith Berzon examined at length the mulatto character in American fiction, culminating in her discussion of the mulatto character as symbolic prototype of the twentieth century's alienated, existential man.[60]

In addition to such use as a symbol for abstract, conceptual structures, miscegenation can also be used thematically as a locus of meaning for examining specific social and political issues. Miscegenation can be the focal point for expounding upon slavery, sectionalism, and racism in particular forms, times, and places, or it can be used to put an issue into larger context as, for example, when Thomas Dixon, Jr., makes turn-of-the-century racism in America part of the world wide conflict between whites and darker colonial peoples. While not excluding comments on interracial sex as a symbol of abstract, conceptual structures (e.g., "alienation"), the second thematic approach—seeing miscegenation as focal point for rhetorical debate about concrete social and political issues—weighs most heavily in the discussions to follow. I organize chronologically, rather than around abstract concepts such as "alienation," in order to foreground the developing pattern of how miscegenation, as presented in the novels over time, relates to a changing society.

The novels taken up clearly relate to specific issues. They are, by and large, examples of what Wayne Booth refers to as overt rhetoric; that is, the narrators and narrative techniques used are reliable guides to the "implied author's" rhetorical intention.[61] For example, set-piece conversations in which several characters represent different points of view on slavery or racism occur in almost every novel examined from *Modern Chivalry* to *The Autobiography of An Ex-Colored Man*. We know the implied author's view because a highly sympathetic character (one for whom the ethical appeal of classical rhetoric has been well developed) delivers it, or the reliable narrator points out the correct view with approval. Readers made uncomfortable by my discussion of an author's rhetorical intention, by the apparent fallacy of confusing a character or narrator with the author, may assume I mean Booth's text-derived "implied author." In reality, for most novels discussed here little difference exists between the values of implied and historical authors.

In addition to its presence as rhetorical theme, miscegenation also presents itself embodied in the concrete choices made by the writer as craftsman, particularly as rhetorical craftsman. Every writer—novelist as well as speechwriter—faces the rhetorical demands of invention, arrangement, and style, and the problem of audience. In the criticism of individual works, I suggest ways in which the subject of miscegenation helps the author meet those demands. In some cases, for example, miscegenation allows a writer to generate a plot or parts of a plot out of stereotyped circumstances associated with the subject, such as the reversal of fortune suffered by tragic mulattoes.

Character development and motivation may also draw upon miscegenation, as when a tragic mulatto feels torn between conflicting black and white heritages.

On a somewhat subtler level, miscegenation may be used as a touchstone to reveal character after the author has prepared us for the proper response. In the novels by Dixon, for example, we know that characters repulsed by the very idea of miscegenation are good, while those who accept it are evil or incredibly foolish. Arrangement of incidents within a plot may derive from an author's rhetorical intention, as when a miscegenetic act is followed by a series of disasters for those involved. Obviously, style choices are guided by rhetorical concerns about the subject, such as the significant animal imagery in a term like "mongrelization" used to mean interracial sex. Finally, the use of certain stereotypes—even certain omissions—can suggest assumptions that the author must believe the audience will share, an indirect but intriguing route to beliefs and attitudes of the popular mind at that time.[62]

Race and the frontier are, in the end, the two great themes unique to American literature. We have been a people divided by race and lured by the frontier, and our literature is obsessed with these native affairs so foreign to European culture. Too much of America's racial story has been a tale of oppression and conflict, the exploitation and rape of one race by another. Miscegenation lies at the core of racism, its hatreds, and its violence, because racists believe in genetic, race-specific qualities of intelligence, morality, and humanity. The story of American miscegenation is our own, not repeated in other mixed cultures. We should listen carefully to the way it is told in the novels that follow.

NOTES

1. James Hugo Johnston, *Race Relations in Virginia and Miscegenation in the South, 1776–1860* (Amherst: Univ. of Massachusetts Press, 1970), pp. 254–55. A 1937 University of Chicago Ph.D. dissertation, Johnston's work was first published in 1970 and is the seminal study of miscegenation before the Civil War. Johnston quotes extensively from court and legislative records related to miscegenation. My

quotations of these records are taken from Johnston and cited parenthetically in this chapter. Throughout this introduction, I am heavily indebted to Johnston in many ways, as anyone familiar with his work will see.

2. Edward B. Reuter, *The Mulatto in the United States* (Boston: R. G. Badger, 1918), p. 112.

3. For fuller discussion of black and white relations with Indians during this period, see Lerone Bennett, Jr., "Miscegenation in America," in *Marriage Across the Color Line*, ed. Cloyte M. Larsson (Chicago: Johnson Publishing Co., 1965), pp. 24–26; and Johnston, pp. 269–92; for a study of the literary treatment of white sexual relations with Indians during the nineteenth century, see William J. Scheick, *The Half-Blood: A Cultural Symbol in 19th Century American Fiction* (Lexington: Univ. of Kentucky Press, 1979).

4. See Jean Fagin Yellin, *The Intricate Knot* (New York: New York Univ. Press, 1972), pp. 3–11; and Houston A. Baker, Jr., *The Journey Back* (Chicago: Univ. of Chicago Press, 1980), pp. 145–47, for their discussions of Jefferson's *Notes on Virginia* as representing colonial belief that blacks were less human than whites.

5. Joel Williamson, *New People: Miscegenation and Mulattoes in the United States* (New York: Free Press, 1980), pp. 42–48.

6. Gunnar Myrdal, *An American Dilemma* (New York: Harper, 1944), p. 56.

7. Bennett, p. 8.

8. Williamson, pp. 33–34.

9. Williamson, p. 28.

10. Johnston, p. 170.

11. Herbert G. Gutman, *The Black Family in Slavery and Freedom, 1750–1925* (New York: Pantheon Books, 1976), p. 19.

12. Quoted by Bennett, p. 12.

13. Williamson, p. 58.

14. Eugene D. Genovese, *Roll Jordan Roll: The World the Slaves Made* (New York: Pantheon Books), p. 418.

15. Bennett, pp. 12–13.

16. Williamson, pp. 75–77.

17. Johnston, p. 236.

18. Genovese, p. 417.

19. Bennett, p. 14.

20. Williamson, pp. 42, 53–56.

21. Bennett, p. 11.

22. Gutman, *Black Family*, pp. 61–83.

23. Genovese, pp. 473–75; John Blassingame, *The Slave Commu-*

nity: Plantation Life in the Antebellum South, rev. and enlarged ed.
(New York: Oxford Univ. Press, 1979), p. 164.

24. Genovese, pp. 484–85.

25. Johnston, p. 248.

26. Catherine Clinton, *The Plantation Mistress: Woman's World in the Old South* (New York: Pantheon Books, 1982), p. 199.

27. Blassingame, *The Slave Community*, p. 156.

28. See, for example, Clinton, pp. 204–11. Her assertion that planters set out to father slaves "for the dollar value of slave offspring" indicates her 1850s mindset, when this practice occurred widely in the upper South. One also questions her implication that the relationship between white females and black male slaves was so thoroughly desexualized that adult black males commonly appeared naked in the presence of white women. Nakedness among prepubescent slave children of both sexes was, of course, common.

29. Genovese, p. 422.

30. Johnston, pp. 264–65.

31. Johnston, pp. 264–67.

32. Susan Brownmiller, *Against Our Will: Men, Women, and Rape* (New York: Simon and Schuster, 1975), pp. 170–73. For a detailed response to the many problems with Fogel and Engerman's *Time on the Cross*, see Herbert G. Gutman, *Slavery and the Numbers Game: A Critique of Time on the Cross* (Urbana: Univ. of Illinois Press, 1975).

33. Genovese, pp. 414–15.

34. Johnston, p. 304.

35. Gutman, *Black Family*, pp. 365–66.

36. Williamson, pp. 88–89.

37. Bennett, pp. 20–21.

38. Genovese, pp. 427–28.

39. For a detailed discussion of race relations in the North, see Leon Litwack, *North of Slavery: The Negro in the Free States, 1790–1860* (Chicago: Univ. of Chicago Press, 1961).

40. For examples and discussion of this problem, see Gutman, *Black Family*, pp. 386–402.

41. Gutman, *Black Family*, pp. 24–28.

42. Genovese, pp. 461–62.

43. George M. Frederickson, *The Black Image in the White Mind* (New York: Harper and Row, 1971), p. 282.

44. W. J. Cash, *The Mind of the South* (1941; reprint New York: Vintage-Knopf, n.d.), p. 118.

45. See Frederickson. In Chapter 6, I summarize his argument in more detail.

46. See Williamson, Chapter 2, "Changeover, 1850–1915" from which I draw the following discussion.

47. Williamson, p. 63.

48. Williamson, pp. 71–75; see also Winthrop D. Jordan, *White Over Black: American Attitudes Toward the Negro, 1550–1812* (Chapel Hill: Univ. of North Carolina Press, 1968), pp. 167–78.

49. Williamson, p. 109.

50. Williamson, pp. 84–85.

51. Williamson, p. 89.

52. Johnston, pp. 215–16.

53. Sociologists and social psychologists have written extensively about the symbolic meaning of white male hostility to sex between white women and black men. Sociologists such as Myrdal see this hostility as displacement from the threat posed by blacks to white males' social status; more Marxian interpreters see this hostility as displacement from the threat of economic competition. Psychological explanations run to such theories as John Dollard's that hostility toward black men having sexual relations with white women stems from the white males' projection of guilt over the "sinfulness" of sex (*Caste and Class in a Southern Town* [Garden City: Doubleday Anchor, 1957]), or Joel Kovel's thesis that the white man suffers from a double Oedipus complex toward both black mammy and white mother, which he resolves by killing the black man who has one and wants the other (*White Racism: A Psychohistory* [New York: Pantheon Books, 1970]). Charles Herbert Stember reviews the traditional psychosocial interpretations and dismisses them all (*Sexual Racism* [New York: Elsevier Scientific Publishing, 1976]). He argues that sexual stimulation and pleasure have a strong cognitive element fed by the inaccessibility of majority females to minority males that makes sex with white women better for black men that it can ever be for white men, hence white male hatred.

54. Williamson, pp. 188–90. In this century, despite a surge in the 1960s, interracial marriages have declined to the point that they represent fewer than 1 percent of existing marriages. Even in this decline, however, white women have married black men much more frequently than white men married black women. A study of mixed marriages in Philadelphia between 1922 and 1947, for example, showed that white women cross married more; in one sample of fifty mixed marriages, forty-four were by white women. More recently, the Civil Rights movement stimulated a 63 percent increase in cross marriages during the 1960s, due totally to white women marrying black men; the number of white men marrying black women actually declined during the same period.

34   Amalgamation!

55. See, for example, Florence Leaver ("Mark Twain's *Pudd'nhead Wilson*," *Mark Twain Journal* 10 [1956]:14) where she says that Twain "initiated" the theme of miscegenation; or Thomas W. Ford ("The Miscegenation Theme in *Pudd'nhead Wilson*," *Mark Twain Journal* 10 [1955]:13) where he says that "Twain considers a theme which was *totally avoided* [italics mine] in nineteenth-century American literature, the subject of miscegenation."

56. Francis Pendleton Gaines, *The Southern Plantation* (New York: Columbia Univ. Press, 1924), pp. 221–22.

57. Francis Pendleton Gaines, "The Racial Bar Sinister in American Romance," *South Atlantic Quarterly* 25 (1926):396–402.

58. Helena M. Smith, "No-Nation Bastards," *Studies in the Humanities* 1 (1969):18–28.

59. William Bedford Clark, "The Serpent of Lust in the Southern Garden," *Southern Review* 10 (Autumn 1974):805–22.

60. Judith R. Berzon, *Neither White nor Black: The Mulatto Character in American Fiction* (New York: New York Univ. Press, 1978), pp. 218–27. For earlier studies of the mulatto character as stereotype, see John Herbert Nelson, *The Negro Character in American Literature* (1926; reprint; College Park, Md.: McGrath, 1968); Penelope Bullock, "The Treatment of the Mulatto in American Fiction from 1826–1902," M.A. Thesis, Atlanta University, 1944, and "The Mulatto in American Fiction," *Phylon* 6 (1945):78–82.

61. Wayne C. Booth, *The Rhetoric of Fiction* (Chicago: Univ. of Chicago Press, 1961), especially pp. 11–22.

62. Peter J. Rabinowitz, "Assertion and Assumption: Fictional Patterns and the External World," *PMLA* 96 (May 1981):408–19.

2
Origins, 1792–1849

As the English novel emerged during the eighteenth century, the genre became the base for an American national literature that developed after the Revolution. Following the war for independence, national pride helped turn American attention from literary models of British life to novels of our own scene and manners. The very earliest American novels, William Hill Brown's *The Power of Sympathy* (1789) and Susanna Haswell Rowson's *Charlotte Temple* (1791), were tales of moral trials in the sentimental, didactic, Richardsonian tradition. Hugh Henry Brackenridge published *Modern Chivalry* serially between 1792 and 1805, a book more in the Fielding tradition, in many ways more satiric fable than novel.[1]

Captain John Farago, the narrator in the Brackenridge book, presents himself as a disinterested eighteenth-century man of reason. During his travels, Farago attends the annual lecture of a local Philosophical Society and is surprised to find Cuff, a black slave, as the orator. Cuff has been sent by his master to counter the argument that "Africans had been once white, had sharp noses, and long hair; but that by living in sunburnt climates, the skin had changed color, the hair become frizzled." Cuff must argue the opposite, "that men were all once black, and that by living in snowy countries, and being bleached by the weather, the skin had gradually become white" (p. 131). Cuff's ludicrous oration is recounted in the broadest dialect, and the narrator's ironic view is made clear when he informs us that a committee of the Society approached "Mr. Cuff" to "request a copy of his oration, that it might be published" (p. 131).

Thus from the very beginnings of our national literature, concern about race and the relationships between races has been present. The origins of racial differences became a serious subject in later, nineteenth-century debate, and the narrator, after returning to his lodging, ponders the question of multigenesis. After dismissing his contemporaries' theories, including Lord Kames' that the building of Babel led to a "confusion of complexions as well as languages," Farago offers his own conclusion:

> I am of the opinion that Adam was a tall, straight-limbed, red-haired man, with a fair complexion, blue eyes, and an aquiline nose; and that Eve was a Negro woman.
> For what is the necessity to make them both of the same color, feature, and form, when there is beauty in variety. . . .
> As God made Adam in his own likeness, so it is to be supposed that Adam begat some in his; and these were red-haired, fair-complexioned, blue-eyed, proportionately featured boys and girls; while, on the other hand, some took after the mother, and became Negro men and women (p. 132).

Perhaps Brackenridge, having observed the common practice of miscegenation on plantations and on the frontiers of slave-holding areas, felt (as does Farago) that this simple, common-place idea provides the most reasonable answer to the question.

Brackenridge was one of very few novelists around the turn of the century. Only some two hundred works of fiction had been produced from 1779 to 1829, and of these only about twenty received any real circulation.[2] James Fenimore Cooper was the best known novelist of this period, and he raised the subject of miscegenation in *The Last of the Mohicans* (1826).[3] In this work, Cora Munro appears to be nothing more than an attractive brunette until Duncan Heyward approaches Cora's father to ask for the hand of his younger daughter, Alice. Colonel Munro mistakenly believes that Heyward is interested in Cora, but is rejecting her because he knows the secret of her heritage. Munro angrily threatens Heyward, who pleads ignorance of the matter. Munro then reveals that Cora is his daughter by his first wife who was "descended, remotely, from that unfortunate class who are so basely enslaved" (p. 172). Heyward insists that he did not know nor would that knowledge have made any difference if he were interested in Cora. At the same time, however, he experiences within himself a consciousness of revulsion based in a prejudice so "deeply rooted as if it had been ingrafted in his nature" (p. 172). Because Heyward's interest does not lie with Cora the problem of her ancestry does not become an important part of the novel. Cooper's brief treatment, however, does introduce one basic quandary to be faced by many white authors writing about miscegenation—how to resolve the dilemma of the white man's attraction to the beauty of the mulatto, and his revulsion at the thoughts of marriage and children of mixed blood.

Cooper does not involve Heyward in this dilemma, but his depiction of Cora does involve the reader. A strong and impressive character, she is far more attractive than her insipid sister Alice, and neither Cora nor her father is ashamed of her heritage. The only times Cora speaks of it are once indirectly when she denounces prejudice (p. 26), and again when she heroically pleads with the Indians to take her and spare Alice, saying that "the curse of my ancestors has fallen heavily on their child" (p. 326). Cooper must have felt the reader's dilemma caused by the attractiveness of Cora, for he apparently experienced the need to resolve it by having her killed (p. 358). In so doing he introduces one of the favorite resolutions of later authors facing the same quandary.

In his introduction to the novel, William Charvat notes Cooper's disapproval of miscegenation, points out that Cooper's evil Indians, the Mingoes, are a tribe of mixed blood (p. xiv), and remarks that Hawkeye rejects the sentimental hope for some kind of relationship between Cora and Uncas after death (p. vi). Granted that Cooper opposes miscegenation, he still creates a problem by making Cora one of the most appealing characters of the novel, despite her heritage. In introducing miscegenation, he presents it as a dilemma of approach-avoidance, a problem having both an attracting and a repelling side.

The other white approach to miscegenation, that it is not a dilemma but an evil to be uprooted at any cost, is introduced nine years later by a Southern author using the pseudonym Oliver Bolokitten. With his work, *A Sojourn in the City of Amalgamation, in the Year of Our Lord, 19—*(1835),[4] we also have the first use of miscegenation for overt rhetorical purposes. This satire not only condemns miscegenation, it also tries to establish the sub-human status of blacks as the justification for slavery. Opening with a quotation on madness from *The Battle of the Books*, the satire is obviously modeled on Swift. It seems inspired at least superficially by the tone of intense revulsion found in the fourth voyage of Gulliver. The narrator, taking a stroll, is mysteriously transported in time into the twentieth century, where he visits the City of Amalgamation. The narrator's observations there constitute a twofold attack on the practice of interbreeding: intellectually he considers it unnatural, and emotionally he finds it offensive.

The intellectual attack is the least developed, consisting of sophistries such as the idea that prejudice has been implanted by the deity and is therefore good (p. 59). The brunt of the attack on miscegenation is emotional and centers on the author's pathological concern with the foul odor attributed to blacks. When the narrator first sees a congregation of mixed couples in church, he describes a device universally used to separate husbands and wives:

It was perfectly original. It seemed composed of fans and little vials ingeniously intermingled. It whizzed round seemingly by a perpetual motion power, and with amazing swiftness: its object being to protect the husbands from those disagreeable evaporations exhaling from the odoriferous spouse which it did by fanning off the offensive air, and at the same time dispensing, by means of the vials, a delightful perfume (p. 17).

Despite such precautions, however, white husbands frequently vomit in public because their stomachs are "too wise to be bamboozled into such mongrel principles" (p. 21). The narrator likens the mixed marriages to the practice of hundreds of residents of the city who "kept manure spread around their houses to convince themselves of its beautiful smell.... [they] slumber with a platter of this excrement smoking before their noses" to overcome their prejudice against its odor (p. 141).

Bolokitten, a textbook anal retentive, could provide a field day for Norman O. Brown or Leslie Fiedler, but of most interest here is the author's tone. The excoriating vehemence of his attack on miscegenation, and on blacks generally, reflects less the period in which it was written than adumbrates the racial bitterness which was to develop in the decade immediately preceding the Civil War and which lasted long after, throughout Reconstruction and on into the twentieth century. The work seems to be one of the generally unsuccessful attempts to establish a taboo against miscegenation both before and, especially, after the Civil War.[5]

In his treatment of blacks, Bolokitten differed markedly from other Southern writers of his time, who were developing the Plantation Tradition in which the best plantation that ever existed, or perhaps one that never did, was proposed as typical.[6] Actually, before 1824, barely a half dozen works of fiction which could be called novels had been produced in the South, and blacks do not appear in any of them.[7] Tremaine McDowell considers George Tucker's *The Valley of the Shenandoah* (1824) to be the prototype of the plantation novel, while Gaines, in *The Southern Plantation*, cites John Pendleton Kennedy's *Swallow Barn* (1832) as the beginning.[8] Either way, blacks were introduced as characters within the Plantation Tradition, which developed around 1830 and paralleled a rise of Southern interest during the same period in the defense of slavery.

Following the passage of the Slave Act (1807) forbidding importation of slaves, attacks on the institution of slavery declined. Moreover, the remaining opposition to slavery was largely limited to the Southern states. In 1827, for example, 106 out of a national total of 130 antislavery societies were in slave states. Significantly, however, by 1837 there was not one left in the South. This change reflects a shift during those ten years in the Southern attitude from tolerating or opposing slavery to fervent defense of it. Among the many factors producing this change were the rapid growth of the cotton industry, Nat Turner's rebellion (1831), the debates in the Virginia legisla-

ture (1831–1832) over plans for partial or total abolition, and the rise of a new, violent abolition movement in the North led by William Lloyd Garrison, whose first issue of *The Liberator* was published January 1, 1831.[9]
It was during this period of change and of developing defense for the institution of slavery that black characters were first being used by Southern novelists, and it is understandable that miscegenation, a significant problem associated with slavery, would not be a topic much favored. McDowell agrees that in this period of growing contention over slavery, authors such as John Pendleton Kennedy, George Tucker, William Alexander Caruthers, Nathaniel Beverly Tucker and others omitted almost totally the unpleasant elements of plantation life, relying on the stereotypic amusing, loyal darky of the Plantation Tradition and avoiding problem areas such a interracial sex. He remarks that interbreeding was mentioned by only one Southern author before 1850, Joseph Holt Ingraham, who eventually avoided the issue.[10] Actually there were two other Southern writers, besides Bolokitten and Ingraham, who at least mentioned the subject before 1850, William Gilmore Simms and Mrs. E. D. E. N. Southworth. Ingraham, Simms and Southworth manage to present the subject in a less bitterly rhetorical manner than the earliest Southern treatment in the Bolokitten satire.
The first Southern novel to incorporate miscegenation after Bolokitten's work is Ingraham's *The Quadroone* (1841).[11] The story is so frivolous that the modern reader finds it difficult to accord it serious attention. McDowell considers the novel a mad Gothic romance and notes that the resolution and recognition scene at the end is "so incredible that it becomes excellent, though unintentional burlesque."[12] Set in New Orleans in 1769, following the Spanish occupation of that city, *The Quadroone* presents Renault and Azelie, supposed quadroon brother and sister, who both feel cursed by their racial lot. The miscegenation theme develops when Renault falls in love with Estelle, daughter of the Spanish governor Osma. Moreover, Azelie loves and is loved by a member of the Spanish nobility, Don Henrique. Adding to her plight, Azelie's corrupt, mulatto "mother" is constantly on the verge of peddling her to one or another

evil and lecherous man. The wild conclusion reveals that both
Azelie and Renault are actually of noble and untainted Spanish
blood, and all ends happily.

Despite the ludicrous quality of the conclusion, as well as
most of what precedes, several factors relate to the development
of miscegenation as a literary subject and bear examination.
Ingraham deals with black/white miscegenation and does so
not in an imaginary place in the distant future as did Bolokitten, but within the historical South. The author of *The Quadroone*, however, mitigates the effrontery of this taboo-trampling
in several ways. The story is set in the past, and, although
New Orleans is a Southern city, it is a city unlike any other
in the South. The author stresses the foreignness of New Orleans, particularly through emphasis on Oriental qualities.
Living quarters are of "Oriental elegance" (I, 81); Spanish war-
riors are compared to "voluptuous Persian princes" (I, 106);
and quadroon women to the harem girls of the "Sultan of the
Orient" (II, 124). These romantic qualities of the distant and
exotic past remove the forbidden subject from the immediacy
of normal Southern life. Moreover, Ingraham neutralizes much
of the poison in the viperous concept of miscegenation by ultimately dodging the issue. Renault and Azelie are not mulattoes; they are white. This motif of misunderstanding and
revelation is used repeatedly by later writers, such as James
Peacocke, Epes Sargent and others, who also touch forbidden
fruit. In addition, Ingraham introduces what is to be another
popular evasion of dealing honestly with racial intermingling
in America: the mulattoes in question do not have a love relationship with Americans but with foreigners.

Linking miscegenation to "foreign" New Orleans is general
practice in many of the works touching the subject. Ingraham
establishes in American literature the convention of quadroon
concubinage in New Orleans and develops many of the literary
details associated with the practice.[13] Renault explains to Don
Henrique the stringent laws against intermarriage and the
resultant system of freed mistresses raising their daughters to
be like themselves, "lamentably adapted to the degraded state
for which they have been so carefully educated" (I, 93). Later
he attacks his "mother" for her "guilty ambition, that, to attain

its end, has degraded female virtue to an article of merchandise, till our sisters are become a proverb and a by-word" (I, 162). Throughout, the scheming mother concerns herself about Azelie's reputation, for "the honor of a quadroone, till she hath her protector, is sacred as a betrothed bride's" (I, 149). Openly admitting and discussing interracial concubinage in New Orleans continues in many novels which are to follow. Every time an evil slave dealer mentions New Orleans in connection with a beautiful slave, he does so with a leer, and the knowing reader gasps at the enticing horror of the slave's fate.

If New Orleans is the accepted setting for enforced concubinage, the actuality of that fate is usually reserved for somebody other than the heroine. With rare exceptions, all the not-quite-fair maidens whom we meet prefer, like their blonde and blue-eyed sisters, death before dishonor. In this Azelie foreshadows all the "tragic octoroons" to come. If, in *Uncle Tom's Cabin*, Cassy will sleep with her owner, Emmaline will not, and she, like Azelie, is more in step with the legions of similarly put-upon young ladies in the works of H. Lord Hosmer, Frances McDougall, James Peacocke, Mayne Reid, Epes Sargent and others. In fact, Ingraham's supposed mulattoes, Azelie and Renault, embody many characteristics that are to become stereotypes in later works, one of which is the highly developed sense of honor, exemplified in Azelie's attitude and Renault's statement that she "shall die by a brother's hand ere she share the fate to which her degraded race is doomed!" (I, 87) Other stereotypic traits of mulattoes introduced by Ingraham are bitterness about their fate (I, 97, 144–145), bravery despite it (I, 26, 28), and, above all, the incredible beauty of the women. When Don Henrique first sees Azelie, two complete pages are devoted to a description of her beauty (I, 81–83), especially dwelling on the glories of her dark hair and eyes. Although not all the later writers are as profuse as Ingraham, no mulatto woman of any importance in a story gets away without at least two or three paragraphs on her slightly dusky charms.

The conventionalized, sexual attractiveness given in novels to the children of miscegenation leads inevitably to situations in which they also must face the racial barrier in seeking and winning love. Mulattoes have other problems which could be, and occasionally are, the focal point of a novel, such as the problem of being accepted by neither their fellow slaves nor their white masters. But many works about mulattoes focus on the theme of frustrated, though mutual, interracial love. Gaines comments that

Universally romantic invention has been challenged by the problem of love and the insuperable barrier. Lacking in the large a community of multiple social gradations as background, American fictionists have found our sharply defined racial restrictions, particularly of white and black, an opportunity for exposition of the general tragedy of caste and for the specific pathos of passion warring with opposeless polity.[14]

In the seemingly hopeless loves of both Azelie and Renault we have the situation outlined by Gaines. Although *The Quadroone* is no *Romeo and Juliet*, undoubtedly Ingraham made a significant contribution by establishing in the American novel the theme of tragic interference with the course of honorable, but interracial, affections.

Within the year following publication of *The Quadroone*, William Gilmore Simms took up the subject of miscegenation, but with an approach far different from concern with the course of honorable affections. When Simms writes of miscegenation in *Caloya; or, The Loves of the Driver* (1841),[15] he introduces a significant new trait in a black character—lust. The object of desire is not a white woman but an Indian; nevertheless the work seems important in a study of white/black miscegenation for having introduced the motif of sexual aggression by a black male. In *Caloya* the black man's sexual desires are treated humorously, but even as a known pro-slavery man, Simms offended many Southerners by writing about the subject at all.[16] In later years the topic of black sexual aggression recurs in the works of Thomas Nelson Page and Thomas Dixon, but in these the treatment is anything but humorous.

In the Simms novella, Caloya is a young, beautiful Indian woman married unhappily to a drunken old Catawba, Richard Knuckles. They camp on the grounds of Colonel Gillison and encounter the slave Mingo, the "driver" or assistant overseer of the plantation. Mingo attempts the seduction of Caloya, who spurns his advances, and he incurs the jealous hatred of her husband Knuckles, who plans to kill Mingo. Caloya, a good woman, tells Colonel Gillison of the plan and he saves Mingo's life.

The development of Mingo as principal character is careful and complete. Although tremendously loyal to his master, Mingo is not of this stereotyped dimension alone. He has shrewd insight into Gillison's character, and he uses this knowledge to his own advantage in minor matters (p. 382). Though given to braggadocio, the driver braves much and perseveres in his pursuit of Caloya, even continuing his quest after being knifed by her husband. Most important to the depth of Mingo's characterization is his frustration. As a driver, we are told, he is accustomed to having his will obeyed, yet with Caloya he cannot work that will: "He fancied that, in pursuit of his desires, were the woman alone concerned, he should have no difficulty, but he knew not what to do with the man. To scare him off was impossible,—to beguile him from his treasure seemed equally difficult" (p. 318). Mingo's growing frustration makes up the core of the story, is the source of tension and interest. Resolution comes with a fitting, but not harsh, chastisement for Mingo's lust and a change of fortune for Caloya; her husband dies and she marries a worthy young man from her tribe.

This early story of miscegenation provides several noteworthy items. Simms caters in two ways to a basic Southern reticence about discussing interracial sex. No actual sexual union takes place, and the relationship exists between black and Indian. But throughout the Simms story, miscegenation performs a basic structural function. The human emotional conflict, both between the characters and within their individual psyches, grows from the sexual conflict between people of different races. We are told that Mingo had been "engaged in sundry liaisons" (p. 411) with other slaves. These affairs annoy his wife, but result in no other adverse effects. Simms implies that within Mingo's own racial sphere his seductions are successful and to some degree acceptable, but once he tries to cross the racial bar he is doomed to failure and frustration. Caloya also suffers because of his attempt; it is only later with one of her own kind that she finds happiness.

In both *The Last of the Mohicans* and *The Quadroone* miscegenation is rather incidental, providing some spicy addition
to the primary adventurous plot. In *Caloya*, however, Simms
uses miscegenation in a basic human situation with believable
characters honestly working out their emotions and lives in
relation to their miscegenetic acts or desires. This kind of approach to miscegenation in the American novel does not really
come into its own until after World War I. In the interim, the
majority of authors writing about miscegenation employ it as
titillative tinsel or as a hard-sell, rhetorical gimmick.

Simms comes back to miscegenation the following year in
Beauchamp (1842),[17] but in this novel he does not move beyond
the superficial employment of it for shock value. In this fictional
account of the famous "Kentucky Tragedy," Colonel Stevens
whispers a secret to Beauchamp concerning Margaret Cooper's
dead child. Enraged by what is said, Beauchamp stabs Stevens
(p. 333). In the actual case on which the novel is based, rumors
circulated for some time that the child in question had been
fathered by a black,[18] so it would seem that Simms toys with
the forbidden theme of black/white miscegenation. Although
the question of interbreeding may have some structural value
in *Beauchamp* because it provides part of the immediate motive
for the killing, it is not developed in any significant manner.

The final work in this early period by a Southern author,
Mrs. E. D. E. N. Southworth's *Retribution* (1849),[19] is a typical
sentimental novel of that time, and miscegenation occurs only
superficially. Mrs. Southworth adds a touch of pathetic spice
to her stew with the sad tale of Minny, a quadroon slave girl
in the household of Colonel Dent. The details of Minny's trial
and tribulations are inserted (pp. 51–69) simply to elicit tears,
for they bear no connection to the main plot of the novel. Minny
plays a small role when Dent's wife accuses him of committing
adultery with the slave (p. 200), but the charge is false and
serves simply as one of many causes for constant arguments
between the Dents. It is not within the novel itself that Minny's
story is significant, but for its historical place in the development of the miscegenation theme. Minny's constant swooning
and the details of her sale in New Orleans are to become generally typical of tragic octoroons, adding further stereotypic

characteristics and situations to those begun by Ingraham concerning miscegenation in New Orleans. More importantly, the significance of Minny's story lies in her origins. She is unknowingly the slave daughter of a wealthy planter who raises her as white. Her slave status comes to light only after her father's death when it is discovered that he had neglected to free her. She is sold into slavery with the breakup of the estate. This reversal of fortune, from the pampered daughter of a wealthy planter to the pitiful object of lust placed on an auction block, is to become the standby of many novels dealing with miscegenation. Unlike later novelists, however, Southworth does not use this situation to condemn slavery. John Herbert Nelson notes that she typically gilds her pictures of antebellum society.[20] In this instance the gold leaf consists of the slaveholding Colonel Dent, who buys Minny only to protect her, treat her well, and eventually free her. Also through Dent's help Minny reunites with her long-lost husband and child. Incidentally, but worth noting, Minny's white husband is foreign, thus following a standard evasion of dealing with miscegenation in America.

The sentimentalized, idealized mixed-marriage with which Southworth rewards her Minny is a long way from the vituperation of Bolokitten. Simms and Ingraham, in line with the direction set by Cooper, fall between the extremes of condemning miscegenation vehemently and not condemning it at all. They imply that the racial barrier should be avoided rather than overcome. Southworth utilizes the subject only for sentimental spice; Ingraham flirts with it for thrills in his wild potboiler, and Simms builds an honest literary work around the problem of interracial sex. By 1850, Southern writers had provided many of the basic characters, situations, and attitudes found in novels of miscegenation, but had generally avoided linking the subject to any specific issue for rhetorical purposes. With the exception of Cooper, however, early Northern authors saw clearly the particular suitability of interracial sex for attacking black bondage in the South.

Until 1850 the majority of American novels dealing in any way with slavery were produced by the plantation romancers who professed to admire the institution; there are only five or

six Northern novels dealing with the subject before that date.[21]
Out of the many plantation novels written, only the three discussed above deal with miscegenation, but out of only a half dozen novels by authors not sympathetic to slavery, two use the theme of racial mixing, Hildreth's *The Slave* and the anonymously published *The Fanatic*. Both of these works use the subject clearly and overtly for a rhetorical attack on slavery.

Richard Hildreth, a Massachusetts native, received his degree from Harvard in 1826 before beginning a career as journalist, abolitionist, and lawyer. Because of ill health, he lived in Florida in 1834–36 where he observed slavery first hand. He published his one and only novel the year he returned north.

Hildreth's *The Slave; or, Memoirs of Archy Moore* (1836) was the first fictive slave-narrative, the first antislavery novel, and the first work to use miscegenation as a basic element in the propaganda attack on slavery. A greatly expanded edition, with identical text to the point where the 1836 edition ends plus a lengthy continuation of the narrator's adventures, was published in 1852.[22] In both editions, miscegenation is intrinsic to the novel's antislavery message. The narrator, Archy Moore, joins Mrs. Southworth's Minny as prototype for the many tragic mulatto figures of the antislavery novels to follow, and Catherine J. Starke suggests that "the tragic mulatto is probably the oldest archetype in our literature."[23] The son of a wealthy Virginia planter and a slave mistress, Archy is rebellious, which he attributes to his white heritage: "though born a slave, I inherited all my father's proud spirit, sensitive feelings and ardent temperament" (p. 10). He is the first of a long line of tragic mulattoes cursed with a "white" spirit in a "colored" body. But Archy Moore is something more than most of the stereotyped mulattoes who follow, suffering as he does the bitter indignity of being "the slave of my own father, the servant of my own brother" (p. 19). Moore's tragedy is not, like that of the characters of *The Quadroone* and the many others who fulfill Gaines' thesis, that of true love frustrated by a racial barrier. Moore is the first to suffer from the self-conscious awareness that his heritage has isolated him from his fellow man. He belongs neither to the ruling white class nor, truly, to the laboring black. His mother's dying speech reveals that such isolation had been the curse of her life; Archy discovers the truth of his own alienation when he first encounters trouble on the plantation and the darker slaves rejoice in his misfortune (p. 35). In many ways Archy is a proto–Joe Christmas, a character often considered the archetypal symbol of modern, alienated man.[24]

The theme of miscegenation shapes Archy's character, and it also plays another important structural role. Much of the plot revolves around actions directly or indirectly related to miscegenation. The most crucial development in the plot, Archy's initial rebellion and attempt to flee, is directly produced by the attempt of Colonel Moore first to seduce (p. 42) and then to rape (p. 129) Cassy, his beautiful mulatto daughter and Archy's half-sister. Archy's violent reaction causes him to be sold, separated from Cassy, whom he loves, and imbued with a lasting hatred for the white race. In the 1852 expanded edition, Archy returns after twenty years, passes for white, and searches successfully for Cassy and their son. By having a character cross the color line, Hildreth introduces the theme of "passing," which is to be of great importance in the novels of miscegenation by later black writers, such as Frank Webb, Charles Waddell Chesnutt and Sutton Griggs. Hildreth also introduces the frequently repeated link of miscegenation to incest.

Hildreth's attitude toward miscegenation emerges in the early edition and shows most fully in the expanded material of the later one. The author obviously does not oppose miscegenation per se; if anything, he seems to approve. The children of miscegenation are superior, not only to their black peers, but to the whites who rule them. Archy is more intelligent, morally better, and even physically stronger than his two white half-brothers. Cassy's "clear, soft olive ... complexion" is "more pleasing than the sickly, sallow hue ... of the patrician beauties of lower Virginia" (p. 32). Hildreth does not attack miscegenation, but slavery and the abuses it makes possible: the sexual advances forced on female slaves (pp. 42, 129, 142, 145–146), the cruel jealousy of white women toward their rivals (p. 142), the sale of a planter's own children (p. 70), and the separation of families (p. 160). In the 1852 continuation, he attacks the hypocrisy of the plantation owner who indulges in miscegenation but refuses to recognize his children (pp. 316–321). In the 1852 edition, as Southworth had three years earlier, Hildreth describes a stereotyped tragic octoroon and her classic coming to awareness only after her father's death (pp. 390–401).

That Hildreth views not miscegenation but slavery as evil shows most clearly in the story of a young planter named Mason, who has inherited a plantation abounding with his father's mulatto children and feels "called upon to act the part, not of a mean, selfish despot, but the head of a family, the chief of a tribe, whose clansmen are his poor relations, who have a family claim upon him" (p. 282). Another character refers to miscegenation as "the means which nature takes gradually to extinguish the inferior race, and to substitute an improved, mixed race in the place of it" (p. 317). Hildreth's novel supports miscegenation but attacks slavery as a system which leads to abuses involving the sexual relationships of the races.

The other antislavery miscegenation novel before 1850 is a less significant work by Reverend Howard Meeks of Baltimore. Published anonymously, *The Fanatic; or, The Perils of Peter Pliant, the Poor Pedagogue* (1846),[25] is primarily a revenge novel dealing with a number of vicious characters surrounding Peter Pliant, a Pennsylvania school teacher transplanted to Maryland. The novel opens with Pliant in prison for abolitionist activities; he has become a "fanatic" about slavery (p. 6). The book develops as a long flashback leading up to the imprisonment of Pliant. The antislavery message is clear; the slave owners are without exception a greedy and cruel bunch. The worst of the lot, a multiple-murderer named Morgan, upon his deathbed blames his evil ways on the corrupting influence of a slave society (p. 71). Structurally, miscegenation provides the basis for the initial rivalry between Morgan and Charles Ashley, another slave owner, and from this rivalry spring the series of murders and acts of revenge which make up the plot. Both men seek to force a sexual relationship upon the beautiful mulatto Hester, who is the slave of Ashley and the half-sister of Morgan (p. 6). As in Hildreth's novel, miscegenation is again linked to incest. Pliant becomes involved through his attempts to aid the beleaguered girl (p. 15). Hester suffers not only at the hands of the men, for example when Ashley attempts to whip her into submission (p. 14), but also from the cruelty of Ashley's wife (p. 15). Hester is morally superior to the whites, declaiming in her time of torment, "I am your slave, sir, but I cannot, will not be your mistress. Kill me, sell me if you will—I consent to death before dishonor" (p. 14). In expressing this preference (and in using these words) she places herself solidly in the ranks of her virtuous sisters, both white and mulatto, marching through the pages of the popular sentimental novels.

The author of *The Fanatic*, however, provides an interesting deviation from both the popular sentimental novels and the antislavery works by introducing to the American novel the black rapist. As aggressive as Mingo had been in Simms' *Caloya*, he stopped far short of rape, but in *The Fanatic*, Ashley, out of revenge, commands his slave Joe to rape Morgan's sister, Arabella. Joe, who has his own reasons for hating Morgan, carries out this assignment—"he wreaked his vengeance" upon her (p. 18). In *The Fanatic*, the barbarous act of rape, whether by master of slave or by slave of mistress, emerges as one more evil growing inevitably out of a corrupt and corrupting system. As in Hildreth's *The Slave*, miscegenation in itself does not come under attack. In fact, Arabella Morgan, who bears a black child as a consequence of the rape, is the one member of the white ruling class who repents her evil ways and settles into a life of benevolent care for her slaves (p. 71). Before *The Fanatic*, the black rapist had been studiously shunned by all writers dealing with miscegenation, and he remained taboo, particularly in other antislavery novels which attempted to portray blacks in the best light possible. The incident in *The Fanatic* appears to be the only occurrence of this black rapist motif until it blooms again in the works of Dixon and is taken up to be denied by the black apologists attempting to counter him.

The first years of the American novel saw miscegenation treated honestly, but they saw the subject used in the most superficial ways as well. Brackenridge and Cooper introduced miscegenation free from propaganda, but it was not long until amalgamation was linked to the great issue of the day—slav-

ery. Within a very few years, the Southerner Bolokitten had
used the subject in a vituperative attack on blacks and oppo-
nents of slavery, and within the following year the Northern
abolitionist Hildreth had produced a skillful assault on slavery
based on the institution's potential for terrible abuses involving
sexual exploitation of slaves and the misery of the children
who resulted. Many of the basic approaches to miscegenation
and the motifs in which it appears were established by the
eight novels before 1850 using the subject, including the approach which was to dominate treatment of miscegenation until after World War I—its exploitation as a powerful and
shocking rhetorical weapon. Cooper had raised an intriguing
human dilemma; Bolokitten and Hildreth contaminated it with
politics before anyone, even Simms, had had a chance to explore
its rich possibilities, and by 1850 the chance was lost. Before
that date, Northern authors almost never wrote of blacks. The
Southern authors who wrote dozens of books in which blacks
appeared forfeited their opportunity to probe the dilemmas posed
by miscegenation because they wished to ignore an unpleasant
subject. After 1850, conflict between the acrimonious attack on
slavery and the bitter defense of it began rising rapidly until
it reached the flood stage of the Civil War, and the novelists
were swept along in the great turmoil of their day. The first
great rush stemmed from the passage of the Fugitive Slave Act
in September 1850. Thousands of Northerners were roused from
apathy, or from opposition to the antics of abolitionists, to active denunciation of slavery. With the publication of *Uncle
Tom's Cabin* (1852) there was no turning back.

NOTES

1. Hugh Henry Brackenridge, *Modern Chivalry* (1792–1805; reprint ed. by Lewis Leary, New Haven, Ct.: College and University
Press, 1965). Hereafter cited parenthetically.

2. Helen W. Papashvily, *All the Happy Endings* (New York: Harper, 1956), p. 2.

3. James Fenimore Cooper, *The Last of the Mohicans*, ed. by William Charvat (Boston: Houghton, 1958). Hereafter cited
parenthetically.

4. Oliver Bolokitten [pseud.], *A Sojourn in the City of Amalgam-*

ation, in the Year of Our Lord, 19— (New York: n.p., 1835). Hereafter cited parenthetically.

5. Cash, pp. 87, 131.

6. Gaines, *Southern Plantation*, p. 35.

7. Tremaine McDowell, "The Negro in the Southern Novel Prior to 1850," *Journal of English and Germanic Philology* 25 (1926), in *Images of the Negro in American Literature* Seymour L. Gross and John E. Hardy, eds., (Chicago: Univ. of Chicago Press, 1966), pp. 56–57.

8. Gaines, *Southern Plantation*, p. 18.

9. Lorenzo D. Turner, *Anti-Slavery Sentiment in American Literature Prior to 1865* (1929; reprint, Port Washington, N.Y.: Kennikat Press, 1966), pp. 47–48.

10. McDowell, pp. 58, 68–69.

11. Joseph Holt Ingraham, *The Quadroone*, 2 vols. (New York: Harper, 1841). Hereafter cited parenthetically.

12. McDowell, pp. 61–62.

13. For further discussion of miscegenation in New Orleans both before and after the Civil War, see John Blassingame, *Black New Orleans, 1860–1880* (Chicago: Univ. of Chicago Press, 1973).

14. Gaines, "Racial Bar Sinister," p. 396.

15. William Gilmore Simms, "Caloya; or, The Loves of the Driver," 1841; reprinted in *The Wigwam and the Cabin*, revised ed. (Chicago: Donohue, Henneberry, 1890). Hereafter cited parenthetically.

16. Jennette Tandy, "Pro-Slavery Propaganda in American Fiction of the Fifties," *South Atlantic Quarterly* 21 (1922):170.

17. William Gilmore Simms, *Beauchamp* (1842; revised ed., Chicago: Donohue, Henneberry, n.d.). Hereafter cited parenthetically.

18. James H. Justus, "The Kentucky Tragedy in Simms and Warren: A Study in Changing Milieux," (M.A. Thesis, University of Tennessee, 1952), p. 36.

19. Mrs. E. D. E. N. Southworth, *Retribution* (Chicago: M. A. Donohue, n.d.). Hereafter cited parenthetically.

20. Nelson, p. 29.

21. Kenneth S. Lynn, "Introduction," in Harriet Beecher Stowe, *Uncle Tom's Cabin* (Cambridge, Mass.: Belknap, 1962), p. vii.

22. Richard Hildreth, *The White Slave; or, Memoirs of a Fugitive* (Boston: Tappan and Whittemore, 1852). Hereafter cited parenthetically.

23. Catherine J. Starke, *Black Portraiture in American Fiction: Stock Characters, Archetypes, and Individuals* (New York: Basic Books, 1972), p. 89.

24. Berzon, pp. 225–35.

25. [Howard Meeks], *The Fanatic; or, The Perils of Peter Pliant, the Poor Pedagogue* (Philadelphia: American Citizen, 1846). Hereafter cited parenthetically. For identification of the anonymous author, see Donald E. Leidell, "The Authorship of Two Anti-Slavery Novels of the 1840s: *The Fanatic* and *Winona*," *Papers of the Bibliographic Society of America* 67 (1973):447–49.

Abolition and Civil War, 1850–65

Despite early novelistic attacks on slavery like Hildreth's *Archy Moore* or *The Fanatic*, the great wave of abolitionist literature did not crest until after 1850. Spiller explains the early paucity of Northern antislavery novels by noting that until at least the 1840s it was considered both bad form and unprofitable to expose the great flaw in the land that prided itself on being the bastion of freedom.[1] With the passage of Clay's Omnibus Bill of 1850, however, Northern sentiment underwent a great change. The original Fugitive Slave Act of February 1, 1793, had long been systematically circumvented in the North by state laws protecting the rights of fugitives. The Fugitive Slave Act of September 1850, however, removed any recourse to basic rights for the fugitive and exerted extreme pressure in favor of the claimant; for example, his sworn statement was legal proof of ownership. For the first time, Northerners could be forced by law to aid in the capture and return of runaways. Northern popular sentiment had long been morally opposed to slavery, but its distance made the situation tolerable, and abolitionists were, in fact, viewed suspiciously as trouble makers. The Fugitive Slave Act, which brought the slavery issue home and rubbed Northern noses in it, galvanized the previously apathetic moral opposition and brought a new respectability to abolitionist feelings. The Kansas-Nebraska Act of 1854, which led to open contention and bloodshed over the issue of slavery in the territories, and the 1857 Dred Scott decision added continuing fuel to the fires of antislavery sentiment in the North.

The popular literature of the 1850s, led by *Uncle Tom's Cabin*, served as the bellows which fanned the blaze into the holocaust of war.

Popular literature from 1850 to 1865, both North and South, became so infected with propaganda that ever since the immediate emotions associated with the Civil War waned, these novels have been read only as embodiments of the opposing views of slavery.[2] As a result of this propaganda struggle, the black character suffered, becoming a living argument for one party or the other.[3] The early Southern romances and later proslavery novelists cast blacks as members of the happy plantation family. As Kenneth Lynn points out, however, they used a familial rhetoric to defend the destruction of families; Harriet Beecher Stowe wisely chose the separation of families as the focal point of her attack.[4] To parallel the Southern stereotype of the happy black member of the plantation family, the Northern antislavery novels produced their own major stereotyped figure, the tragic mulatto, a character for whom the joys of family life are destroyed, or nearly so, because of his or her racial mixture.

The course of proslavery literature in the thirty years preceding 1865 is best summarized by Margaret Butcher:

The point is that though these early writers—Kennedy, Simms, and such Virginia writers as W. A. Caruthers and John Esten Cooke—sustained the sentimental and unrealistic plantations, they were not seeking self-justification. Writing in the romantic tradition of the antebellum years, at a time when romanticism was moving toward its national climax, the Southern romantics were portraying the idyllic life of the agrarian South, in which the Negro slave was a colorful native background figure. In the years immediately following *Uncle Tom's Cabin* the tone of Southern fiction turned to frank propaganda.[5]

But in the crush of propaganda "answers" to *Uncle Tom's Cabin* only two proslavery authors used miscegenation to defend the peculiar institution.

The first open apologist for slavery to use miscegenation is Dr. James S. Peacocke of Mississippi in his novel *The Creole Orphans* (1856).[6] By 1856, several abolitionist works had attacked miscegenation under slavery; Peacocke undertakes not only to defend slavery but specifically to combat the growing popularity of attacking slave owners for their interracial licentiousness. Being the good propagandist that he is, Peacocke employs the basic rhetorical device of seeming to grant the opponent's argument, at least up to a certain point, before proceeding to demolish its value. He depicts the relationship between a planter and quadroon mistress, showing the possible problems involved, but blames the actual development of problems on misunderstandings and on scheming Yankees.

The novel opens with Charles Ormond's purchase of a beautiful young quadroon in Jamaica. The scene shifts to ten years later in New Orleans, where Ormond and the quadroon Marie are seen sharing a warm, loving relationship (pp. 10–11). Reflecting on the situation, Ormond defends his miscegenation with a glowing tribute to Marie and their children, expressing his determination to marry her:

As to the sin of living so in this pseudo-marital manner—that is for churchmen to decide. There are many who do it. It is custom, and custom calls it honorable. Yet I owe it to her; to her whose heart is as warm as the sunbeams of her own bright isle. I owe it to my children, the cherubs with their soft, warm smile, and happy laughs, and loving kiss. I owe it to them and I'll do them justice at any rate (p. 11).

Through procrastination and a sensitivity about the publicity involved, however, Ormond neglects marrying Marie for several years. Their slaveholding friends graciously accept her; their only concern is that something might happen to Marie and the children if Ormond should die unexpectedly (pp. 89–90). During a later visit to Jamaica it is revealed that Marie is not, after all, a quadroon, and immediately Ormond and she marry (pp. 175–179). After their return home, they spend contented years together until their eventual deaths. In school in Paris, the daughters Zoe and Estelle are by now eighteen and sixteen years old. After Ormond's death, a Mr. Talbot, an unscrupulous Yankee cousin whom Ormond had befriended and given a position years before, lays claim to the estate and seizes it. Because Ormond's marriage was never publicized, everyone assumes that the children are still legally slaves. Talbot sends his equally despicable Yankee friend, Stamp, to Paris to seize the girls. Returned to New Orleans, the young women are held at the mercy of Talbot and Stamp until the truth outs, the scoundrels are killed, and the children come into their rightful inheritance.

Rhetorical concerns clearly dominate this melodramatic story. It was published four years into the propaganda war touched off by *Uncle Tom's Cabin*, and Peacocke intimately involves miscegenation with proslavery polemics. The author deals with interracial sex on three levels directly tied to his defense of slavery and slaveholders. On the first level, he attempts to establish as the basic Southern attitude the moral judgment that miscegenation is wrong. Ormond is a man emotionally committed to miscegenation. He loves Marie and their children; his total concern is for their happiness and welfare. Despite these feelings, however, he reveals during an initial reverie on how much he loves Marie: "Yet—yet, the feeling. The dark tinge from Africa—can it be so, a Quadroon!" (p. 11) The Southerner's adverse opinion of miscegenation is illustrated even more clearly when Ormond discovers that Marie is not of mixed blood:

The shame spot was now removed forever. His heart was light already—happiness! His Marie had parents to whom she could look back without shame—with pride. The blot on his children's name could now be removed forever; there was no blood in their veins but what was pure—no attainting stream to poison life to the core (p. 177).

The inference is not difficult to draw. If Ormond, a Southern gentleman totally committed to what he believes is miscegenation, can, in his inmost essence, feel that it is wrong, then we can logically expect that a Southern gentleman not so committed would condemn the practice outright. Contrary to Northern charges that slaveholders are eager practitioners of miscegenation, we are urged to believe that Southerners view it as "shame," which does indeed "poison life to the core."

Having established by implication that Southerners condemn miscegenation, Peacocke also implies on the next level that the Northern charges are totally groundless, that the prac-

tice does not really exist. *The Creole Orphans* presents the basic
situation of many antislavery novels: a plantation owner purchases a beautiful quadroon, makes her his mistress and has
children by her. For over half the novel the reader, along with
Ormond, Marie and the other characters, accepts the relationship as being interracial; every indication points to it as such.
Abruptly, however, one discovers that all the evidence is wrong;
the slave mistress is actually white; the affair is not miscegenetic. Again, the implication is clear. If this so absolute instance proves upon close investigation to be false, cannot we
assume that other, perhaps the great majority of alleged cases
of miscegenation in the South are also mistakes? The argument
grows stronger when we look at the role played by the Yankee,
Talbot. Even before Ormond's death, Talbot discovers the papers proving Marie's untainted ancestry (p. 237). But he destroys them (p. 260) and continues to promote the belief that
the relationship is miscegenetic. A Yankee, then, to further
his own selfish ends, falsely claims that a Southerner practiced
miscegenation. It seems likely that Peacocke intended readers
to make the same judgment about the claims of Northern antislavery novels.

On the final level, abandoning the defensive posture, Peacocke assigns miscegenation a primary role in his offensive
thrust at those who attack slaveholders as sexual exploiters of
the helpless. Southern miscegenation is a key point in the attack on slavery because, in the interracial relationship, the
slave status of the woman puts her totally at the mercy of the
white male. Crying out against the degradation of helpless
females has great emotional appeal, and Northern novelists
did not fail to take advantage. But Peacocke's work throws the
burden of sexual exploitation on the Yankees. When a Southern
gentleman, Ormond, discovers a beautiful, helpless female slave,
he buys her out of kindness (p. 5). She becomes his mistress
out of love (p. 10), and their relationship lasts a lifetime filled
with mutual respect. Confronted with a similar situation, Yankees Talbot and Stamp react in a dramatically different manner from the Southern gentleman. When Stamp arrives from
Paris with the girls, he locks them in a New Orleans hotel and
attempts to rape Zoe, but is fortuitously interrupted (p. 317).

Talbot then arrives and the two men begin plotting to force themselves on the unwilling girls. Hoping to weaken the girls' resistance, Talbot resorts to bringing in a prostitute from the streets to live with and influence Zoe and Estelle. Later we discover that this Yankee whore is, in fact, Talbot's sister (p. 351). Talbot finally tries to rape Estelle, and when she fights him off he screams, "You shall either submit, or I'll put you up to auction and sell you to the highest bidder—for you are my slaves!" (p. 327) In all, about forty-five pages (pp. 312–357) are devoted to Yankees making sexual demands on helpless slave women. The Northern attacks on slaveholders as sexual exploiters can now be seen in a new light. The accusations are, Peacocke seems to suggest, nothing less than projections of the Yankees' own evil desires.

The last proslavery author before 1865 to write about miscegenation is Mrs. G. M. Flanders, whose novel *The Ebony Idol* (1860)[7] appeared on the eve of the Civil War. Unlike Peacocke, who shadows his attack on the North in implication, Flanders carries the offensive openly into the heartland of the enemy. The setting is New England where unscrupulous Yankees and a renegade slave plan amalgamation. A foolish young minister in the New England village of Minden takes up the cause of abolition and gains support among the less stable elements of his congregation. They import a fugitive slave, Caesar, who is placed on a farm owned by Mr. and Mrs. Hobbes, a dandy pair deserving of each other's villainies. This charming couple attempts to force their adopted daughter Mary to wed Caesar, but eventually the town regains its senses and the marriage is prevented. Like Peacocke, Mrs. Flanders is harsh in dealing with Yankee miscegenators.

The man initially responsible for all the trouble is the Reverend Cary, who is swayed by the emotionalism of an abolitionist meeting. However, his wife, a level-headed woman, thinks him crazy (p. 15). The author quickly expresses her low opinion of the other agitators. Mr. and Mrs. Hobbes and Miss Dickey, a spinster, work hard for the formation of a society to aid a fugitive slave, but are also the only people in town who refuse to help a poor local widow (pp. 41, 49). Later, because he fears possible antiabolition reaction, Mr. Hobbes refuses to pick up the fugitive at the railroad station. After a nasty argument between Hobbes and his wife revealing the depth of their selfishness, she has to perform the task her cowardly husband fears (pp. 112–113).

Caesar, the willing agent of the would-be amalgamation, is also subject to the author's wrath. Introduced when Mrs. Hobbes picks him up, to win her sympathy the fugitive immediately begins relating false tales of his suffering as a slave (p. 117). He continues deliberately lying to the townspeople for his own advantage (p. 137) and prepares to go on a hopefully lucrative tour, presenting a sensational, but totally false, antislavery lecture written by a white abolitionist (pp. 206–208). Caesar differs significantly from the black stereotypes generally presented by earlier Southern writers. He contains elements of evil, cunning, and lust which foreshadow the black monsters of Thomas Dixon. Caesar lies constantly, refuses to work because he is "free" (p. 141), and generally behaves grossly and obnoxiously (p. 143). The depths of his villainy are sounded at the conclusion when we learn that Mary, the Hobbes' adopted daughter, had been stolen years before as a child from her parents' Southern plantation by Caesar, who sold the infant to a couple headed North (p. 256).

The author clearly indicates that the intended miscegenation is highly unnatural. Mary in no way desires the match and abhors Caesar; her foster parents have decided to compel the marriage for selfish reasons. Hobbes has political ambitions and feels that marrying his adopted daughter to a black will endear him to the growing number of abolitionists (p. 166). The only character in the novel, besides the lecherous Caesar, who seems honestly to believe in miscegenation, is the rather demented Miss Dickey, who wants to crown Caesar with a wreath of white and black roses "to intimate . . . the future amalgamation of the races!" (p. 105) Miss Dickey's nephew remarks that if they really wanted someone willing to marry the black, they should have asked her (p. 180). In short, Flanders argues that miscegenation results from black lust, Yankee unscrupulousness, and the confused erotic desires of loveless old women.

The Ebony Idol merits some attention for its significant treatment of miscegenation on the symbolic level. In an important

adumbration of post-Reconstruction novels, Mrs. Flanders introduces to the literature of miscegenation what W. J. Cash
calls "the Southern rape complex."[8] This complex identifies the
South with Southern womanhood, so that the rape of a Southern woman symbolizes the rape of the South. Even though
raised in New England, Mary is by birth a Southern lady and
as such is far superior to the other girls of Minden—"delicate,
kind, generous and intelligent" (p. 204). The author stresses
that all these valuable assets are purely hereditary. Mary not
only symbolizes the South, she also personifies the South's natural, hereditary superiority to the North, where people are
oblivious to the importance of aristocratic breeding. On the
very eve of war, the air abounding with constant talk of the
coming strife, the symbolism of Mary's impending forced marriage (rape) is clear. Just as she must marry a black against
her will, so also is the North going to force the loosening of the
blacks' depravity, symbolized in Caesar, upon the South.

Yet, with war looming darker overhead every day, Flanders
sees one last shaft of light. The good people of the North can
still reject those leaders of the attack on the South and its
institutions—the misguided idealists, suggested by Cary, and
the unscrupulous, self-seeking politicians like Hobbes. Symbolically, the light of truth and peace breaks forth in the novel
when the sensible people of the town revolt against the idea of
the forced marriage. They seize Hobbes, tar and feather him
and make him renounce forever the doctrine of amalgamation
(pp. 220–221). Cary's punishment is suitably milder; he loses
his congregation (p. 235). Mary weds a young Southern gentleman conveniently staying in Minden, and all ends well for those
on the side of slavery, racial purity, and general good sense.
But in reality, racial purity did not exist, slavery was not good
sense, and Mrs. Flanders' vision proved faulty. The fury of the
storm that burst swept away forever the Old South and the
"peculiar institution" on which it was based.

The fictive vision of novelists opposing slavery was not always very accurate either, yet it managed to sway the mass of
popular feeling in the literary battles preceding the military
ones. Unlike the proslavery forces, who generally avoided the

subject of miscegenation, the abolitionist writers used it as a major piece of heavy artillery in their attack. The basic ammunition was the sorrowful story of a tragic mulatto, ironically a character prefigured by the proslavery Mrs. Southworth's pitiful Minny in *Retribution*. The tragic mulattoes, near-white heroes and heroines, are the offspring of a white father and mulatto mistress; they are of superior beauty; suffering and degradation are heaped upon them, but the indomitable spirit of the white father rises in revolt. As Sterling Brown points out, in Mrs. Stowe's novels the proud, adventurous, nonsubmissives are mulattoes: Eliza and George Harris, Cassy, Harry Gordon. There is, however, at least one major difference, according to Brown, between the stereotyping of Northern novelists and that of Southern writers:

Where proslavery authors had predicted a different set of characteristics for the Negro, a distinctive sub-human nature, and had stereotyped in accordance with such a comforting hypothesis antislavery authors insisted that the Negro had a common humanity with the whites, that in given circumstances a typically human type of response was to be expected.... The stereotyping in abolitionary literature, therefore[,] is not stereotyping of *character*, but of *situation*.[9]

Actually, however, stereotyping of character is found as well as stereotyping of situation. Nonstereotypic characters in stereotyped situations occur only in the best of the antislavery novels, as Richard Beale Davis points out in commenting on Mrs. Stowe's work.[10] In the flood of lesser books, the character of the tragic mulatto is often as strong a stereotype as is the plantation darky of the proslavery novels.[11]

There are several theories for the immense popularity of the tragic mulatto in antislavery literature. John Herbert Nelson sees the attempt to appeal to a common humanity as the reason for the extensive use of the tragic mulatto, a bit of reverse racism anchored in the idea that a nearly white person enslaved was more pitiable than a pure African similarly situated.[12] Nelson's rationale has been generally accepted by the critics following him, including Brown and Berzon. Brown adds the possibility that because of Victorian gentility the abolitionist writers were wary of dealing directly with the practice of concubinage and made use, instead, of the offspring of illicit unions to make their point about sexual exploitation of slaves.[13] This conclusion hardly seems tenable, given the large number of antislavery novels which very explicitly present the practice of concubinage itself. Jules Zanger offers a reader-centered, rhetorical analysis of the tragic mulatto's popularity that I summarize here before discussing the antislavery novels which employ this stereotype.[14]

According to Zanger, by far the most popular of the tragic-mulatto type in abolitionist fiction is the "tragic octoroon," a character possessing certain stereotypic qualities and appearing in certain stereotypic situations. She is a young, beautiful girl having only a trace of "black blood," who was raised and educated as a white lady in her father's household. Her condition radically changes when her father dies unexpectedly, and it is revealed that she is a slave whom he neglected to free properly. Sold into slavery to pay her father's creditors, she is victimized by a low-class slave dealer, or Yankee overseer, who tries to rape her; she is loved by a young Northerner or European who wishes to marry her. Occasionally she escapes to a happy marriage; more often she dies tragically. Her relationship to the conventional ingenue "victim" of sentimental romance made her a perfect object for sympathy and moral indignation for Northern readers accustomed to idealized and sentimentalized heroines. Noting that modern critics have attacked the stereotyped figure of the tragic octoroon, Zanger points out that they have failed to consider, and give credit to, the effectiveness of the quadroon in serving the basic rhetorical purposes of the writers. He refutes Nelson's idea that the appeal is based solely on racial snobbishness, although this is a part, and explains that the plight of the octoroon evoked a variety of responses from Northern audiences. Zanger's four main points follow.

The tragic octoroon primarily appeals to the Northern readers' sense of moral superiority. The South could always answer attacks on slavery with accusations about sweat shops, but had no counter-attack for the purely Southern tragic-octoroon situation. It is an attack primarily on the slave owner rather than on slavery. The charge of sexual looseness was very serious in this period, and the existence of an octoroon provides living proof of the sinfulness of three generations of whites. Another appeal to a sense of moral superiority lies in the tragic octoroon's being threatened by a would-be rapist, usually a Yankee. Critics have traditionally maintained that the evil Yankee overseer is meant to appease the South in hopes of reconciliation. Zanger believes that while the use of the Yankee overseer may, in part, have been intended to soothe Southern readers, that detail also had a propaganda effect in the North. Identifying the most detestable character in the novel as a Yankee suggests that Northern moral superiority is shared only by antislavery Northerners: a Yankee who accepts the idea of slavery becomes worse than a Southern slave owner; he becomes a Simon Legree.

The use of the brutal overseer in tragic-octoroon plots serves another rhetorical purpose. The popular literature of the day relied on aristocratic and sentimentalized heroes and heroines. The Southern Gentleman and his Lady were accepted as an ideal. Use of the overseer showed that even the conventional, noble and kind master of proslavery literature was helpless to protect his slaves, even his slave daughters, because they were property and, as such, could be attached for debt and sold to the worst slave driver. Thus the reading public can maintain its beau ideal but see his irrelevance to the moral question of slavery as a legal institution.

Finally, an important appeal to Northern readers lay in the sudden, horrible reversal of the tragic octoroon's fortunes. On the imaginative level this presented a real threat to the reader. The audience for these novels was largely middle-class and female, women almost literally as dependent upon the head of the household as the octoroon was upon her master/father. The antislavery propagandist worked upon the readers' own dread of the life they would lead if something unexpected, such as a bank failure or a foolish speculation, destroyed their provider. Zanger thus attributes the tremendous popularity of the tragic octoroon to the effectiveness of this figure as a multilevel rhetorical device.

Although the tragic octoroon figure constitutes the most pop-

ular form miscegenation takes in antislavery novels, not all
the authors used it or relied solely upon it. Of those who did,
some emphasized different aspects of the stereotype for different rhetorical purposes. All the novels shared the basic purpose
of attacking slavery, but some used miscegenation for the specific point of advocating colonization, others for attacking the
Fugitive Slave Act, or some for condemning slavery primarily
because it encouraged miscegenation. Each of the novels selected for extensive discussion from the group of abolitionary
novels published between 1850 and 1865 illustrates a different
aspect of the many-pronged attack. We have seen that among
Northern writers using miscegenation, the propaganda assault
on slavery was present from the beginning; in the 1850s the
assault move into high gear. Leading the charge, and by far
the most impressive of these abundant antislavery novels, is
Harriet Beecher Stowe's *Uncle Tom's Cabin* (1852).[15]

Because of the novel's moral didacticism and homiletic tone,
Vernon L. Parrington long ago called Mrs. Stowe a preacher.[16]
Severn Duvall suggests that her homily preaches the error of
Southerners who defend slavery as a patriarchal system.[17] *Uncle Tom's Cabin* actually presents slavery as the antithesis of
a patriarchal system, showing that slavery destroyed families—black ones through sale and separation, white ones indirectly through miscegenation. Miscegenation plays a
secondary role, but the subject is handled here better than in
most antislavery works, giving the novel a key place in the
history of miscegenation in American fiction.

Although introduced early (p. 15), referred to throughout,
and used to provide material for the conclusion, miscegenation
does not play an intrinsic structural role in the main plot of
Uncle Tom's Cabin. The principal actions of the story are the
parallel but opposite journeys of Tom southward to a slave's
death and of George and Eliza northward to freedom and a new
life. These main strands of action are generated, not by miscegenation, but by the primary theme, the separation of families. Tom's journey begins when he is separated from Aunt
Chloe and his children; George and Eliza's begins when she
refuses to be separated from her son, Harry, and flees. Although
Cassy, Simon Legree's mulatto mistress, the mulatto girl Em-

maline, and their situation are important toward the end of
the novel, they are in no way causal factors in Tom's suffering
and death. Cassy's link to the main action is more coincidental
than anything else; she happens to be present on the plantation
where Tom ends his days, and she happens (rather unbeliev-
ably) to be Eliza's mother.

Although not a significant factor in the main plot, miscegenation holds thematic importance in the book. Cassy and her
story serve as a shocking subplot to drive home the point of
the main action—the horror of the separation of families. Not
only are Cassy's children taken from her, they are used to force
her submission to the sexual desires of a man she detests (p.
374). The terrible separation of Tom from his family, or that
of little Harry from Eliza, for the money necessary to maintain
the Shelby home pales by comparison to the callous brutality
of a man who would forcibly separate a mother from her children in order to fulfill his licentiousness, and the degradation
of the legal system allowing this horror is held up for illumi-
nation. The full tragedy comes to fruition when Cassy later
bears another child by a man who loves and is kind to her, but
she murders the infant with laudanum and tells Tom "it is one
of the few things that I'm glad of now" (p. 375). The subsequent
sexual exploitation of Cassy by Simon Legree is, in the context
of what she has already suffered, merely a minor evil possible
under the slave system.

The three important mulatto figures, Cassy, George and Eliza
Harris, are all representative of the tragic-mulatto type, with
the characterizations of George and Eliza more heavily dependent on the stereotype than that of Cassy. George, like
Archy Moore, has inherited from his white father intelligence
and "a high, indomitable spirit" (p. 114). It is this spirit that
drives him to rebellion. He does, however, encompass more
than just the stereotypic qualities. He expresses concern with
the problem of the black person as an individual, asking who
he is and what has made him this way, questions which will
recur and dominate much of twentieth-century fiction.[18] Moreover, at the very end of the novel George expresses an idea
that is to be developed by later black writers: that the mulatto
should not seek to pass or integrate, but should identify with

the black race and work for its betterment—to his father he was "no more than a fine dog or horse; to my poor, heartbroken mother I was a child" (p. 444). Eliza suggests the female variety of tragic mulatto; the novel opens with the slave trader's attempt to purchase her for the New Orleans market (p. 8). But, unlike most of her fictional sisters who show courage only at the raping point when they take their death-before-dishonor stand, Eliza does not passively allow herself or her family to be trucked around like so much baggage, nor does she run off to the woods at the edge of the plantation and there wait patiently to be recaptured. In the face of danger to her child, she rises to meet it in heroic fashion, leaping the ice floes of the Ohio to safety.

Cassy, although caught in the classic situation of the tragic octoroon, breaks completely free of the mold. Educated in a convent as her white father's legitimate daughter, she discovers after his funeral that she is a slave, that he had intended to free her but had neglected to do so. She is purchased by a young planter whom she loves passionately and by whom she has two children. After seven years of happiness, the young man is led astray by his cousin, who takes possession of Cassy and her children to cancel her lover's gambling debt. The cousin had carefully planned the sequence of events leading to the forced sale so that he might possess Cassy himself. This is the wretch who uses Cassy's children as a club to force her submission. One day, seeing her son being beaten and being unable to help him, Cassy attempts to murder the man responsible. For this she is sold again, this time to Captain Stuart, who treats her kindly and by whom she has the child that she kills. After Stuart's death she is sold again, eventually winding up as the mistress of Simon Legree (pp. 371–375).

Cassy serves the propaganda purposes of the tragic octoroon as outlined by Zanger, but she is leagues apart from the fainting, sentimental creatures, concerned only with preserving their virginity, who ordinarily fill the role. Edmund Wilson has compared Mrs. Stowe's *Uncle Tom's Cabin* to what Zola was soon to do,[19] and in the character of Cassy we can see a mastery of realism. Her world view is, above all, realistic. She submits to force, both the moral force of the threat to her children and the physical force of Legree, when there is no alternative, but she is pragmatic, not cowardly. When she sees that her submission does not protect her children, she tries to murder her hated owner (p. 375). Having learned the harsh lesson of the fate in store for slave children, she courageously kills her infant son to protect him from that fate (p. 375). In this and other actions we see her as a believable human being, a product of her experiences. The horror of her life has beaten her down; she is a drunkard and has streaks of insanity (p. 379). She has become brutalized: when she first talks of Emmaline she says, "and now, he's got a new one,—a young thing, only fifteen, and she brought up, she says, piously. Her good mistress taught her to read the Bible; and she brought her Bible here—to hell with her!" (p. 369), concluding that there is no God, "there's nothing here, but sin and long, long, long despair!" (p. 371) Later, Cassy advises Emmaline to submit to Legree and to deaden herself with drink as she has done (p. 386).

Despite her degradation, the old vitality, the old courage is not completely dead in Cassy. It is reawakened by the example of Tom's strength. Quite realistically, when Cassy decides once again to act, her first thought is to murder Legree (p. 406). When Tom convinces her to take Emmaline and flee instead, Cassy shows ingenuity and resourcefulness in devising the scheme for their escape, playing on Legree's fear of the garret and avenging herself by driving him to drink and the edge of insanity (p. 435). Cassy, the most artistically developed of the tragic octoroons, becomes a living character of great power and truth.

As developed in the character of Cassy, the theme of miscegenation serves the purpose of reinforcing the separation-of-families theme in the main plot, but it also develops to some extent the mulatto as a symbol of alienation. George Harris' questioning about identity introduces the idea, and it recurs about half-way through the book in the character of Rosa, the near-white maid in the St. Clair household. Rosa is unpopular with the other servants and one attacks her, saying, "you seem to tink yourself white folks. You an't nerry one, black *nor* white, I'd like to be one or turrer" (p. 245). Cassy, however, is the clearest symbol in *Uncle Tom's Cabin* of alienation. As a beautiful, aristocratic woman of education and refinement she belongs to the world of the white ruling class, but she is rejected by that world because of her black ancestry. At the same time her refinement keeps her outside the world of the black slave class to which she belongs by law. When she is sent to the fields one day by Legree, the black hands exult in her punishment and hope to see her flogged (p. 360). Her refinement, moreover, isolates her from Legree, a crude and brutal man. In her isolation she has turned inward, to drink and borderline insanity. Only establishing a link to another human being, at first with Tom and then with Emmaline, saves Cassy. She symbolizes both the destructive suffering of, and the only way to salvation for, man alone. It has been said that the black character in American literature has reversed itself from the stereotype of the plantation darky to the archetype of suffering, alienated man in the best works of the twentieth century.[20] The roots of this reversal are found in Hildreth's Archy Moore, but the first growth is in Mrs. Stowe's Cassy, and the first budding is found in her character Harry Gordon in *Dred*.

Uncle Tom's Cabin is important in the history of American novels about miscegenation not simply because it presents a more artistic handling of the materials than its contemporaries but because it provides the definite beginning of a literary tradition. Richard Beale Davis points out that there is a continuation of the plantation tradition in popular literature from Kennedy's *Swallow Barn* to Margaret Mitchell's *Gone With the Wind*, but that Mrs. Stowe, using the same or similar scenes and characters, enlarged "the dimensions of the form, particularly on its darker and moral side." He traces the development of the patterns set by Mrs. Stowe, including miscegenation, through Twain and Cable to the Southern Renaissance in the twentieth-century works of Paul Green, Erskine Caldwell, Lillian Smith and, particularly, Faulkner and Warren.[21] This germinal role of *Uncle Tom's Cabin* in the treatment of miscegenation by American novelists is forcefully stated by Severn Duvall:

Certainly no modern reader of *The Grandissimes* and *Madame Delphine*, of *Light in August, Absalom, Absalom!*, and *Go Down, Moses* can escape the conclusion that miscegenation is still a crucial theme, or that the patriarchal legend still establishes its ironic patterns through the collateral genealogy of black and white.... Other writers, far more talented and much closer to the scene, have taken up the themes of Mrs. Stowe. But however lurid and glaring it may seem to the sophisticate of today, however crude its appeal, *Uncle Tom's Cabin* still knifes to the heart of the matter.[22]

Even more significant in the development of the miscegenation theme is Harriet Beecher Stowe's *Dred; A Tale of the Great Dismal Swamp* (1856).[23] In comparing this work to *Uncle Tom's Cabin*, Gaines notes a greater consciousness of the tragedy of mixed blood in *Dred*.[24] The story primarily concerns Harry Gordon, the mulatto half-brother and slave of Nina and Tom Gordon. Harry works to preserve the plantation for his beloved sister Nina, but after her death it falls to their degenerate brother Tom, who hates Harry and attempts to destroy him. Harry and his mulatto wife Lisette are forced to flee to the Great Swamp and the protection of Dred, a mystic black who preaches revolution and is modelled on Nat Turner.[25] Eventually, Dred is killed, the other fugitives decide to flee rather than fight, and they escape to freedom in the North. Throughout his struggle, Harry is aided by Clayton, the fiancé of Nina. The theme of miscegenation exists in the parallel branches of the Gordon family: the mulattoes Harry and his sister Cora, and the white Tom and Nina. Nina is unaware of her relationship to Harry, but both he and Tom know. Nina serves as a control over Tom, preventing his worst excesses (I, 179), but after her death the novel resolves to its essential structure: the struggle between good and evil, symbolized by Harry and Tom respectively. This conflict is further symbolized in sexual terms by Tom's miscegenetic desire to possess Harry's wife (I, 172–173, 179; II, 262).

Tom, the representative of evil, is supported in his depravity by the legal system of the slave states, and this legal system becomes the primary object of attack for the novel's rhetoric. In a subplot involving the mulatto Cora and her white husband, the legal system allows Tom to reach out as far away as Mississippi to have her seized as a slave after her husband's death

(II, 88, 203). The totality of evil involved strikes us when Cora, like Cassy in *Uncle Tom's Cabin*, kills her children to prevent their becoming slaves (II, 205). The legal system also supports evil when it usurps the will of Harry's dead father by holding the slave's free papers to be worthless (II, 139). Moreover, the system forces an essentially good man, Clayton's father, into a morally reprehensible judgment because he is sworn to uphold the law. Because the law continually supports evil, Clayton separates himself from it by resigning from the bar. That Southern law supports evil is made clear through the lawyer Jekyl, Tom's constant companion and advisor in all his nefarious schemes.

Following Nina's death, the novel polarizes between the forces of good and the forces of evil when the struggle reduces to the Great Dismal Swamp versus the plantation house. The representatives of virtue, a racially mixed group composed of Dred, Harry and Lisette, Clayton, the old black Tiff and the two white children he cares for, all gather in the swamp, where they are hunted by Tom, Jekyl and others who are based in the manor house (II, 288).[26] The novel, then, is a classic example of the battle of good and evil represented by two characters, intensified by the fact that they, like Cain and Abel, are also brothers. Notably, as in *Othello* or *Benito Cereno*, the traditional symbolic values of black and white have been reversed. But the theme of good and evil and the rhetorical attack on the legal system of the slave states should not overshadow our concern about the historical development of American miscegenation novels. Severn Duvall sees in *Dred* a reversal from the dramatic emphasis on black Uncle Tom in Mrs. Stowe's first novel, to a consideration of the psychological complications of miscegenation.[27] This concern is largely worked out in the character of Harry Gordon.

As in *Uncle Tom's Cabin*, the characters in *Dred* often rise above being mere stereotypes. Like Sam in the earlier novel, Tom Gordon's slave Jim is used to show the falsity of the white conception of blacks. Jim's buffoonery and incompetence fit the image whites created of their slaves, but in reality these behaviors serve to cover his aid to the fugitives in the swamp (II, 307). Dred, as Edmund Wilson points out, represents Old Testament wrath in contrast to the Christlike figure of Uncle Tom.[28] Actually, Dred's stern righteousness is superseded by the New Testament spirit of love, of moderation, seen in Clayton, Tiff and Lisette. Harry is torn between the two. Dred appears to him in times of trouble like a beckoning dark angel, calling to the hatred and revenge lying deep in Harry (I, 242, 329). Harry's dilemma is that of the divided heart, of being torn between his innate goodness and the sense of decency, justice and Christian love given him by his white training, and the hatred engendered in him by his treatment as a black slave. This inner conflict is symbolized in his sense of alienation, of not totally being one thing or another, of not feeling that he belongs anywhere:

I'm just like the bat in the fable; I'm neither bird nor beast. How often I've wished that I was a good, honest, black nigger, like Uncle Pomp! (I, 76)

Mrs. Stowe, posing this dilemma, created characters, first George Harris and Cassy and then Harry Gordon, who know the terrible anxiety of alienation, who wander in the existential wilderness of knowing one's real isolation from our fellow humans. Having posed the dilemma, however, Mrs. Stowe fails to face it very bravely. Being a good Christian, she believes in heaven and brings little pieces of it to earth to solve her problems. For George, Eliza and Cassy heaven comes in the form of Liberia, for Harry and Lisette it is Canada. From the moment the decision is made to flee the swamp (II, 302), Harry and his wife drop into the background; eventually they are dismissed with a single line telling how well they prospered on the settlement Clayton establishes in Canada (II, 331). Harry had resolved nothing before slipping from view; we are to believe his problems are dissolved by the simple expediency of moving him to Canada. Mrs. Stowe fails to fulfill what she began, but she does begin something. The relationship between miscegenation and the theme of alienation is continued in the American novel by George Washington Cable, Charles Waddell Chesnutt, James Weldon Johnson, William Faulkner, Robert Penn Warren and such recent authors as James Baldwin, William Styron, and Ralph Ellison.

One of the few novels of miscegenation in which the question of where the mulatto belongs is never raised, even implicitly, is Mayne Reid's *The Quadroon: or, A Lover's Adventures in Louisiana* (1856),[29] published the same year as *Dred*. Born in Ireland, at twenty Thomas Mayne Reid traveled to New Orleans and worked his way northwest as a hunter, trapper, and Indian trader. Later he spent three years as a literary acquaintance of Edgar Allan Poe in Philadelphia, fought and was wounded in the Mexican War, and compiled an output of nearly seventy novels and romances before his death in 1883 in England. In Reid's one antislavery novel, the mulatto Aurore knows her slave status and accepts her position. Her education and the nature of her relationship with her mistress Eugénie Besançon, however, fully qualify her to live as the wife of the young Englishman who loves her, and eventually Aurore moves easily into that role. The complications of the plot arise from external barriers keeping the lovers apart.

The novel argues the rhetorical point that bankruptcy and debt can force the sale of slaves despite the best intentions of their owner, a fictional situation popular in antislavery novels and true to the actual economic life of plantations.[30] The narrator-hero, a young Englishman, rescues Eugénie in a steamboat and becomes her guest. He meets Eugénie's maid and close companion Aurore with whom he falls in love, but complications exist because Eugénie is in love with him. Eugénie loses the plantation through the deliberate mismanagement of her lawyer, Gayarre, who purchases Aurore for himself despite the narrator's efforts to prevent it. But putting her own feelings aside, Eugénie aids the narrator in rescuing Aurore and, after establishing ownership, frees her so the quadroon and the Englishman can marry.

The plot of the novel develops from the desirability of the quadroon Aurore. Eugénie mistakes the narrator's intentions because he visits her frequently for an excuse to be near the beautiful slave (p. 123). Gayarre brings about the loss of Eugénie's estate because it is the only way he can obtain Aurore for himself (p. 141). A subplot involving miscegenation also parallels to some extent the main action. A slave named Scipio had expressed his fears to the narrator that the overseer Larkin wanted his daughter Chloe (p. 117). Just after interrupting Gayarre as the lawyer suggests to Aurore that she become his concubine (p. 141), the narrator interrupts the beating of Scipio by the overseer hired by Gayarre (p. 158). Scipio had discovered Larkin trying to rape Chloe and had attacked him (p. 162). Gayarre in the drawing room relies on words, while his overseer in the slave quarters uses a club, but miscegenation forced in either manner is harshly condemned. The narrator confronts each man in his own style, driving Gayarre verbally from the room (p. 143) and knocking Larkin unconscious (p. 160).

This defender of mulatto womanhood expresses an interesting attitude toward miscegenation. Unlike the lover of a tragic octoroon who ordinarily becomes enamored of her while ignorant of his beloved's background, the narrator here is fully aware of Aurore's heritage and status, yet proclaims, "What was it to me? Why should I care for customs and conventionalities which I at heart despised?" (p. 104) He pursues his aims in secret, thus allowing Eugénie's misjudgment, only because he fears the greater difficulty of achieving his desire if others were to discover it. When Aurore confronts him with the legal fact that they cannot marry in Louisiana, he declares he will nick her and suck her blood so that he can swear that he, too, has African blood in his veins (p. 148). The novel is unique because both parties to a voluntary miscegenetic affair are aware of the situation. The usual approach is to have the truth revealed only after the attachment has been formed, leading to an inner conflict for one or both of the people involved. In *The Quadroon* the problems are all external and straight-forward— for example, how to raise money for Aurore's purchase or how to effect her escape. Eugénie's mistaken love and the possibility of jealousy toward her slave rival are elements which would lend themselves to significant development, but which fail to achieve this because of the point of view used. Through the first-person narrator we can only see Eugénie's actions, and never experience her thoughts and emotional conflicts. Thus she becomes a one-dimensional figure of unbelievable selflessness, rather than the woman struggling with herself that she might have been. *The Quadroon* is perhaps most significant because it deals extensively with the taboo of miscegenation without occasioning any psychic conflict in its characters.

The problem of inner conflict between love and rejection of miscegenation is an important element in *Neighbor Jackwood* (1857),[31] by John T. Trowbridge. At twenty-one, John Townsend Trowbridge left New York for the literary center of Boston, where he became a full-time writer, well-known for his popular boys' stories. Published under the pseudonym Paul Creyton, which Trowbridge later dropped, *Neighbor Jackwood* is a propaganda attack on the Fugitive Slave Law. The mulatto heroine, Charlotte Woods, has escaped to Vermont, and the plot revolves around her attempts to avoid exposure and seizure as a fugitive slave. To the rhetorical appeal of the poor fugitive has been added the considerable appeal of the tragic octoroon—even the minister who had preached against harboring fugitives in defiance of law is struck by her helpless beauty and undergoes a conversion (p. 328). Charlotte's tragic-octoroon story of sudden slave status, sale, attempted rape, and final escape is told in a flashback (pp. 360–374), but the main plot also depends on miscegenation. Throughout most of the novel, the other characters know nothing of her background except for one man who constantly uses his knowledge as a threat, trying to force her sexual submission, until she flees the safety of the Jackwood's home for Canada (p. 184). The miscegenetic love affair between Charlotte and Hector Dunberry, a neighbor of Jackwood's, forms another essential element of the plot. The interest in this relationship heightens when she refuses Hector's proposal, referring to a mysterious "gulf" between them (p. 109). When the affair has progressed to a point demanding some kind of consummation, Charlotte tells Hector the truth and he temporarily rejects her (p. 166). The resolution comes when Hector finally does marry her, goes South, purchases her freedom and returns in time to prevent her being taken away as a fugitive.

Except for her stereotypic death-before-dishonor stances (pp. 369, 373, 388), Charlotte's characterization does not depend much on the tragic octoroon. Throughout most of the novel, the reader knows nothing about her background, and finds her an agreeable, resourceful character rather than a typic figure. The

author's attitude toward miscegenation seems quite approba-
tory; when Hector finally rescues her and announces their marriage, the narrator exclaims "and she, who was so late a thing,
a slave, a chattel, rode out of the jubilant throng *a soul, a
woman, a wife loving and beloved*" (p. 397, italics in original).
Although approving the miscegenation, Trowbridge deals with
the human problems of inner conflict and family dispute which
arise. Hector agonizes through the night following Charlotte's
revelation and flees, rejecting her, when he cannot face the truth
(p. 166). Later, when he has come to terms with himself, seeks
her in Canada, and marries her, he has to face the anger and
rejection of his father (p. 263).

The main thrust of the novel is not, however, so much toward
problems in human relationships as it is an attack on political
ones—the institution of slavery and particularly the Fugitive
Slave Law. In the end, it is a story of how the good Northern
people rally one by one behind Charlotte in her battle with the
despicable slave catchers. *Neighbor Jackwood* demonstrates
the successful adaptation of the tragic-octoroon motif to a setting and rhetorical purpose other than the standard Southern
plantation and general attack on the evils of slavery in the
South. By locating the action in New England and forcing a
spectrum of Northern characters to cope with their individual
moral dilemmas created by the Fugitive Slave Act, Trowbridge
plays effectively on the popular sentiment that had been growing steadily for seven years in the North against the hated law,
a sentiment that had been further inflamed by the Dred Scott
case of the same year in which the novel was published.

The most fully developed example of the tragic-octoroon situation, H. L. Hosmer's *Adela, The Octoroon* (1860),[32] also has
a particular rhetorical point to make. Hezekiah Lord Hosmer
emigrated from upstate New York to Toledo, Ohio, where he
settled as editor of the *Toledo Blade* in 1844. In 1860, he em-
braced Lincoln and the Republicans, and published his only
novel, from which Dion Boucicault is said to have taken part
of the plot for his famous play, *The Quadroon*. In Hosmer's
novel, Adela's father dies, leaving her at eighteen in possession
of the plantation. She has two suitors, evil Henry Westover,
whom she despises, and honorable Frank Thornton, whom she

finds attractive. She attempts to manage the plantation for the benefit of the slaves, freeing many, but an old debt brings court action, revealing that Adela is herself an octoroon slave, and she is sold to the corrupt Henry Westover. Helped to escape by a slave uprising, she flees to California and there marries Thornton. The point of the novel is not only that slavery is wrong, but that blacks simply cannot live in a white society. The strongest subplots deal with two groups of slaves freed from Adela's plantation. One group tries to live in the North and suffers continuously (pp. 61, 270ff., 361). The other group travels to Liberia where they find acceptance (p. 237), intellectual achievement (pp. 242–243), true Christianity (p. 250), fame (p. 295) and lasting happiness (p. 383). This polemic emphasizes colonization as the only real solution to the problems of slavery.

Structurally, miscegenation underlies the whole of the main plot. Westover discovers the secret of Adela's status and uses it to bring about her downfall so that he may possess her sexually (p. 201). Several other major incidents involve miscegenation and indicate two different ways in which the slave system brings about evil consequences. Tragedy results from the actions of George Tibald, a neighboring planter, who forces himself on slave mistresses. He sells one of his daughters over the protest of her mother (p. 45), who later kills herself (p. 78). We also learn that Tibald has had a baby by one of his slave daughters, who then died of shame and sadness, taking her child with her (p. 318). Once again, the shock value of miscegenation has been augmented by connecting it with incest. Juxtaposed to this tragic story of incest is the account of Zilpha, another beautiful slave sold by Tibald in New Orleans, who is frustrated because she is *not* being used sexually: "She knew that she could in no other way shake off the thraldom, and avoid the drudgery incident to her condition; and it was from a desire for freedom, that she was willing to submit to the degrading penalty, by which alone, it could be obtained. To find herself installed as a chambermaid only, when she expected to be mistress, was a great disappointment" (p. 311). Accordingly, Zilpha makes herself obnoxious enough to be resold and this time is successful in becoming a concubine (p. 313). The narrator wonders if any beautiful slave has the moral courage to resist the path Zilpha chooses (p. 315).

In addition to driving the action of the novel, miscegenation plays a role in characterization. Adela is quite stereotypic; she has nothing much to individualize her, and she has her best scene facing Westover, dagger in hand, proclaiming death before dishonor in the best tradition of tragic octoroons. Tibald's characterization is also affected by the theme of miscegenation. In some ways he is not a totally evil man; he gives Adela extensive help with her legal problems before he learns the truth about her heritage (p. 282). Tibald, however, suggests the dehumanizing effects of slavery on the class of owners. The totality of power, in his case the power to fulfill his sexual desires, corrupts and destroys. The author opposes miscegenation within the slave system rather than the practice per se. Tragedy flows from forced relations and corruption from voluntary ones, which are voluntary only to the extent that the alternative is a life of drudgery. But the miscegenetic marriage of Adela and Frank Thornton creates a happy resolution for the plot.

In its only approach to literary art, the novel provides the high irony of Tibald's throwing Frank Thornton out of his home because Tibald "will have nothing to do with a man who seeks to wed a slave" (p. 373). Aside from this one bright spot, the novel is pedestrian, highly propagandistic, and important mainly as the most extensively developed example of the tragic-octoroon motif, with the whole novel instead of just a brief section devoted to the evolution of the standard events in the life of a tragic octoroon.

If Hosmer's *Adela* addresses the dehumanizing effects of slavery on owners, the next novel presents the attempts of white owners to dehumanize black slaves. Mrs. Metta Victoria Victor was already well known as a New York temperance novelist when she married Orville James Victor, the creator of the "Beadle's Dime Novels" series. Her *Maum Guinea, and Her Plantation "Children"* (1861),[33] was one of the most successful dime novels ever, selling more than 100,000 copies in this country alone. Set in the South, the novel attacks slavery, but with emphasis on something more basic and common to the North as well as to the South—white indifference to black humanity.

Essentially the story involves Philip Fairfax, his fiancée Virginia Bell, their respective servants Hyperion and Rose, and Maum Guinea, the cook on the Fairfax plantation. Philip and Virginia are to wed, and Hyperion and Rose wish to be married on the same day. Before this can happen, however, Virginia's father agrees to sell Rose to satisfy a debt, and her new owner, Mr. Talfierro, intends to make her his mistress. To avoid this, the young slaves flee in the company of their confidante, Maum. The situation is resolved when Captain Slocum, the white husband of Maum's quadroon daughter Judy, arrives to purchase Maum. The fugitives return to a happy ending with both marriages taking place and Maum's removing to New York to live with her daughter and Slocum.

Basically, the novel compares love relationships between the planters with those between the slaves, like the parallel wedding plans of Philip and Virginia and of Hyperion and Rose. Subplots are introduced through the device of the slaves gathering in Maum's cabin to tell stories about themselves, and in the most important stories the parallel between the planters and slaves is maintained. Sophy tells the tale of losing her children by having them sold away from her, and of her husband's later murdering their owner's children during Nat Turner's rebellion. Maum's story relates her life with her husband Jackson, comparing it to the marriage of Dudley Gregory, her first owner, by whom she had her daughter Judy.

In both the main plot and the slaves' stories the point is identical: whites fail to understand that blacks share the same human feelings. Philip and Virginia readily accept the necessity for the sale of Rose. Philip tells Hyperion that he will find another girl and should not worry about it, never realizing that his slave could feel about Rose the way he feels about Virginia (p. 78). The lack of feeling allows the sale of Rose despite her love for Hyperion and brings miscegenation into the main plot through the relationship Talfierro expects to force on her. We learn that miscegenation is even more involved when we discover that Hyperion is Colonel Fairfax's son and Philip's half-brother (p. 131), which also reveals the full degree of white insensitivity.

The most rhetorically effective story is that of Maum at age sixteen and of her affair with Dudley. The happiness she felt in being with Dudley and later in the birth of their child (pp. 145–146) explodes because of Dudley's white inability to conceive of her capacity for human feelings. For several months after the baby is born, he simply ignores them both. When Dudley accidentally encounters her and the child, he remarks that the baby is "good property" and will "sell for a t'ousand dollars by the time you're ready to wean it," and laughs as he walks away (p. 147). Maum fears greatly for her baby, but, significantly, she also says of the incident that "I loved young massa—loved him jus' as well as w'ite folks love—mighty sight better dan de most. I 'dored the very yearth he trod on—and it broke my heart to hab him speak so to me" (p. 148). Deeply hurt by the rejection of her love, Maum seeks revenge when Dudley marries a young white woman. While perhaps incredible that a slave would dare such an affront to her master, Maum's method of revenge is believably human. All the servants are assembled to meet the new mistress. As she passes Maum and Judy, Dudley's bride stops to comment on the beauty of the little girl and asks Maum if she is hers. Maum replies, "Yes, mine and Massa Dudley's" (p. 151). This indiscretion provokes in Mrs. Gregory a violent and undying jealousy, which she attempts to satisfy when Judy reaches fifteen by selling her to a man desiring a mistress. But Maum and Judy manage to flee on the ship of the sympathetic Captain Slocum instead. Maum is recaptured and knows nothing of her daughter's fate until Slocum arrives at the end to resolve all difficulties.

In her depiction of Judy's marriage and of Maum's love for Dudley, the author reveals a sympathy for miscegenation accompanied by love. The rhetorical attack is not on miscegenation nor even on the system of slavery so much as on the planters themselves. Victor condemns their total disregard for their slaves' humanity, and with the condemnation a threat is implied by showing that the blacks are indeed human. Sophy's story of Nat Turner's rebellion and the murder of her master's children (pp. 90–99) immediately precedes the happy scene when Philip and Virginia receive parental consent to their marriage and begin a blissful discussion of wedding plans (pp. 101ff). Their elaborate wedding, a symbol of genteel Southern life, becomes a semi-transparent overlay covering the hostility and horror beneath, revealed in the slaves' stories told in the dark of night before the glimmering fire in Maum Guinea's cabin, and glimpsed in the gentle cook's occasional flashes of private rage—"Curse 'em, I say! Curse 'em all—buyer, seller, de whole w'ite race!" (p. 73) The blacks reveal their humanity in the intensity of their love, of Hyperion and Rose for each other, of Maum Guinea for Dudley, but establishing their human capability to love clearly establishes also their human capability to hate.

J. R. Gilmore's *My Southern Friends* (1863)[34] also uses the potentially terrible results of miscegenation for its rhetorical attack on slavery. The narrator Edmund Kirk, the pseudonym under which the novel is published, travels in the South and loans a planter named Preston money to buy a mulatto, Phyllis, and her children, saving them from being taken to New Orleans. Kirk later learns that the children are Preston's and that he has another mulatto child, Selma, whom he and his wife are raising with their children as a legitimate daughter. Preston's wife dies and he remarries, later sending Selma to Boston for her education, where she meets Kirk's adopted son Frank. The young people fall in love and are to marry. Preston dies; Selma returns home and is seized as a slave by the second wife, who has learned the truth. Selma is rescued by her legitimate half-brother Joe, and they wait for her fiancé Frank to arrive. When he does, now aware of Selma's background, he is greatly disturbed. Following a long, unrecorded conversation between them, she commits suicide and he goes insane.

In addition to the basic role of miscegenation in the main plot, the theme also dominates subplots. After Preston's death, his second wife intends to marry a neighboring planter named Dawsey. Dawsey, who has numerous mulatto children by his slaves (p. 217), beats one slave to death because she refuses to submit to him (p. 221). Preston's legitimate son Joe has a baby by the slave girl Rosey, discovering only later that she is his half-sister (p. 229). Another subplot involves a conflict between Frank Kirk and his real father, John Hallet. In this, Hallet attempts to buy Selma from the second Mrs. Preston to make her his mistress (pp. 269–270), but he is forced to abandon his scheme (p. 279). Structurally, then, the theme of miscegenation is an intrinsic element of the complexly interwoven plot and subplots.

The most interesting thing about this novel is Gilmore's relatively blatant appeal to the reader's prurient interests. While most of the novels discussed rely on euphemism and avoid direct, imagistic presentation of the sexual, Gilmore goes much further. Discussions of selling women in New Orleans and of the purpose for which they are intended abound in many novels, but *My Southern Friends* presents a more realistically crude element. A slave trader, joking about not wanting a young slave's children because he intends to sell her in New Orleans, says, "What'll one o' them young bloods want o' them? They goes in fur home manufactures" (p. 14). Attempting to sell another young woman, a trader is reported by the narrator to lift the girl's dress and claim she is " 'good at nussin', wet or dry. Good at breedin' too; hed two young'uns a'ready. Ye kin * * * * *.' (The rest of this discourse will not bear repeating)" (p. 62). At another sale, a trader presents a young mulatto woman in chains:

"Ye haint seed half of har yit. I doan't want ter sell ye a damaged article. I want ter show ye she's sound's a nut—*ye won't pay my price ef I doan't.* [Ital. in original] Look a thar, now," and with a quick dextrous movement, he tore open the front of her dress * * * *. The poor girl, unable to use her hands, bent over nearly double (p. 72).

A row of asterisks does not today appear particularly daring, but this passage depicts the sexual exhibition of slave women more graphically than most other abolitionist novels. Catherine Clinton even argues that such debasement of black women under slavery, the use of chains and whips by white men to dominate them, contributes to the prominence of bondage and punishment themes in contemporary American pornography.[35] In any event, Gilmore's use of offensive detail supports his

attitude that miscegenation is an opprobrious affair. Rhetorically, he builds this argument by demonstrating that only tragedies are associated with the practice, from the beating death
of the slave girl who refused Dawsey, to the suicide and insanity
of the main characters involved in a miscegenetic affair, and
the horror of incest for Joe and Rosey. The potential for developing the human problems present, particularly Frank's agonizing conflict, goes unfulfilled, and the novel remains
essentially propaganda, relying on the appeal of the tragic-
octoroon motif and the shock value of some scenes to make the
rhetorical point that miscegenation is a tragedy which exists
only because of slavery. In two other novels by Gilmore, *Down
in Tennessee* and *Among the Pines*, minor incidents involving
miscegenation are used to convey the same idea.[36] In one, a
character says, "You know the black does not seek the white,
but the white the black. Free the black, give him control of his
own person, and amalgamation will totally cease." Kirk, again
the narrator, responds, "I think so; and that, to me, is one of
the strongest reasons for abolishing slavery."[37]

The last novel about miscegenation to appear before the end
of the Civil War is Epes Sargent's *Peculiar: A Tale of the Great
Transition* (1864),[38] which has been called the most effective
antislavery novel written during the conflict.[39] Sargent, the descendent of Massachusetts governors, worked as a journalist and
literary editor in Boston and New York. In his only novel, the
two main plot lines are built around both an actual tragic
octoroon and a false one. A successful New Orleans businessman named Vance has devoted himself to aiding fugitive slaves,
because as a young man he had suffered the tragic loss of the
beautiful slave he married. Estelle was raised as white in a
convent, but upon her father's death she discovers she is a slave
and becomes a servant in the house where Vance lives. Purchased by the villain Ratcliff, she turns to Vance for aid. He
helps her escape, hides her, and when he falls ill she nurses
him back to health. They fall in love, are married, and Estelle
becomes pregnant. Discovered by Ratcliff, she is seized, and
when Vance tries to rescue her he is captured also. In another
exceptionally graphic scene of sexual violence, Vance in chains
is forced to watch Estelle stripped and beaten; she later dies

in his arms as a result of the whipping. The other plot line involves Clara Barstow, daughter of wealthy Northern parents killed in a Mississippi steamboat explosion when she was three. The child was presumed lost but actually was rescued and sold as a slave. Ratcliff purchased her and placed her in a boarding school. Fourteen years later he comes to claim her as his slave and mistress. She is finally rescued by Vance and returns North to claim her inheritance, there becoming engaged to a war hero.

The superiority of *Peculiar* as a rhetorical work lies in both the bitterness of the author's attack and the careful arrangement of the book. For example, the reader's response to Estelle is considerably greater than to the ordinary tragic octoroon, who usually suffers only a certain amount of debasement and, at worst, suicide. The reader follows Estelle, however, through the tender growth of her love for Vance (pp. 118–126), and the joy of her pregnancy (p. 127). The particular brutality of her murder (p. 137), contrasted to these preceding scenes of domestic bliss with Vance, makes a shocking and powerful indictment of the slave system. Structurally well-balanced, the book provides the happily resolved story of Clara as both a counterpoise and a foil to the tragedy of Estelle. Miscegenation itself is accepted; the brief marriage of Vance and Estelle is ideal, and Vance expresses the opinion that "the French Quadroons are handsome and healthy, and are believed to be more vigorous than either of the parent races from which they are descended." He goes on, however, to attack vehemently the hypocrisy of men who keep colored mistresses and cry out against amalgamation (p. 149). Although the most effective of the antislavery novels relying on the theme of miscegenation, the book contributes little to the historical development of the theme, except that it employs both of the basic resolutions for the dilemma of interracial love—death and the revelation that no taint exists.

The novels discussed thus far have all contributed something new to the literary treatment of miscegenation or, at least, have been good examples of a standard approach. There were rhetorical antislavery novels between 1850 and 1865, such as the two by Gilmore not discussed, which use miscegenation very incidentally and which seem for other reasons to merit little attention. Such a book is Frances McDougall's *Shamah in Pursuit of Freedom; or, The Branded Hand* (1858),[40] a wild, epistolary novel distinguished mainly by its lack of readability. An incident involving potential incest and daughter-selling is thrown into the gallimaufry of antislavery leftovers for shock value (pp. 162–165), and a tragic-octoroon story suddenly boils up at the end. An earlier epistolary novel by Emily Pearson, *Cousin Franck's Household; or, Scenes in the Old Dominion* (1853),[41] is somewhat better; the dominant concern, however, is not with miscegenation but with the problem of slave-breeding for profit.[42] The mulatto half-sister of the plantation mistress tells her story to the narrator (pp. 105–122), heightening revulsion at the practice of using slaves as a revenue source by revealing that the human products are sometimes the children or brothers and sisters of the marketing agents. Historically, about this time Virginia and Kentucky slaveholders did increase greatly the export of slaves, particularly mulattoes, to the new slave states of Texas and Arkansas.[43]

Another novel making very incidental use of miscegenation is Mrs. Harriet Stephens' *Hagar the Martyr* (1855).[44] The author disapproves of slavery but her main concern is with defending women who have borne illegitimate children. At the beginning of the novel there is strong suggestion that Hagar is the daughter of a mulatto, but no further reference to this occurs until the wild climax some thirty years later when someone tries to seize Hagar as a slave. Her natural mother, not a mulatto, is coincidentally present to prove the falsity of the charge.

Two Men (1865),[45] by Elizabeth Barstow Stoddard, provides welcome relief from the above potboilers. Jason Auster is married to Sarah Parke, the only daughter of a wealthy family. Over the years, Jason loses his youthful idealism and becomes a hard businessman, accumulating substantial wealth. The Austers have a son, Parke, and also raise a girl named Philippa, who had been left with them by Sarah's wandering cousin, Osmund Luce. A mulatto woman, Mrs. Lang, and her two beautiful daughters arrive in the New England town of Crest, where the Austers live. Parke, who is about twenty at this time, gradually becomes involved with the older girl, Charlotte. When she becomes pregnant, Parke announces he will marry her.

Philippa, who loves Parke herself, is outraged, but Jason quietly approves his son's action. Before Parke can fulfill his pledge, both his mother and Charlotte fall sick and die, Charlotte while giving birth to a still-born infant. Parke has Charlotte and the baby buried in the family plot and leaves for South America with Osmund Luce. Before he departs, Philippa tells Parke of her love, and Parke admits he did not love Charlotte but now feels unworthy of Philippa.

With his wife Sarah dead and Parke gone, a singular change comes over Jason. He reveals to Philippa that he had hated Sarah for years and felt his life totally empty. Now he declares his love for Philippa and asks her to marry him. For months she coldly rejects the older man, often taunting him by speaking of her love for Parke, but slowly she begins to see Jason as a kind and sensitive man. When Jason is found mysteriously wounded (there is a suggestion of attempted suicide), Philippa nurses him back to health and tentatively offers her love. Jason is cautious and leaves for some months, but when he returns they are married. The novel ends with Parke in South America contemplating going home. Osmund Luce tells him if he does it will be to find Jason and Philippa together, a suggestion Parke refuses to believe possible.

In this novel, miscegenation functions primarily as a catalyst. Parke's miscegenetic affair forces him to face adult responsibility, and the breakup of the Auster family as a result of the affair frees Jason from his self-imposed isolation and the frustration of an empty life. Characterization is affected two ways by the subject of miscegenation. Charlotte and her family are basically stereotyped mulattoes with little individualism, except for her sister Clarice, who expresses hostility toward Parke (pp. 147, 163). The other characters—Parke, Philippa, Jason and Sarah—are all tested and judged by their reaction to the catalytic miscegenation. Parke is a spoiled child, pampered by his mother (p. 159), and his feelings for Charlotte are based in pride and possessiveness (pp. 158–159). In spite of not wanting to marry Charlotte, Parke decides he must fulfill his moral obligation to her and takes the first step toward breaking free of immature self-centeredness and accepting adult responsibility (pp. 168–169). He reveals his newfound strength when

Charlotte's death frees him; he insists on showing the open respect he would have shown his wife and buries her in the family plot (p. 210). The townspeople react with mixed emotions of contempt and admiration, but Clarice's former hostility turns to grudging respect (p. 211).

Jason and Parke for the first time become close and develop respect for each other (p. 212). Jason had been driven into the isolated, hollow world of business when his wife rejected him in favor of her son. Now Jason is drawn back into emotional contact with his family by the crisis of Parke's miscegenetic affair. Jason's basic decency and strength are the sources of Parke's ability to treat Charlotte properly (pp. 173, 185). By supporting his son, Jason frees them both from the domination of Sarah and sets the stage for his own renewal of interest in life after she dies. Sarah cannot change from the total, smothering devotion to Parke which alienated Jason and almost ruined the boy. She cannot face his involvement with another woman—she has hated Philippa for years (pp. 62, 159)—and collapses before the reality of his intended marriage to Charlotte, preferring to give up life rather than give up her little boy. Philippa also fails the test presented by the crisis. Her reaction is selfish and hysterical (pp. 176–177); when she encounters Charlotte Lang, Philippa is childishly cruel to the girl (p. 181). Philippa's selfish, possessive, and immature love for Parke is essentially similar to his feeling for Charlotte. Parke, however, has now achieved the beginnings of manhood and goes out into the world. Philippa is still a selfish child, and Jason, whose mature objectivity and love had aided his son, now faces the task of helping Philippa grow up. As end result of the miscegenetic affair, Parke finds his manhood and begins life, while Jason is rewarded by finding fulfillment in love after years of empty duty.

The novel is notable for psychological insights into the relationship of the father and son with each other and with Sarah, but it is also notable for the astounding objectivity with which the subject of miscegenation is handled. In 1865, with Emancipation and the beginnings of Reconstruction, the Southern fear of amalgamation was receiving wide attention, but Mrs.

Stoddard presents miscegenation in a matter-of-fact manner, seemingly unaffected by the controversial nature of the subject. Miscegenation occurs in the novel because it makes Charlotte more alluring and pitiful; it makes Parke's stance a little braver. The essential story, though, is that of the scion of a wealthy family's getting a girl from across the tracks in trouble; that she is a mulatto is almost incidental.

Wife of Richard Henry Stoddard, a popular poet and New York literary editor, Mrs. Stoddard was a remarkable novelist. Too grimly realistic for popular taste, her three novels were praised by Hawthorne and should become better known now that she has been "rediscovered" by literary scholars and part of her work made generally available again.[46]

During the period 1850–1865, apparently only four novels by black Americans saw print. Two were abolitionist attacks on slavery. Somewhat surprisingly, the other two were set in the North, generally ignored slavery, and focused instead on the hate-filled racism and destructive prejudice found in the "free" states.

Clotel, or, the President's Daughter (1853), by William Wells Brown, is the first known novel by an American black. Brown, the author of an 1847 slave narrative, had been a successful abolitionist sent to England to raise support. In the year after *Uncle Tom's Cabin* made abolitionist fiction popular, Brown gathered some previous pieces on a "white" slave woman into his novel.[47] Published in London, the novel received little circulation in the United States until an American edition appeared in 1864, under the title *Clotelle; A Tale of the Southern States*.[48] The idea for the original novel was based on a rumor circulated by Garrison's *The Liberator* that a slave daughter of Thomas Jefferson had been sold in New Orleans.[49] In the first American edition, the principal changes were dropping any reference to Thomas Jefferson and making the title character's father a fictitious United States Senator.[50] It appears that many details of the plot were taken from an 1842 short story by Lydia Maria Childs, "The Quadroons," published in *The Liberty Bell*, Boston.[51] The basic situation in both works is similar to an incident in Walt Whitman's temperance novel

Franklin Evans, also published in 1842, in which a brief interracial marriage, a result of Evans' drunken rashness, is destroyed by an interloping white woman.[52]

Despite the existence of possible literary sources, the incidents of the novel were drawn largely from Brown's own experience. Similar to the situation in the novel, Brown's mistress, Mrs. Young, hated him because he was her brother-in-law's son and bore the family resemblance. Once he was even mistaken for her son by a visitor. Again, Brown observed a slave, Cynthia, be forced to become the mistress of a slave trader who later sold her and their children. Brown also saw his mother whipped and his sister sold away. When he and his mother attempted an escape to Canada, they were recaptured and she was sold in New Orleans.[53]

In Brown's first American edition, the basic story is of Senator Harry Linwood, his mulatto mistress Isabella and their daughter, Clotelle, a stereotypic tragic octoroon. All is well for many years until Harry tires of Isabella and marries a white woman. His new mother-in-law, Mrs. Miller, discovers his other family and insists that they be disposed of. Isabella is sold in New Orleans, later escapes and seeks Clotelle, only to fail and commit suicide (p. 52). Meanwhile, Clotelle discovers she is a slave, is brutally treated by Mrs. Miller (p. 41), and is herself eventually sold in New Orleans (p. 74). She is finally rescued by a white Frenchman, Antoine Devenant, who marries her and takes her to Europe. Years pass, Devenant dies and Clotelle re-encounters Jerome, a black she had known and loved as a slave. They marry, and in Switzerland they stumble upon her aged father, who has been driven insane by guilt over his daughter's fate. Clotelle nurses him back to health, and Harry resolves to return to Virginia and free all his slaves.

Structurally, miscegenation drives both the development of the plot and the characterization of Isabella and of Clotelle, who are created according to stereotyped qualities of the tragic mulatto. They leave little impression on the reader except as things, beautiful and mistreated. The actions of the novel evolve from the separation of Isabella and Clotelle and their subsequent sales. The adventures of the two women result from this separation, as does Harry's decline into drinking (p. 44) and eventual insanity. The motivating force behind the separation is not Harry's rejection of Isabella for another, but the hatred toward Isabella and Clotelle of Mrs. Miller (p. 38). The source of this hatred is her sexual jealousy of slave women because of her husband, who is described as "bankrupt in character, and debauched in body and mind, with seven mulatto children who claim him as their father" (p. 38). Thus the key incidents of the plot are motivated by a problem arising from miscegenation.

Counter to one critic's belief that no argument is made in the novel for or against miscegenation,[54] the author's attitude toward it seems clearly negative. Nothing but tragedy flows from the practice: Isabella commits suicide, Harry is driven to drink and the edge of total insanity, his wife dies of melancholy, Mrs. Miller is burned to death. Clotelle does find happiness, but not in her miscegenetic marriage to Devenant. She achieves true happiness only after his death and her subsequent marriage to Jerome, who, it is stressed, is "pure African" (p. 57). While not openly opposing miscegenation, the first black American novelist does set the pattern which later black writers follow of advocating that mulattoes identify with their black heritage rather than with their white. This idea develops as the solution of black authors to the problem of where the mulatto belongs. Except for this sense of mulatto loyalty, *Clotelle* explores no other new aspects of miscegenation, and the elements of potentially broad human problems presented—the rejection of a woman by a lover who grows tired of her, the bitter jealousy of another—are distinctly undeveloped and lost in the wash of antislavery propaganda.

In contrast to Brown, Martin Delaney produced not the typical abolitionist novel but a revolutionary call for slaves to rise against their masters. His *Blake; or, the Huts of America* appeared serially in two parts: Part I in the New York *Anglo-African Magazine* between January and July, 1859; Part II in the New York *Weekly Anglo-African Magazine* between November 1861 and May 1862.[55] Delaney's life as a free black in Pittsburgh and Philadelphia created his bitterness and hostility toward the white-dominated world and he sought colonization in East Africa, Central or South America as the only way to freedom for all blacks.[56] Born in 1812, at twenty-seven

he risked his freedom by extensive travel in Mississippi, Louisiana, Texas, and Arkansas before returning to Pittsburgh to
become co-editor of Frederick Douglas' *North Star*. A self-ed-
ucated man, Delaney was accepted at Harvard Medical School,
but student protests there against admitting a black caused
Harvard officials to withdraw their acceptance.[57] The travels
by Henry Holland (Blake) from plantation to plantation, car-
rying his message of revolution to the slaves, suggest Delaney's
own Southern journey.

When the novel opens, Henry is married to Maggie, the beautiful mulatto daughter of their master, Colonel Franks. Early
in Part I, Maggie rejects her father's incestuous advances, and
he sells her. Spurred by this atrocity, Blake escapes and travels
to promote a slave uprising throughout the South, eventually
(in Part II) ending up in Cuba. As part of his rebellion, Blake
openly breaks with and speaks against Christianity, reflecting
the actual disenchantment among slaves in the 1850s with a
church controlled by the slave owners that preached the idea
of total obedience to the slaves.[58] Miscegenation is a minor,
although outrageous, concern in this sometimes fragmentary,
disjunctive novel. But Delaney clearly opposes the practice as
he opposes all things white.

Delaney's bitterness against white prejudice in the North
was well founded. Northern, white, abolitionist authors found
it easy to assume a position of moral superiority to Southern
slave owners, but apparently found it almost as easy to overlook
the essential hypocrisy of much of their own rhetoric. Two little-
known novelists, from their perspective as blacks living outside
the slave states, saw that the hypocrisy which allowed slavery
to exist in the self-proclaimed land of the free ran deeper than
the contradiction between the national constitution and the
laws of one section allowing some men to enslave others. The
truth of their vision can be seen in that the problems which
they took up pen against still persist more than a century after
the Emancipation Proclamation.

Frank J. Webb, in his novel *The Garies and Their Friends*
(1857),[59] shows that the problems surrounding miscegenation
go far beyond the tragic octoroon on the auction block, that
mixed marriages in the North can occasion as much suffering

as enforced concubinage in the South, that mulattoes every-where suffer their particular agony, whether as slaves of their own fathers or as slaves to the secrets of their own hearts.

In her preface to the original edition, Harriet Beecher Stowe tells us that Webb was a young black from Philadelphia (p. v), but the novel is dedicated to Lady Byron by "her grateful friend, The Author," (p. iii), so he apparently lived in England, where the novel was published. In the preface to a facsimile reprint, Arthur P. Davis discusses several important points about the work. Davis notes that Webb's work is technically far superior to William Wells Brown's *Clotel* and that *The Garies and Their Friends* is significant for several "firsts." It is the first novel to tell about the lives of free blacks in the pre-Civil War North, the first to treat in depth a mixed marriage, the first to include a lynch mob, the first to treat ironically problems of the color line (as Charles Waddell Chesnutt does later), and the first to make passing for white a major theme, which it is throughout later black literature, especially during the Harlem Renais-sance (p. ii). Davis also calls attention to the totally middle-class concern of the novel, a concern which continues as a char-acteristic of black novels until the 1940s. Webb's work is a black version of the American dream of material success. The characters seek money and the position and power it can pro-vide, but not in an adumbration of "black power"; their pride is in class, not race; they would prefer to be white, but they clearly oppose passing for white because it leads to insecurity rather than success (pp. v-vi).

As Davis indicates, the plot develops by tracing the fortunes of two families, the "mixed" Garies, who, with one exception, are destroyed by prejudice, and the dark-skinned Ellises, who achieve a reasonable degree of happiness (p. iv). Mr. Garie, a white Georgia planter with a mulatto wife and children, moves to Philadelphia to escape danger to his family in the South. The Garies become acquainted with the Ellis family and with a fabulously wealthy black named Walters. Mr. Stevens, an unscrupulous white neighbor of the Garies, organizes a mob attack on the black homes in the city so that the destroyed property may then be purchased cheaply, a fictional version of the race riot on July 7, 1843, when white mobs stormed through the black section of Philadelphia, clubbing and beating blacks, burning homes, forcing hundreds to flee. As a result of this violence, and threats of more, propertied blacks were forced to sell at a loss to white investors.[60] In the fictional attack, Mr. and Mrs. Garie are killed and Mr. Ellis is invalided for life. Walters comes to the aid of both families. Emily Garie is raised as colored with the Ellis family, while Clarence Garie is sent to a boarding school where he passes for white. Eventually, Emily and Charlie Ellis marry happily, but Clarence dies of a broken heart after his secret is betrayed to his white fiancée and she rejects him. The novel makes its point primarily through the parallel between the sons of each family—light-skinned, weak Clarence Garie and strong, dark Charlie Ellis.

While young, both boys are exposed to prejudice. The whites in Georgia will not associate with the Garies. When they move to Philadelphia, Emily and Clarence are put in school with white children, but their neighbor Mrs. Stevens discovers the truth and forces the teacher to expel them (pp. 156–160). The narrator comments that Clarence "was beginning to learn the anomalous situation he was to fill in society" (p. 157). Charlie's education is also interrupted, but by his parents' putting him into service with a wealthy white family, where he gets into trouble and is sent to the country with a kindly white woman, Mrs. Bird (pp. 69–95). Charlie suffers from prejudice at the hands of Mrs. Bird's white servants (pp. 141–146) and is rejected by a white academy where she tries to enroll him. But Charlie remains undaunted and attends Sunday school instead, where he impresses everyone with his intelligence (p. 243). In addition to their educational difficulties, the boys share a further parallel when both their fathers are destroyed by the mob. Mr. Garie is killed outright (p. 223); Mr. Ellis is physically and mentally incapacitated for life (pp. 218–219). The scenes of violent horror in the city immediately precede Charlie's rejection at the white academy in the country, rhetorically linking "little" acts of discrimination to their logical end in mass murder.

The thematically significant contrast between Clarence Garie and Charlie Ellis develops after the riot, when each boy heads down a different path to his destiny. Charlie, now the man of his family, looks for work, answering an advertisement by letter and receiving an interview with a pair of business partners. The attack on Northern prejudice is made clear when the Southern partner wants to hire the boy but the Northern partner refuses (pp. 288–292). Despite this and other rejections (pp. 294–298), Charlie perseveres and finally obtains work as an engraver's apprentice (p. 308). Concurrently, Clarence and Emily Garie are the subject of debate between their father's lawyer, who wishes to pass them as white, and Mr. Walters, who believes that fear of discovery destroys those who try to pass (pp. 274–276). They decide that Emily will stay with the Ellis family, but Clarence will be sent to a white boarding school, and he is well-coached to keep his heritage a secret (p. 279). Unlike Charlie with his trials, Clarence settles quickly into a pleasant life at the school, free at last from prejudice (p. 284).

The narrative shifts to a time several years later when both Charlie and Clarence are engaged to be married. Charlie will marry Emily Garie, and they fill the discussions of their wedding plans with anticipation of domestic bliss (pp. 340–343). Clarence, however, is engaged to a white girl, Anne, whose family despises blacks, and the parallel discussion of wedding plans finds Clarence filled with secret horror (pp. 334–336). Clarence suffers the anguish of deciding to confess his secret to Anne but of failing to do so out of fear (p. 331). He suffers guilt when joining in her family's anti-black remarks, feeling his mother will rise from her grave to curse him (p. 325). In all, Walters' prophecy has come true; Clarence is being destroyed by his secret. Charlie and Emily marry happily (p. 375), but Clarence is betrayed and Anne's father drives him away (pp. 351–354). Clarence has received a large inheritance but is now left rich and friendless: "He was very wretched and lonely: he felt ashamed to seek the society of colored men now that the whites despised and rejected him, so he lived apart from both classes of society" (p. 381). In the end, he goes home to Emily and Charlie to die (p. 391).

The point of the novel seems clear: open prejudice is a physically destructive force, but one which can be fought; the secret guilt and fear in attempting to pass as white are spiritually destructive and cannot be conquered. Prejudice operates openly in the mob's sacking, burning and killing. But prejudice in even its most violent forms can be fought, as Walters shows by converting his home into a fortress that is besieged by the mob and defended in a manner reminiscent of a medieval castle under attack—the black defenders drive the white rioters from the doors by pouring boiling water on them (pp. 204–214). Walters' money enables him to defend himself and all those who flee to his protection against the overt violence of prejudice. But Clarence Garie's money is no defense against the spiritually destructive force of his fear. There is no way this terror can be fought:

I dare not tell—I must shut this secret in my bosom, where it gnaws, gnaws, gnaws, until it has almost eaten my heart away. Oh, I've thought of that, time and again; it has kept me awake night after night, it haunts me at all hours; it is breaking down my health and strength—wearing my very life out of me; no escaped galley-slave ever felt more than I do, or lived in more constant fear of detection: and yet I must nourish this tormenting secret, and keep it growing in my breast until it has crowded out every honorable and manly feeling; and then, perhaps, after all my sufferings and sacrifice of candor and truth, out it will come at last, when I least expect or think of it (pp. 324–325).

Clarence accurately predicts both the way his secret will be revealed and the ultimately degenerative effect of the concealment. When he encounters a man who he knows recognizes and will betray him, Clarence collapses in a faint (pp. 346–347). His death a few weeks later is caused by no particular physical ailment, just the debilitation brought on by years of hidden fear and the melancholy of a broken heart.

The novel offers multiple examples of how to fight prejudice— the stories of Walters, Charlie Ellis, and others who conquer its effects by the middle-class virtues of hard work, courage, and money. The book is not an abolitionist novel because it practically ignores slavery; at one point Stevens has the opportunity to seize the Garie children as part of their dead father's estate, but has no interest in doing so (p. 260). The lessons are about the free black and Northern prejudice, with a major concern for the problem of what the mulatto light enough to pass for white should do. Clarence Garie himself provides the answer in his letter to Emily saying that he is coming home to die: "If my lot had only been cast with yours—had we never been separated—I might have been today as happy as you are" (p. 381).

The problem of the Garies' mixed marriage underscores the author's concern for the proper role of the mulatto. From the time of her marriage, Mrs. Garie's life is one of unrelieved suffering, in Georgia from her fears for her children (pp. 54–57), in Philadelphia from the insults of whites like Mrs. Stevens (pp. 130–132). The prejudice against a mulatto trying to live openly in a white world is further emphasized by the legal impossibility of their marrying in Georgia and the refusal by one white minister to perform the service in Philadelphia (p. 137). Moreover, after her horrible death in the process of giving birth to a dead child while hiding in a woodshed from the mob that had just killed her husband (pp. 223–225), Mrs. Garie suffers the final insult of being refused burial beside her husband in a white cemetery (p. 233).

The tragedy of Mrs. Garie's miscegenetic marriage evolves slowly over the years; the tragedy of Clarence's attempt to pass for white eats away at him until his loss of love in a miscegenetic affair destroys him. The only mulatto who survives and achieves happiness is Emily, and she does so by rejecting both the path of her mother and that of her brother. She neither attempts to live openly as a mulatto in a white world nor to pass secretly for white. She instead rejects her white heritage entirely, seeking nothing from the white world and turning for her destiny to life as a black. In so doing she sets the pattern for nearly all mulatto characters drawn by later black authors.

The mulatto heroine of Mrs. H. E. Wilson's *Our Nig* (1859)[61] also chooses to live and marry black, but without Emily's success. Frado, a mulatto girl aged six, is abandoned by her parents at the wealthy Belmont home in a Northern city. Most of the family are kind to the child, but she is brutally overworked by Mrs. Belmont, who sees her as merely a source of free labor. By age eighteen Frado, or "Nig" as she is called by Mrs. Belmont, physically exhausted and ill, becomes a ward of the county. One woman with whom she stays while convalescing teaches her to read and write. Once well, Frado marries a black man,

Samuel, and they return to Singleton, her mother's original home. When she becomes pregnant, Samuel deserts her. Finally we learn that Frado has found a useful article to manufacture, and by selling it is caring for herself and her child. A similar statement is found in the preface, where Mrs. Wilson says that she is writing to support herself and a child. Further evidence of the autobiographic nature of the novel is provided in an appendix (pp. 138–141), containing three letters which attest to the truth of the story and the good character of the author, urging purchase of the book. The exceptional realism of the plot in the great age of the sentimental novel would also seem to indicate that the events are factual autobiography.[62]

The novel, a denunciation of the hardships and prejudice encountered by Frado, shows no concern for the problem of slavery. The only mention of it is in connection with Samuel, who claims to be an ex-slave, but who, when he deserts Frado, admits that he had always been free and was just making abolition lectures for money (p. 128). The rhetorical attack is leveled at the prejudice generally prevalent around Frado, from her experience as a school child (p. 31) to the indifferent way she is passed around as an unwanted burden by the county (pp. 124–125). The prejudice described in the novel not only affects Frado, but earlier wears down her mother, leading her to abandon Frado as a child. The story of Frado's mother, Mag Smith, makes this novel especially interesting to a study of miscegenation, because she is the first white female character to enter a miscegenetic marriage with a black male.

Mag is a lower-class woman who initially thought she could better herself through an affair with a wealthy man, but he abandons her and she bears a baby who dies (pp. 1–6). Viewed as an immoral person, Mag is rejected by the town and lives a few years on the brink of starvation. The only person who helps keep her alive is a kindly, black cooper named Jim. Sexually attracted by her fair skin and straight hair, Jim thinks to himself, "She'd be as much of a prize to me as she'd fall short of coming up to the mark with white folks. I don't care for things past. I've done things 'fore now I's 'shamed of. She's good enough for me, anyhow" (p. 11). Jim goes to see her just as winter sets in; secretly glad to discover that she has no wood or food, he decides to propose:

> "Well, Mag," said Jim, after a short pause, "you's down low enough. I don't see but I've got to take care of ye. 'Sposin we marry!" Mag raised her eyes, full of amazement and uttered a sonorous "What?"

Jim quickly convinces her and the narrator tells us:

> He prevailed; they married. You can philosophize, gentle reader, upon the impropriety of such unions, and preach dozens of sermons on the evils of amalgamation. Want is a more powerful philosopher and preacher. Poor Mag. She has sundered another bond which held her to her fellows. She has descended another step down the ladder of infamy (pp. 12–13).

Structurally, the miscegenetic relationship of Mag and Jim is the basis for the ensuing actions of the plot. Frado and another child are born to them, and are the living symbols of Mag's awful violation of taboo. The narrator says, "She was now expelled from companionship with white people; this last step—her union with a black—was the climax of repulsion" (p. 15). After Jim's death, Mag's situation becomes increasingly desperate until she takes up with an unsavory character who proposes that they abandon the mulatto children and move on to where Mag's crime will not be known. She acquiesces, leaving Frado on the Belmont doorstep (p. 22).

Frado, as a mulatto, is subject to the particular mania that white America has for insisting on the negritude of the mulatto.[63] The kind of treatment Frado receives at the hands of Mrs. Belmont doesn't result from the girl's being part black, but rather from her not being black enough. Mrs. Belmont's use of her as a virtual slave and her insistence on referring to Frado only as "our Nig" both epitomize her desire to deny that the girl is not purely black, to deny the existence of miscegenation or mulattoes. This attitude is best symbolized in Mrs. Belmont's continually forcing Frado to work unshaded in the sun to darken her skin (p. 39).

In addition to physical mistreatment, Frado, like the alienated mulattoes of Harriet Beecher Stowe, suffers the fate of not belonging. First rejected by her white mother, she is pushed into the white world of the Belmonts. She lives in their home but does not belong there, any more than she belongs to any of the places where she is shifted about as a ward of the county. When she leaves the white world, she experiences symbolic rejection by the black world because her husband deserts her. In the end, Frado becomes another of Helena Smith's "no-nation bastards."[64]

The Garies and Their Friends and *Our Nig* present some interesting variations, foreshadowing later works, on the treatment of miscegenation in novels published between 1850 and 1865. Both books free the subject from the limiting context of slavery, which often clouded the issue by suggesting that the only real problem faced by mulattoes was enslavement. Harry Gordon, for example, is a well-drawn figure of alienation, but Mrs. Stowe unrealistically resolves his crisis by simply freeing him. The symbolic link between miscegenation and the theme of alienation cannot come to its fullest development until twentieth-century novels when the context of slavery has been forgotten, as, for example, in *Light in August*, where Joe Christmas, although free, drives himself to destruction trying to discover where he belongs. Similarly, Clarence Garie and Frado are both free, but their isolation and lack of identity exist anyway. Mrs. Wilson introduces another interesting motif, the willing sexual relationship between a white woman and a black man, which continues to occur before World War I only in novels written by other blacks, such as Charles Waddell Chesnutt, James Weldon Johnson, and Oscar Micheaux. Not until 1932, when Faulkner depicts the sexual relationships of Joe Christmas, first with a white prostitute and later with Joanna Burden, does a white novelist treat this subject. Even after Faulkner, the topic has remained largely the concern of black authors, receiving important consideration in such major novels as Ralph Ellison's *Invisible Man* and James Baldwin's *Another Country*.

The majority of novels printed between 1850 and 1865 use the subject of miscegenation only to attack or defend the legal institution of slavery and, with the exception of Mrs. Stowe's work, ceased to be of any importance at the demise of that institution. But *The Garies and Their Friends* and *Our Nig*, despite being polemical works, focus their concern not on slavery but on the more basic issue of racism, thus foreshadowing the concern for the next fifty years of most novels in which miscegenation appears.

NOTES

1. Robert E. Spiller, et al., eds., *Literary History of the United States*, 3rd ed., rev. (New York: Macmillan, 1963), p. 565.
2. Herbert Brown, *The Sentimental Novel in American, 1789–1860* (Durham, N.C.: Duke Univ. Press, 1940), p. 245.
3. Nelson, p. 73.
4. Lynn, p. viii.
5. Margaret Butcher, *The Negro in American Culture* (New York: Knopf, 1956), p. 155.
6. James S. Peacocke, *The Orphan Girls: A Tale of Southern Life* (Philadelphia: John E. Potter and Co., 1880). *The Creole Orphans* was reprinted under different titles and this was the edition used. Hereafter cited parenthetically.
7. Mrs. G. M. Flanders, *The Ebony Idol* (New York: Appleton, 1860). Hereafter cited parenthetically.
8. Cash, p. 118.
9. Sterling Brown, "Negro Character as Seen by White Authors," *Journal of Negro Education* 2 (1933):194.
10. Richard Beale Davis, "Mrs. Stowe's Characters-in-Situations and a Southern Literary Tradition," in *Essays in Honor of Jay B. Hubbell*, ed. by Clarence Gohdes (Durham, N.C.: Duke Univ. Press, 1967), pp. 108–125.
11. For a full discussion of the tragic mulatto character, see Berzon, 99–116. According to Joel Williamson, the historical evidence suggests that while octoroons were accepted as white during much of the slavery period, in the years just before the Civil War a "whitening" of slavery took place as the South moved toward the "one drop rule" and the economic demands of slavery on the frontier drew in more and more mulattoes; see his *New People*, especially pp. 63–75.
12. Nelson, p. 84.
13. Sterling Brown, "Negro Character," p. 193.
14. Jules Zanger, "The 'Tragic Octoroon' in Pre-Civil War Fiction," *American Quarterly* 18 (1966):63–70.
15. Harriet Beecher Stowe, *Uncle Tom's Cabin; or, Life Among the*

Lowly, ed. by Kenneth S. Lynn (Cambridge, Mass.: Belknap, 1962). Hereafter cited parenthetically.

16. Vernon L. Parrington, *Main Currents in American Thought* (New York: Harcourt, 1930), II, p. 371.

17. Severn Duvall, "Uncle Tom's Cabin: The Sinister Side of the Patriarchy," *New England Quarterly* 36 (1963); reprinted in Gross and Hardy, pp. 167–69.

18. Davis, p. 115.

19. Edmund Wilson, *Patriotic Gore: Studies in the Literature of the American Civil War* (New York: Oxford Univ. Press, 1962), p. 8.

20. Seymour L. Gross, "Introduction: Stereotype to Archetype: The Negro in American Literary Criticism," in *Images of the Negro in American Literature,* pp. 25–26.

21. Davis, pp. 108–09.

22. Duvall, p. 180.

23. Harriet Beecher Stowe, *Dred; A Tale of the Great Dismal Swamp,* 2 vols. (Boston: Philips, Sampson and Co., 1856). Hereafter cited parenthetically.

24. Gaines, *Southern Plantation,* p. 39.

25. Yellin, p. 146.

26. Such "maroon camps" of escaped slaves were common. See Blassingame, *The Slave Community,* pp. 209–15.

27. Duvall, p. 170.

28. Edmund Wilson, p. 37.

29. Mayne Reid, *The Quadroon; or, A Lover's Adventures in Louisiana* (New York: Robert M. DeWitt, 1856). Hereafter cited parenthetically.

30. Blassingame, *Slave Community,* 173; Gaines, *Southern Plantation,* p. 149; Genovese, p. 351.

31. John T. Trowbridge, *Neighbor Jackwood* (Boston: Lee and Shepard, 1885). Hereafter cited parenthetically.

32. H. L. Hosmer, *Adela, The Octoroon.* (Columbus, Ohio: Follet, Foster and Co., 1860). Hereafter cited parenthetically.

33. Mrs. Metta Victoria Victor, *Maum Guinea, and Her Plantation "Children"; or, Holiday Week on a Louisiana Estate: A Slave Romance* (New York: Beadle and Co., 1861). Hereafter cited parenthetically.

34. Edmund Kirk [J. R. Gilmore], *My Southern Friends* (New York: Carleton, 1863). Hereafter cited parenthetically.

35. Clinton, p. 229.

36. Edmund Kirk [J. R. Gilmore], *Among the Pines; or, South in Secession-Time* (New York: G. P. Putnam, 1862); *Down in Tennessee, and Back by Way of Richmond* (New York: Carleton, 1864).

37. Gilmore, *Down in Tennessee*, p. 220.

38. Epes Sargent, *Peculiar: A Tale of the Great Transition* (New York: Carleton, 1864). Hereafter cited parenthetically.

39. Lorenzo Turner, p. 108.

40. Frances H. McDougall, *Shamah in Pursuit of Freedom; or, The Branded Hand* (New York: Thatcher and Hutchinson, 1858). Hereafter cited parenthetically.

41. Emily C. Pearson, *Cousin Franck's Household; or, Scenes in the Old Dominion* (Boston: Upjohn Ford and Olmstead, 1853). Hereafter cited parenthetically.

42. Gaines, *Southern Plantation*, p. 41.

43. Williamson, pp. 56–59.

44. Mrs. Harriet M. Stephens, *Hagar the Martyr; or, Passion and Reality, A Tale of the North and South* (Boston: W. P. Fetridge and Co., 1855).

45. Elizabeth Barstow Stoddard *Two Men* (New York: Bunce and Huntington, 1865). Hereafter cited parenthetically.

46. Elizabeth Stoddard, *The Morgesons and Other Writings*, ed., with an Introduction, by Lawrence Buell and Sandra A. Zagarell (Philadelphia: Univ. of Pennsylvania Press, 1984).

47. Yellin, pp. 160–76.

48. William Wells Brown, *Clotelle; A Tale of the Southern States* (1864; reprinted with an Introduction by Maxwell Whiteman, Philadelphia: Albert Saifer, 1955). Hereafter cited parenthetically.

49. Whiteman, "Introduction," p. vii.

50. Maxwell Whiteman, *A Century of Fiction by American Negroes, 1853–1952: A Descriptive Bibliography* (1955; reprint Philadelphia: Albert Saifer, 1968), pp. 12–13.

51. William E. Farrison, *William Wells Brown, Author and Reformer* (Chicago: Univ. of Chicago Press, 1969), pp. 249–250.

52. Walt Whitman, "Franklin Evans; or the Inebriate," in *The Early Poems and the Fiction*, ed. by Thomas L. Brasher (New York: New York Univ. Press, 1963), pp. 204–229.

53. Ronald T. Takati, *Violence in the Black Imagination: Essays and Documents* (New York: G. Putnam's Sons, 1972), pp. 215–21.

54. Margaret Butcher, p. 156.

55. Martin Delaney, *Blake; or, the Huts of America* (1859–62; reprint, Boston: Beacon Press, 1970).

56. Takati, pp. 83–90.

57. Yellin, pp. 192–98.

58. Blassingame, *Slave Community*, p. 86.

59. Frank J. Webb, *The Garies and Their Friends* (1857; reprinted

with an Introduction by Arthur P. Davis, New York: Arno Press and *The New York Times*, 1969). Hereafter cited parenthetically.

60. Litwack, pp. 100–01.

61. Mrs. H. E. Wilson, *Our Nig; or, Sketches from the Life of a Free Black in a Two-Story White House, North. Showing that Slavery's Shadow Falls Even There* (Boston: George C. Rand and Avery, 1859). Hereafter cited parenthetically.

62. Some time after I completed my analysis of *Our Nig*, Henry Louis Gates, Jr., published a reprint edition (New York: Random House, 1983) with an introduction in which he establishes the book as the first American novel by a black woman. I had concluded from internal evidence that the novel was autobiographical, that the author was a black female; Gates presents a tale of fascinating literary detective work that traces the external evidence and firmly establishes Mrs. Wilson's identity.

63. John G. Mencke, *Mulattoes and Race Mixture: American Attitudes and Images, 1865–1915* (Ann Arbor, Mich.: UMI Research Press, 1979), pp. 1–28; see also Jordan, p. 178.

64. Helena Smith, p. 18.

4
Reconstruction and After, 1866–90

Even before the Emancipation Proclamation and the end of the Civil War, the program of Reconstruction had begun in the conquered border states. Following the capitulation of the Confederacy, a moderate plan for re-establishing the Union was pursued throughout the South by Presidents Lincoln and Johnson. This "presidential" Reconstruction came to an end with the Reconstruction Acts of March 1867, when Congress wrested control of the program and divided the South into five military districts. All the states were re-admitted to the Union by July 1870, but with governments largely unpopular and supported by Northern military presence. It was not until 1877, with the withdrawal of the last Federal troops from Louisiana, that the era of Reconstruction came to a close.

During the actual period of Reconstruction, the literary battle over slavery had already ended and with that cessation had come a virtual halt in novels about miscegenation. Jay B. Hubbell notes that Southern writers were largely cut off from both publishers and a market in the late 1860s, and that the writings they produced were frequently defensive,[1] which quite naturally precluded mention of miscegenation. According to Hubbell, with the war won and slavery abolished, Northern literary crusaders seemed content, and the barrage of novels attacking the South ended abruptly. Leftover crusading drives were often rechanneled into work with the Freedmen's Bureau or into schools for the newly freed blacks. Many Northern writers even had a positive desire for reconciliation with the South; Hubbell cites correspondence from Oliver Wendell Holmes to the Southern editor Alexander P. Morse in 1868 and from John Greenleaf Whittier to the Charlestonian writer Paul Hamilton Hayne in 1870 as examples of the desire among men of letters for resumption of good relations. By the late 1870s, the Northern reading public had gone beyond simple reconciliation and had become enamored of the South as presented by a new generation of Southern writers; again according to Hubbell, the South had become the most popular setting for American fiction by the 1880s.[2]

Francis Pendleton Gaines discusses the resurgence of the romantic Plantation Tradition novel, noting that only a few inveterate crusaders such as Albion Tourgée attempted to counter the re-edification of the antebellum South.[3] With the North no longer seeking to attack Southern race relations and the South actively rebuilding the myth of the idyllic plantation, the subject of miscegenation almost disappears from American novels during Reconstruction and the years following until 1890. Only a handful of authors turned to miscegenation, as their abolitionist predecessors had, for material to counter the new literary flood of whitewashed cabins, dancing darkies, and moonlight on the magnolias.

Waiting for the Verdict (1867)[4] by Rebecca Harding Davis, precedes the rebirth of the Plantation Tradition and addresses the post-war problems of equal rights and opportunities for blacks both North and South. Born 1831 in Pennsylvania, Mrs. Davis lived in Alabama and Virginia before establishing herself as a short story writer, first published by Lowell in the *Atlantic* in 1861. After her marriage, she lived in Philadelphia where she wrote nine novels, including *Waiting for the Verdict*. In the main plot, Rosslyn Burly, an illegitimate white child, rises above her humble background as a Philadelphia street urchin and marries a wealthy, class-conscious Southern Unionist named Garrick Randolph. In a parallel story, a mulatto slave-boy is purchased by a Quaker woman, who raises the child and educates him in Europe. He returns to Philadelphia as a famous European surgeon, Dr. Broderip. Broderip loves Margaret Conrad, the daughter of one of his white patients, but she rejects him when he reveals his true heritage. He resolves to give his life to the cause of his black brothers and goes to a hero's death leading a black unit in the Civil War. In a complicated attempt to save his family lands before the war, Garrick Randolph had betrayed an old slave's trust and sold him off to die. Later driven by guilt, Randolph returns south to save the old man, which he succeeds in doing. Guilt also forces Randolph to view life from a new perspective; his attitudes toward blacks and his class-consciousness are modified and brought into conformity with Rosslyn's liberal views, in a manner not unlike Miss Ravenel's famous conversion in another novel published the same year.

Miscegenation plays a minor role in the main plot involving Rosslyn and Randolph, but it is a major element in the subplot. Both Dr. Broderip and Margaret Conrad are lonely people who have no love interest until they meet. Broderip dedicates himself to his work but suffers from the lack of personal fulfillment in his life. He attempts to fill the emptiness by doing much charity work and by adopting an orphan (p. 111), but he is continually racked by desire for a "normal" life, something even his Quaker benefactress believes will always be denied him (pp. 115–120). Broderip slowly develops in his feelings for Margaret, whose life, given over to caring for her blind father, is also isolated and unhappy. He initially plans to tell Margaret about his heritage, but as he is about to begin before proposing, a black servant approaches Margaret with a note. She shrinks from the servant "instinctively" and handles the paper as if it were contaminated. Feeling now that the truth would only cause her pain, Broderip proceeds to break off their relationship rather than to propose as he had intended (pp. 199–201). This situation presents a classic example of difference in race as the impenetrable barrier looming in the path of true love.

Later, Broderip, goaded by the marriage of Rosslyn and Randolph, decides it is unfair that he should be denied the chance for a family that other men take for granted (pp. 238–240). He re-establishes his relationship with Margaret, intending to marry her without revealing the truth. On the day he means to propose again Broderip rides through the black section of Philadelphia, feeling a kinship with the down-trodden blacks and aware that they are desperately in need of aid, but saying to himself that he "has turned his back on them with the rest, a cheat and a coward" (p. 291). Broderip faces the basic dilemma of the mulatto light enough to pass; he must choose to be either black or white; there is no middle ground in America. This dilemma is presented symbolically that evening when Broderip's brother Nat arrives at his house gravely wounded and seeking aid. In his operating room, tending to the needs of his black brother, Broderip looks through a window into another room and sees Margaret standing there. On one side of an invisible but nonetheless real barrier lies his wounded race in desperate need of his help, on the other side the white world and the fulfillment of his personal desires. Torn between the two, Broderip at first decides to kill Nat on the operating table, but instead is overcome by the need to free himself from the lie he has lived. He goes to tell Margaret the truth, knowing that she will never marry him (pp. 297–304). Rejected by Margaret and denounced by all but one or two old friends, Broderip throws himself into the task of raising and training black troops. He envisions himself as a Moses figure, born a slave but educated by the ruling class which he later rejects to lead his people into the promised land of freedom, and goes off to war to die (pp. 316–324). Broderip's tragic course demonstrates the moral view that the mulatto cannot live in the white world, neither secretly nor openly, and find happiness.

In addition to its function in the subplot, miscegenation seems of some importance in characterization as well. Both Broderip and Randolph somehow lack strength, the first weakened by his frustrating secret, the second by his obsession with class and his failure when his honor is tested in the land matter. Broderip, though a mulatto, is the stronger of the two; when he is tempted to kill his brother and deceive the woman he loves, he rejects the temptation and acts honorably. Randolph succumbs to his temptation; only when he is driven by guilt to seek the old slave whom he had betrayed is he purged and made whole. Rosslyn, the strongest of them all, sets the example for the other two. At age nine she accepts openly the stigma of her illegitimacy rather than try, like Broderip, to live a lie (pp. 24–25). Later she freely confesses her background to Randolph, the man she loves, despite her knowledge of his feelings about class and breeding (pp. 222–232). The point behind these parallels seems to be that while the white characters are rewarded, sooner or later, for telling the truth and acting honorably, the mulatto who does the same is rejected in love, abandoned by society, and doomed to no honorable course in life except the path to a martyr's death. The author does not, however, suggest that hiding the truth and passing for white is a viable course, either. Broderip's secret almost destroys him spiritually before he reveals it. It seems there is no hope for mulattoes; the only solution lies in avoiding the miscegenation which produces them. At least this inference appears to be the author's suggestion when characters we are led to admire most, such as Rosslyn, speak out strongly against amalgamation (pp. 346, 354–355).

The significance of this novel lies in its use of the tragic mulatto figure for the first time to focus on the plight of postwar, freed blacks. If society rejects Broderip, a nearly white, educated, talented man, what will be the fate of the four million new freedmen severely disadvantaged by their heritage of slavery? Davis poses this question in the character of Broderip's newly freed nephew, Tom. Tom and his mother, Anney, are introduced as they travel unceasingly through the chaos of the war zone searching for Nat. Young Tom is crippled, stunted in growth, but very brave and clever (pp. 267–268). At the end of the novel, Anney expresses her fears concerning Tom's future to Rosslyn, questioning whether white society will decide he can be a man or insist he must be a beast, saying there are four million others also "waiting for the verdict" (p. 354). Tom's symbolic handicap represents the damaging effects on blacks of three hundred years of slavery, while his intelligence and bravery represent the potential of his race. But Broderip's fate seems to foreshadow ill; the narrator intrudes in the last line of the novel to say that the people he died for are still "waiting for the verdict" (p. 361). Davis does not answer the question she raises, but revives the old abolitionist device of using a near-white character to elicit sympathy for blacks in general. The novel also illustrates what Gaines believes to be the general tendency in stories of miscegenation after the war: immorality, which was given great play in abolitionist works, is abandoned in the postwar era in favor of the tragedy of tainted blood, of hope being dashed against the bars of convention and ending in despair.[5]

The conflict between hopeful love and the strictures of society also resolves itself tragically in Anna E. Dickinson's novel, *What Answer?* (1868).[6] Dickinson had a national reputation before the war as an abolitionist speaker, cultivated by leading radicals who called her their Joan of Arc. Her success faded rapidly after the war, however, and she tried writing plays and this one novel in an effort to regain her audience. When her bid failed, she spent the last forty years of her life as a recluse. In the novel, Willie Surrey, a wealthy young New Yorker, meets and falls in love with beautiful Francesca Ercildoune from Philadelphia. Very shortly, however, she mysteriously breaks off their relationship; Surrey leaves for duty in the war, which has just begun. Two years later, wounded and promoted to general, Surrey visits Francesca in Philadelphia, where she again rejects him. He leaves, but then learns that she is a quadroon and has been rejecting him out of love in order to protect his future. Willie returns, restates his love and pledges his willingness to accept all consequences. They travel to New York and marry, but the Surrey family rejects them. Willie plans to raise a freedman's brigade but is caught in the New York draft riots at the home of black friends and is mortally beaten trying to defend them. Francesca, searching the streets for him, finds Willie almost dead, and is shot just as she reaches him. They lie dying in the street together. The novel ends on a compensating happy note with the marriage of their good friends Jim and Sally Given and the developing friendship of Francesca's brother Robert with Willie's cousin, Tom Russell.

The subject of miscegenation forms the basis of the main plot, which is, aside from Willie's battle experiences, the story of his love for Francesca. The incidents of the plot come from the barriers placed in the way of this interracial love. The first problem arises when Willie tells Francesca of a black man who had been fired by his father, but hesitates out of modesty to add that he has since been supporting the man. Francesca becomes angry, feeling that Willie is insensitive, and breaks off their relationship (pp. 60–61). Later she berates herself for being a fool, saying that she must remember that happiness is not meant for her (p. 73). Willie attempts to re-establish their relationship, writing to her from the army, but she returns his letters unopened (p. 98). When he sees her in Philadelphia she tells him to leave, that she does not love him (pp. 138–139). The obstacle which she creates at this time derives not from her racial sensitivity but from her love for him. Willie's aunt had visited Francesca, learned the truth, and insultingly demanded that Francesca give him up. Francesca replied that Willie loved her as a person and that when he learned she was a quadroon it would make no difference. The aunt feared that she might be right and changed her tactics, arguing that if Francesca really loved Willie she would not destroy him. Francesca was convinced by this idea to return Willie's letters and to reject him when he visited (pp. 151–159).

Both the internal force of her love and the external force of society's condemnation work to create the barrier. Once Willie convinces her of his love and willingness to accept the consequences, the bars to their happiness become wholly external. Willie's parents bitterly oppose the marriage and viciously reject him (pp. 184–185). Society at large joins in the condemnation; newspaper articles attack him under headlines such as, "Miscegenation. Disgraceful Freak in High Life. Fruit of an Abolition War" (p. 190). Society's unreasoning condemnation is symbolized by Willie's murder at the hands of a mob enraged by his association with blacks, and by Francesca's tragic death which follows (pp. 260–268). The author vehemently declares that the worst part of the draft riots was the cruel persecution of blacks by the mobs roaming the streets (p. 257). The same prejudice that condemned the marriage of Willie and Francesca motivates the antiblack violence that kills them.

In addition to supporting the plot, miscegenation is also important in the characterization of the Ercildoune family members. All three are people of superior appearance, abilities, and moral strength, typical characteristics of earlier tragic mulattoes. Moreover the father and Robert believe in total allegiance to their people. Mr. Ercildoune had been raised in England free from the effects of prejudice, but when he came back to America his white wife was arrested for violation of anti-amalgamation laws, his home was burned, and one son was killed before they fled back to Europe (pp. 174–175). After raising his remaining children, however, he returns with them to America because, he says,

I had wealth, education, a thousand advantages which are denied the masses of people who are, like me, of mixed race. I came here to identify my fate with theirs; to work with and for them; to fight, till I died, against the cruel and merciless prejudice which grinds them down (p. 176).

The son, Robert, is also motivated by racial allegiance. Despite the daily prejudice and discrimination against blacks that he encounters in the army, he is determined to fight for the freedom of his racial brothers (pp. 164–168), which he does with incredible heroism until severely wounded (pp. 226–227). Francesca's attitudes are also shaped by her being mulatto, although she does not devote her life to the cause as do her father and brother. She attends a boarding school where she successfully passes for white, but for her graduation speech she delivers an impassioned anti-American denunciation of slavery (p. 41). Initially, she rejects Willie because of her racial sensitivity, and her tragic death seems predetermined by her heritage.

As in *Waiting for the Verdict*, the mulatto characters are used to elicit sympathy for blacks in general. In an ending which looks suspiciously like that of the earlier book by Mrs. Davis, a question is posed for the reader when Robert Ercildoune, the mulatto war hero, is turned away from the polls on election day, 1865. Ercildoune asks Tom Russell when will the "war" be over, and the narration ends with a challenge to the reader: "this question must be answered—it is asked by both the living and the dead who fought for liberty" (p. 298).

In many ways *What Answer?* is an undistinguished polemic for the rights of freed blacks, but it is of significance in the history of the miscegenation theme because of the author's implied attitude. Nowhere does Mrs. Dickinson openly advocate miscegenation; indeed, she provides the stock resolution for a miscegenetic affair by having it end tragically. There are, however, several indications that she may be looking to miscegenation as the answer for the problem of race prejudice. Willie's crude and boorish aunt, in her insulting attack on Francesca, puts forth the generally accepted idea that "quadroon, mulatto, or [N]egro, it is all one" (p. 153). Jim Given, a sympathetically portrayed character, advocates an opposite view, one that seldom appears in novels of miscegenation. Jim argues that if one believes in the superiority of Anglo-Saxon blood, he must believe that in anyone mostly Anglo-Saxon that blood will dominate what little Negro admixture there is; he argues, simply, that a mulatto is white, not black (p. 196). Jim also answers the standard charge that miscegenation is unnatural. When someone insists that "an instinct repels an Anglo-Saxon from a Negro always and everywhere," Jim replies:

Instinct, hey? I'd like to know, then, where all the mulattoes and the quadroons, and the octoroons come from. . . . 'Twan't the abolitionists; 'twas the slave holders and their friends that made a race of halfbreeds all over the country; but, slavery or no slavery, they showed nature hadn't put any barriers between them (pp. 194–195).

Dickinson also shows a positive attitude toward miscegenation by making Mr. Ercildoune's mixed marriage successful and in making both the children superior people. Willie unhesitatingly marries Francesca, and both these marriages are extremely happy except for the tragic problems caused by society's prejudice. The author's favorable attitude toward miscegenation seems to be suggested when Francesca corrects Willie's aunt, who calls her a "mulatto," by the proud rejoinder that she is a "quadroon" (p. 153). Her answer implies a sense of degree, of evolution through racial mixing to a level, perhaps at the quadroon, where a being uniting superior qualities of both races is produced. Wide-scale miscegenation would, then, do more than just solve the problem of racial prejudice; it would advance humanity toward perfection.

Widespread interbreeding to produce a superior race is exactly the course advocated by the journalist David Goodman Croly in a social tract called *Miscegenation*, published four years before Dickinson's novel. Croly coined the word "miscegenation," and it first appeared in this work.[7] The common contemporary term for interracial sexual relations was "amalgamation"; indeed, "miscegenation" did not become general until much later in the century. The announced reason for the new word was to have a term free from the negative connotations of "amalgamation." Because Dickinson used Croly's term (for example, in the newspaper headline on p. 190) long before it was popular, it seems quite possible that she knew his work and subtly advocated the idea that interbreeding was the ultimate solution to the postwar race problem. Actually, according to George M. Frederickson, Croly was aided by another New York *World* journalist named George Wakeman in perpetrating an elaborate political dirty trick. The pamphlet advocating "miscegenation" appeared anonymously on the eve of the 1864 election and was believed to be the work of a Republican abolitionist. Despite denunciations by Republican politicians and reservations by the abolitionist press, the work by the two Democratic journalists blackened the Republican image by suggesting that the party supported the incredibly radical position of being "pro-amalgamation." While the hoax failed to do serious political damage to Republican candidates, it revealed the range and depth of antiamalgamation feelings by the wide negative reaction stirred up.[8] It also provided us with a coinage that became our standard word for interracial sex and intermarriage.

Fourteen years after Dickinson, the anonymous author of *Subdued Southern Nobility* (1882),[9] who states that he is one of that group, also turns his attention to the race problem. Spanning the era before, during, and after the Civil War, the book attempts to counter the flood of sentimental novels revitalizing the romantic Plantation Tradition in the post-Reconstruction period. The attitudinal changes necessary for whites if the race problem is to be solved are illustrated by the history of the main character, Rick Gonzales. Gonzales evolves from an impassioned defender of slavery in youth to a man devoted to the care and education of freed blacks following the war. The ultimate symbol of his conversion is Gonzales' willing marriage to a quadroon who had once been his slave. Miscegenation plays a significant role in both the main plot, the development of Rick's attitude, and in the subplot involving a Virginian named Alfred Hastings, whom Rick befriended but later learned not to trust.

Rick's conversion actually begins when he meets a Northern abolitionist, Rose, whom he falls in love with and marries. He is also strongly influenced by a quadroon, Dolores, who had been brought from Cuba by Rick's father and introduced to him as the daughter of an old friend (p. 23). His father and the darkly beautiful girl share a close relationship, especially during the old man's final illness (pp. 27–30). After the father's death, Dolores tells Rick that she is actually a quadroon and a slave, whom his father had taken in when her parents died in Cuba. We see Rick's proslavery attitude when he becomes enraged at having been deceived into treating a slave as an equal, even eating with her. Angrily he decides to sell her in New Orleans as a concubine in order to punish her, but relents when he remembers his promise to his dying father that he would care for the girl (pp. 41–43).

Alfred Hastings also wants to marry the abolitionist Rose, and Rick decides to eliminate him as a rival, while fulfilling his promise to care for Dolores, by offering her $10,000 to marry Alfred. Dolores, willing to do anything to escape from slavery and be established as someone's legitimate wife, quickly agrees (pp. 57–58). Rick is, essentially, still treating her as a thing to be bought or sold, to be used for his convenience. When avaricious Alfred meets Dolores and learns she has a $10,000 "dowry," he immediately "falls in love" and they are married within a month (p. 79). Rick first shows an awareness of her humanity when his second thoughts about Alfred's unscrupulous character prompt him to warn Dolores and to promise his help if she ever needs it; he even shakes her hand (p. 79).

The subplot about the marriage of Alfred and Dolores is used to denounce unreasoning prejudice, the hypocrisy of slave owners concerning miscegenation, and the general cruelty of the slave system. Dolores is content with her lot until she becomes pregnant and the fear of atavism wears her down (p. 104). The baby is white, however, and Dolores rejoices, but her fear of exposure grows worse because it would also affect her daughter (p. 108). The gnawing secret of the mulatto passing for white has its standard effect of mental and physical debilitation; Dolores in a delirium reveals her secret to Alfred (pp. 109–115). Alfred had been perfectly happy with his beautiful wife and new daughter, but his unreasoning prejudice takes over, driving him to the decision that he must kill Dolores and the baby in order to eliminate the "stain on his honor" (p. 116). Ironically, one of the first things Dolores had learned about her new husband was that he had already fathered one child by a mulatto slave (p. 84), which throws into relief the hypocrisy of the "honorable" slave owners who practiced miscegenation but were revolted by intermarriage. Dolores and her baby escape, but encounter incredible hardships and dangers at the hands of various slave owners and traders, surviving their flight to the safety of Rick's Mississippi plantation only through the aid of slaves along the way (pp. 130–206). Dolores recounts her harrowing tale to Rick and his wife, Rose, and finishes by declaring that she will devote herself to her mother's race, which had saved her. This story provides the final incentive for Rick to turn completely against slavery (p. 200–210).

Having devastated the myth of the happy slave "befo' de wah," the author turns his attack in the latter part of the book against postwar Southern attitudes toward blacks. During the war, Rick removes his wife, Dolores, and the baby to Italy for his wife's health, but Rose dies there and he returns to Mississippi with Dolores and her child just before the collapse of the Confederacy. They suffer greatly, as do the slaves, from the rapaciousness of defeated Rebel soldiers, and are forced to flee to New York (pp. 250–301). At the end of the war they return to Rick's plantation, where they establish a school to educate the freed blacks (p. 343). Neighboring whites are exploiting the blacks' ignorance and do everything possible to thwart Rick's efforts (p. 347). A Yankee physician, Dr. Ohlsen, joins forces with Rick, and the local mood becomes increasingly ugly, culminating in the lynching of two blacks educated at Rick's school (p. 361).

A principal source of the hostility (and much of the author's message) is that Rick has great financial success while the other whites starve because they refuse to aid the blacks and thus help themselves to become re-established (p. 348). The theme of racial harmony, of the necessity of working together for mutual success, is driven home when a yellow-fever epidemic strikes. The townspeople are saved only by the efforts of Rick, Dolores, her now grown daughter Rose, Dr. Ohlsen and the blacks educated at Rick's school, who readily volunteer to nurse former malefactors (p. 375). Alfred arrives during the epidemic, seeking Dolores out of guilt and repentance, which suggests the proper attitude for former slave owners who had mistreated their charges (p. 382). But he dies, allowing Dolores and Rick, who had long been in love, to marry at last. The miscegenetic marriages of the quadroon Dolores to her former owner and of her octoroon daughter Rose to the Yankee doctor seem to symbolize the harmony—black and white, North and South—which the author sees as necessary for the salvation of the diseased South, just as this cooperation had saved the now grateful town from the sickness affecting it.

The characterization of Dolores depends to some degree on stereotypic mulatto qualities, such as her superior beauty, moral strength, agony in attempting to pass for white, and resolve to dedicate herself to the betterment of her race. Generally, however, she is not a typical tragic-mulatto character, and in the differences lie the contributions which this novel makes to the development of the miscegenation theme. In one important deviation from the stereotype, Dolores does not suffer a tragic end because of her miscegenation. Miscegenation had frequently been used symbolically before to represent the tragedy of slavery, and by Mrs. Flanders in *The Ebony Idol*, it will be recalled, to represent the impending rape of the South, but in this novel intermarriage becomes for the first time a joyous, hope-filled symbol of future interracial harmony. The other significant difference in Dolores' experience is how the problem of crossing the color line is resolved. In most cases mulattoes find tragedy or unhappiness while living in the white world, discovering peace of mind only when they return to living as a black, dedicated to their people. Dolores and her daughter marry across the line but resolve the conflict between the white world and the need to serve their people by bringing their white partners back with them to join in the cause. The theme of the novel, symbolized by these marriages, is that no racial problem remains insoluble for the white South if it will only follow the radical conversion in attitude undergone by Rick Gonzales.

A much less ambitious novel, Margaret Holmes Bates' *The Chamber Over the Gate* (1886),[10] largely separates miscegenation from both slavery or racism as social problems. While serving with Union forces during the war, Stephen Gatsimer had married an octoroon slave, but remained ignorant of her background until her death some years later. Their child, Coral, is raised in Indiana by Stephen and her mulatto grandmother, June. Stephen's brother Hugh is a selfish and corrupt man. Letty, their younger sister, is the central character, and the novel follows her growth into an intelligent, independent woman who lovingly accepts the truth about her niece. During the course of events, Coral also learns the truth when her mother's white half-brother arrives from the South. She bravely accepts a future life devoid of normal expectations of marriage and family, and fades from the plot.

Miscegenation serves an interesting, catalytic function in the novel. Stephen's miscegenetic secret provides Hugh's first opportunity for villainy—anonymous blackmail of his brother— beginning the development of Hugh's character toward its ultimately evil end. Miscegenation also functions to show the basic goodness of other characters by their reactions to the truth. Letty's reaction, for example, first indicates the positive direction her character development will take.

Most notable about the novel is the lack of sensationalism in treating miscegenation. Even Hugh's concern, aside from a few racial slurs (pp. 14–15, 49) limits itself to the financial advantage he derives from the situation rather than encompassing any real feeling of racial outrage. The author reveals certain obvious prejudices of her own by attributing stereotypic racial characteristics to Coral and June (pp. 47–52) and by making atavism the reason why Coral must never marry (p. 142). Generally, however, she treats her mulatto characters with sympathy and attempts to give them real dignity (pp. 328–344). The mulatto characters do not provide a platform for discussion of race or miscegenation as social issues, but rather are seen as individuals creating private problems within a single family. Because of this approach, the novel does not exaggerate or sensationalize the subject of miscegenation, but neither does it contribute much to the historical development of it, except to demonstrate that even in a period of intensifying racial hostility the subject can be handled, as it is here, without recourse to excess.

Albion Tourgée's *A Royal Gentleman* (1881),[11] first published in 1874 as *Toinette*, by "Henry Churton," focuses on the problem of white attitude as the main barrier to progress in the South during Reconstruction. Most novelists writing about Reconstruction, both North and South, were concerned with restoring national harmony and easing sectional hostility by creating a widely popular body of palliative fiction. Tourgée alone reports the era from the viewpoint of a Radical Republican, and is the only writer who was an active politician in the South during the carpetbag regime. Born in Ohio, Tourgée was wounded twice during the Civil War and spent time in a Confederate prison camp. He moved to Greensboro, North Carolina, in 1865 and entered politics. In 1868, he was elected a judge of the State Supreme Court, where he earned a reputation as a partisan jurist. Tourgée defends Radical Republicans from as strong a bias as other writers had for attacking them.[12] *A Royal Gentleman* was his first novel and sets the pattern for a lengthy career in political fiction demanding equal rights and opportunities for black Americans. The following treatment of the novel is heavily indebted to a discussion of the work by Theodore L. Gross.[13]

The dominant theme, stated by Tourgée in the preface, is a concern with the lingering, unconscious effects of slavery, rather than the obvious ones, and with how these unconscious effects are destructive to racial harmony and equal opportunity for freed blacks (pp. iv–v). Tourgée abandons the antislavery theme of physical cruelty to blacks and emphasizes the rigid caste pride of the Southern aristocracy that makes white adaptation to the postwar status of blacks impossible. In order to present his message, the author creates characters who represent various groups, summarizing in them the whole Southern society before and after the war. Tourgée builds the plot in which the characters operate around the miscegenetic relationship of a Southern gentleman and his mulatto mistress.

The story of Geoffrey Hunter, "a right royal gentleman" in the eyes of the county (p. 12), opens in 1858. Hunter, well-educated and devoted to intellectual and aesthetic pleasures, epitomizes Southern aristocracy (p. 22). A pretty, fourteen-year-old mulatto named Toinette is his serving girl, and she becomes the representative of the slave in Tourgée's polemic. To amuse himself, Hunter decides to dress Toinette as a lady and to educate her accordingly, much as he might decide to train a favored pet (p. 40); he even considers freeing her once she is properly prepared (p. 51). Toinette exhibits much intellectual curiosity and great capacity for learning (pp. 75–78). Inevitably Toinette grows up; her refinement and beauty have a disturbing effect on Geoffrey, a man much too aware of his social position to fall in love with a slave. But he does not reject her love for him and they begin a sexual relationship—"a light thing" to Geoffrey but not to Toinette (pp. 159–161). Shortly before the war, he frees Toinette and establishes the girl, now pregnant, in Ohio (p. 248). Intended by Tourgée to be the representative of all Southern gentlemen, Geoffrey throws himself into the forefront of the debate for secession and is among the first to enlist (p. 256). Toinette, representing freed slaves, becomes a respected teacher (p. 311), demonstrating the capacity that exists in slaves and needing only education to be fulfilled. Moreover, she drives herself incessantly at self-improvement from a need to become Geoffrey's equal, so that when the war is over and slavery is dead, he may marry her (p. 317). In so doing, she seems to represent the hoped-for equality and harmony between former slaves and former owners that will occur when the slaves reach their full potential through hard work and education.

Near the end of the war, Toinette leaves her son with friends and goes to seek Geoffrey (p. 319). She finds him, wounded and blind, in a hospital and becomes his nurse, but he does not recognize her (pp. 330–337). While convalescing, Geoffrey notes that his devoted nurse reminds him of Toinette, whom he remembers only as "one nigger Lincoln didn't get a chance to free" (p. 365). Suddenly he realizes that she is Toinette and demonstrates by his reaction Tourgée's point, that former masters cannot accept the equality of their former slaves:

He saw it all now. Strange he had been such a fool. The jade had taken his name, and passed for a widow—and a white woman too! Probably called her brat Hunter!... Geoffrey Hunter's face showed the most extreme disgust. It actually sickened him that a free nigger should impose on him.... "God! If I had not happened to have been here, she might have married some [sic] of these good, impressionable fellows!" Geoffrey Hunter's face grew white with horror as he contemplated this fearful contingency (pp. 368–369).

In his anger, Geoffrey decides to expose her to the other Confederate officers whom she has been nursing in the ward. When she enters the room, he yells at her, " 'I say, you girl, Toinette! Toinette!' Five years were brushed away in a second.... She started, and answered instantly with the inimitable and indescribable intonation of the slave—'Sir?' " (p. 378). In so debasing her, Geoffrey, the formerly kind master, loses something of his status as a gentleman, because he is responding to the past, as is Toinette, in an altered situation where such an action is no longer proper.

When Hunter learns that Toinette had arranged the operation which restored his sight, he feels badly, comparing it to the way he felt once when he beat his dog for wakening him before he realized that the dog was warning him of a fire (pp. 382–383). Softened by this feeling, Hunter later wishes to resume their antebellum relationship when he returns home and finds Toinette occupying their former house, which she now owns. This desire to go back to the past creates the conflict, symbolically portrayed in Geoffrey and Toinette, between the defeated land and slave owners and the newly freed, educated, equal blacks. Geoffrey openly professes his love for Toinette and recalls the "dear old times" (pp. 438–439), but, despite his admitted love, when she says all has changed he becomes angry: "You expect me to marry you, perhaps?" (p. 440) He tells her to be "reasonable," that freedom has not made her white: "You are not a lady, and need not try to act the part of one" (p. 442). Geoffrey cannot recognize that Toinette is a lady and more than his equal; while he degenerates into bewailing the insurmountable obstacles to his love, she calmly arranges to go abroad and raise their son properly. Hunter simply cannot rise above his past, his now misguided pride. Toinette and her son watch him ride away into the gathering darkness (p. 444), a symbol of the future in the South, just as the miscegenetic marriage which never took place would have been a symbol of the harmony that could have existed between black and white if the Southern aristocracy had been able to discard the unconscious attitudes preventing it. Tourgée emphasizes his theme by the letter which Toinette leaves behind for Geoffrey, in which she says she first became free in the secret room when they shared love as equals, and that he is "a slave, now, bound with the sinful chains which generations of slavery have forged" (p. 463).

Tourgée reinforces the idea that Hunter's problems derive from the past by the story of Toinette's mother, Belle. Woven into the novel in a series of complex and awkward flashbacks, the parallel tale of Belle and her white lover, Arthur Lovett, ends tragically when Belle kills him because he is about to marry a white woman. The inability of both Arthur and Geoffrey to defy tradition is the same; the difference between Belle's tragic fate and her daughter's chance for a new life is simply that times have changed—Toinette is free and has the opportunity to develop her inherent potential.

Tourgée does not appear to favor miscegenation; rather it seems to be treated as one of the many evils growing out of slavery. The affair of Belle and Arthur Lovett ends in murder and suicide and if Toinette's affair does not end tragically, it does not end happily, either. Tourgée does see miscegenation, however, as a convenient metaphor for racial harmony in the South, but unlike the more optimistic author of *Subdued Southern Nobility*, he does not see the symbolic marriage taking place. Hunter's degeneracy prevents the marriage, just as the degeneracy of the Southern aristocracy in general prevents racial harmony in the postwar era. Toinette intends to rear their son so that "he may be worthy of his father at his best," and takes Geoffrey's sword to give the boy when he is old enough to be told the story of his father's bravery during the war (pp. 465–466). Tourgée implies that the aristocrats of the Old South were at their best when they fought heroically for a lost cause, but that the inability to adapt to an altered world has robbed them of their former nobility.

Tourgée returns to the theme of miscegenation with *Hot Plowshares* (1883),[14] the last novel in a cycle of works dealing with Reconstruction. Actually, the book does not treat the Reconstruction period but attempts to provide the background for the conflicts of that time by giving a review of the antislavery struggle from 1848 to the beginning of the war. Moreover, the story does not involve any real miscegenation, only the suspicion of it.

Merwyn Hargrove and his daughter Hilda have settled in New York's Mohawk Valley, but he still owns land and slaves in the South. Constant and confusing hints abound concerning some dark secret involving Hargrove's dead brother. Hilda grows up and attends a boarding school, but while she is there her father dies and papers surface indicating that Hilda is really the daughter of his brother and a mulatto (p. 452). From here on the novel depends upon the standard nineteenth-century story devices of uncovering the protagonist's true genealogy and the theme of rightful inheritance.[15] The revelation of Hilda's "taint" serves as a test of the humanity of each character, depending on whether the character rejects or stands by her. Hilda eventually proves she is Merwyn Hargrove's daughter (p. 572), and finally that the woman whom her uncle married was not a mulatto after all (pp. 601–602). Prolix and contrived, the novel has little significance except that it reveals Tourgée's antipathy to miscegenation. Merwyn Hargrove converts from defending slavery (p. 145) to advocating abolition, but still shudders at the thought of racial mixing (p. 272). Hilda never believes she is of mixed blood, but as long as she feels there is the slightest possibility, she will not consider marrying her white fiancé (pp. 465–471). Over-all, the novel is simply a tract establishing the evils of slavery as the source for the evils of Reconstruction.

In *Pactolus Prime* (1890),[16] Tourgée once again takes up the theme of miscegenation, but again fails to achieve any significance in this his final work concerning blacks in America. Theodore Gross calls the novel "moralistic and homiletic ...

static and pedestrian," and says that "the book that proved to
be Tourgée's valedictory to his struggle for the Negro's intellectual freedom ... is a novel of a bitter man, written in bitter
language."[17] Tourgée directs his bitterness at both Christianity, which had allowed slavery and continued to allow the subjugation of freed blacks (pp. 45, 67), and the failure of Northern
politicians to fulfill the obligation of educating freedmen (p.
133). The novel is little more than a collection of set piece
diatribes by the central character, Pactolus Prime. Most of the
complications in the plot, however, derive from the practice of
miscegenation.

Pactolus Prime, a black bootblack in Washington's best hotel,
is known to be wealthy and politically so well-informed that
members of Congress regularly consult him for advice (pp. 20–
26). He has a very light-skinned mulatto assistant, Ben, and
supports a young white woman, Eva Collins, and her white
maid, Mrs. Macey. Late in the novel, Prime is killed in an
accident and his diary is discovered, explaining the complex
background for many confusing events in the main plot (pp.
290–323). Prime, the son of his master and a mulatto slave,
was once light enough to pass for white. As a young man he
fell in love with Mazy, a beautiful mulatto, but she had an
affair with his white half-brother and bore a son, Ben. After
the war, in which Prime had fought as a white in the Federal
Army, he returns home, takes Mazy and her son to South Carolina, where they are married and pass for white. They have
a daughter, Eva, but Prime is mysteriously shot and left for
dead. A long course of treatment by a doctor using silver prep-
arations causes argyria, a permanent, dark discoloration of the
skin. When he returns home, Prime discovers his half-brother
living with Mazy, so Prime steals his daughter and takes her
to live in Washington. Years later, Mazy and her son Ben arrive
there; he hires Ben and places "Mrs. Macey" as maid for the
unsuspecting Eva, who believed herself to be the daughter of
Prime's old master.

Miscegenation appears most significantly in the theme of
"passing." Prime had passed for white until it became impossible for him and had helped many light mulattoes to pass,
including his wife and daughter (p. 303). He insists that Ben,

who wishes to be a lawyer and help his people, instead accept enough money to settle in the West as a white (p. 40). When Ben argues, Prime insists he must become white for his children's sake, that it would be better to kill them than to have them known to be black, and Ben is crushed by the truth of what Prime says (pp. 46–47). The argument seems reinforced by Eva's fate. She had passed unknowingly for years, but when she discovers the truth she decides to live it openly. Society, however, will no longer accept her, as she learns when she is abandoned by her fiancé. She resolves her dilemma by entering a convent where, as "Sister Pactola," she devotes herself to work among blacks (pp. 355–359).

The theme of passing dramatizes Tourgée's despairing conviction that there is no hope of equality for blacks in America. He had long before called his crusade for civil rights in the South "a fool's errand" and had finally concluded that there was no hope in the North either. The blacks were condemned to inferiority, and the mulatto light enough to pass had the choice of either deception or ignominy. Tourgée's bitter despair was a product of the conditions which prevailed by the 1890s: the successful disenfranchisement of blacks in the South, the rise of Jim Crow, the re-establishment in fiction of the Plantation Tradition, and the loss of Northern idealism concerning the welfare and fate of blacks. By 1890, the verdict sought by Mrs. Davis in 1867 had come in; the question asked by Mrs. Dickinson in 1868 was answered. Black Americans and their sympathizers knew now that Emancipation had meant neither freedom, equality, nor acceptance as human beings.

NOTES

1. Jay B. Hubbell, *The South in American Literature, 1607–1900* (Durham, N.C.: Duke Univ. Press, 1954), p. 710.
2. Hubbell, p. 700–01.
3. Gaines, *Southern Plantation*, pp. 62–89.
4. Rebecca Harding Davis, *Waiting for the Verdict* (New York: Sheldon and Co., 1867). Hereafter cited parenthetically.
5. Gaines, *Southern Plantation*, p. 159.
6. Anna E. Dickinson, *What Answer?* (Boston: Ticknor and Fields, 1868). Hereafter cited parenthetically.

7. David Goodman Croly, *Miscegenation: The Theory of the Races, Applied to the American White Man and Negro* (New York: H. Dexter, Hamilton and Co., 1864), pp. 1, 11, 20.

8. Frederickson, pp. 171–74.

9. *Subdued Southern Nobility: A Southern Ideal* (New York: Sharps Publishing Company, 1882). Hereafter cited parenthetically.

10. Margaret Holmes Bates, *The Chamber Over the Gate* (Indianapolis: Charles A. Bates, 1886). Hereafter cited parenthetically.

11. Albion W. Tourgée, *A Royal Gentleman* (1881; reprint, Ridgewood, N.J.: Gregg Press, 1967). Hereafter cited parenthetically.

12. Theodore L. Gross, *Albion W. Tourgée* (New York: Twayne, 1963), p. 7.

13. Theodore Gross, *Tourgée*, pp. 37–47.

14. Albion W. Tourgée, *Hot Plowshares: A Novel* (New York: Fords, Howard and Hulbert, 1883). Hereafter cited parenthetically.

15. Theodore Gross, *Tourgée*, pp. 108–109.

16. Albion W. Tourgée, *Pactolus Prime* (1890; reprint, Upper Saddle River, N.J.: Gregg Press, 1968). Hereafter cited parenthetically.

17. Theodore Gross, *Tourgée*, p. 133.

5
Broader Concerns, 1880–1914

During the same period when Tourgée and other reformers began to lose hope, when white racists used miscegenation as a terrible threat, and black writers sought to counter their awful charges, a small number of white novelists took up the subject to write about miscegenation in a context broader than the immediate status of blacks in the post-Reconstruction South. Novels of miscegenation by George Washington Cable, William Dean Howells, Bliss Perry, and Ellen Glasgow acknowledge the evils of slavery and post-war racism but also work with other fundamental human relationships and difficulties, of which enslavement, discrimination, and miscegenation may serve as useful symbols.

Tourgée was a Northerner who had participated in the Reconstruction government of the South. Cable, a native of New Orleans and a Confederate veteran, was a Southerner, but one who came to share Tourgée's despair over the treatment of Southern blacks in the post-war decades, eventually leaving the South to reside in Northampton, Massachusetts. A crusader for reform, Cable rejected the cavalier ideal of the neoplantation romancers, the sanctity of the "one drop rule," and the idea of racial stereotypes, arguing that each black, like each white, was an individual. His major novel, *The Grandissimes* (1880),[1] is a *Kulturroman*, but in this clash between an old and a new society, while race may be a central issue, the novel is above all a study of character, of individual human beings caught up in a changing tide of events.[2]

The Grandissimes is a complicated story of two old Creole families, including the colored branches, and of their interrelationships. Involved with both families, Joseph Frowenfeld is an American immigrant to New Orleans at the time of the Louisiana Purchase. The Creoles react to change in ways dependent upon their individual characters, some acting well, some self-destructively, while Frowenfeld is seen by Richard Chase as a "Jamesian Yankee," a man enlarged and humanized by contact with an old, rich, corrupt society.[3] Frowenfeld opens an apothecary, where he comes to know various members of the Grandissime family and the last survivors of the rival DeGrapions, a widow named Madame Aurore Nançanou, and her daughter, Clotilde, with whom Frowenfeld falls in love. The principal Grandissimes are patriarchal Agricola Fusilier de Grandissime and his nephew, Honoré, to whom the rest of the numerous family have entrusted the care of their properties and businesses. Honoré has a mulatto half-brother also named Honoré and designated by Cable as "free man of color" (fmc). With the exception of Honoré, the Creoles are exemplified by Agricola: reactionary, inflammatory, and closed-minded to the point of insanity on any question of race. Their long-fixed way of life and attitudes, however, are threatened by the effects on New Orleans of the arrival of American control in 1803.

The fortunes of the Creoles had declined over the years, and when the story opens the Nançanou women are penniless, while the financial solvency of the Grandissimes depends solely on the profits from one estate. This plantation had belonged to the DeGrapions but came into Agricola's possession after he killed Aurore DeGrapion Nançanou's husband in a duel. The long feud between the families had worsened when Agricola forced the marriage of his mulatto slave, Palmyre Philosophe, to an enslaved African prince, Bras Coupé. Palmyre is the half-sister of Aurore, and Agricola outraged her father by marrying the illegitimate daughter to a black. Bras Coupé is long dead, but Palmyre, now free, hates Agricola because he had degraded her and destroyed any chance that her love for white Honoré might be fulfilled. Honoré actually loves Palmyre's half-sister, Aurore. Honoré Grandissime, fmc, loves Palmyre passionately, but she rejects his suit despite the immense wealth which his white father had bequeathed him.

White Honoré progressively incurs his family's wrath by open cooperation with the despised new American government, and the breaking point is reached when he decides that the wrongs done by Agricola to Aurore and her daughter must be righted. Honoré returns their estate, the one source of financial stability for all the Grandissime holdings. Honoré Grandissime, fmc, offers to rescue the family fortunes by entering a business partnership with white Honoré on a basis of equality under the name, "Grandissimes Bros." Honoré gratefully agrees, but Agricola and the others are outraged. The culmination comes when Agricola slaps his mulatto nephew, and the free man of color kills him, something Palmyre had been trying to do for years. The two mulattoes flee to France, but Palmyre continues to reject Honoré, fmc, and he commits suicide in Bordeaux, where Palmyre lives on for twenty years, supported by a generous allowance from white Honoré. The novel concludes with the engagement of Frowenfeld to Clotilde and of Honoré to Aurore.

Miscegenation plays an important role in this complex plot involving three interrelated conflicts: the feud between the Grandissime and DeGrapion (Nançanou) families, the breach between the white and mulatto elements of New Orleans society, and the clash between the old Creole way of life and the new American presence. Miscegenation is not involved in the last, but is basic to the development and resolution of the other conflicts.

The feud between the Grandissimes and the DeGrapions had its origin in a miscegenetic affair involving an Indian princess (pp. 27–28), and continued in one form or another for generations. The period of open hostility began when Agricola forced Palmyre to marry Bras Coupé despite old DeGrapion's threat to kill anyone who gave his illegitimate daughter to a black (pp. 229, 241). Aurore's husband attempted to fulfill the vow for her father and was killed by Agricola (p. 39).

In addition to its role in the origin and development of the feud, miscegenation is also a key in the resolution; the first step toward reconciliation is taken because of confusion arising from miscegenation. Aurore and her daughter are evicted by a note from their landlord, signed "Honoré Grandissime" (p. 82), and Aurore decides to appeal to him (p. 86). Actually, her landlord is the free man of color, but Aurore mistakenly goes to white Honoré, who, taken by her beauty and plight, begins the aid which leads to the return of her lost property and their marriage (pp. 155–157). Honoré, fmc, a product of miscegenation, kills Agricola, thus removing the chief cause and irritant of the feud. Moreover, final reconciliation between the families comes when Agricola reveals on his deathbed that twenty years earlier he and DeGrapion had secretly pledged the union of Honoré and Aurore (p. 434).

If miscegenation is important in the rivalry between the families, in the conflict between white and mulatto society it is the very core. The refusal of the Creoles to recognize their own children, brothers, and sisters, the refusal to admit the humanity of the mulattoes, create this breach. A duality exists here—irreconcilable conflict between people bound by ties of family and love—that creates great power in the novel. For example, DeGrapion gives Palmyre to Agricola because Aurore loves her too much, and he fears that his mulatto daughter dominates his pure white one (pp. 75–76), but DeGrapion's pride in his blood is outraged by Palmyre's forced marriage to a black. Palmyre, in turn, hates Agricola and tries to murder him (pp. 125, 415). She finally triumphs when Honoré, fmc, carries out the deed for her. But as deeply as Palmyre hates one white Grandissime, just as passionately she loves another (p. 188). Honoré does not return her love, but he also suffers the wrenching effects of divided loyalties produced by a society having miscegenation as a way of life. After ten years of fraternal intimacy with his half-brother in Paris, Honoré is forced upon their return to New Orleans to deny the free man of color. Earlier, their father had also been forced to deny his oldest son and to put aside the woman he loved; he was able to show his feelings only in death by leaving his fortune to the mulatto son (pp. 138–139). Unfortunately, love alone cannot bridge the chasm between Creole and mulatto. Palmyre's love goes unfulfilled, and Honoré's attempt at reconciliation with his brother ends in disaster. The feud between the rival families ends in union; the conflict between old and new diminishes as one by one the Grandissimes accept the American government (p. 208), and the Creole belle, Clotilde, marries the American businessman Frowenfeld. The resolution of the conflict between white and mulatto, however, comes not in reconciliation but in murder, flight, and suicide.

The conflicts of the plot are, in many ways, outgrowths of the characters who are, in turn, products of the caste system resulting from the important social fact of miscegenation. Both white and mulatto figures in the novel are shaped by miscegenation and its consequences on their lives. Palmyre reminds us of Mrs. Stowe's Cassy; both characters depend on the abolitionist tragic-octoroon stereotype for their beauty and role as victim, but differ sharply from the stereotype in their strength and refusal to acquiesce in their fate. Philip Butcher says that Palmyre is a direct opposite to Cable's other mulatto women, 'Tite Poulette and Madame Delphine, in her feline barbarity and ability to hate.[4] Chase explains that Palmyre's hatreds result from distortion of her strongly passional nature produced by social injustice.[5] The injustice results from the caste system based on miscegenation. Like earlier tragic octoroons, Palmyre seeks to marry white and believes that she has a rightful place in the white world to which she is related.

Unlike the tragic mulatto characters of some black authors, Palmyre is not torn apart by inner suffering and conflict,[6] nor does she show any allegiance to the suffering blacks. She is consistent in rejecting her marriage to Bras Coupé and in rejecting the love of Honoré, fmc. Palmyre achieves a kind of salvation, if only a wealthy exile, by the consistency with which she battles the fate conceived for her in the miscegenetic caste system of New Orleans. She begins by dominating her white half-sister (pp. 75–76), later seeks revenge for her forced marriage by urging Bras Coupé to insurrection (pp. 238–239), terrifies Agricola into freeing her (p. 189), and dedicates her hatred to his ruin (p. 239). She pursues her planned destruction of Agricola, who is really a symbol of the society that oppresses her, both directly by knife attack (p. 125) and indirectly by voodoo (p. 415). Palmyre is unable to obtain the love of Honoré, but she is, in the narrator's words, a woman who had "stood all her life with dagger drawn" (p. 173), and by this fierce strength escapes the oppressed state which society had decreed for her. William Bedford Clark calls her "a terrifying personification of the spirit of righteous wrath."[7]

The foil to Palmyre's struggle for freedom is the paralyzed will and passivity of Honoré Grandissime, fmc.[8] Wealthy and educated, the equal of his white half-brother during their ten years in Paris, Honoré, fmc, lacks Palmyre's desire for freedom and accepts the strictures of the caste system when he returns to New Orleans; although he is Frowenfeld's landlord, for example, he will not sit when he visits the white man in his shop (p. 53). Frowenfeld asks the mulatto why, with his education and wealth, he does not devote himself to his people's cause, only to receive the negative response that slaves have no cause; they lost it in Africa. Frowenfeld then says that Honoré, fmc, is the worst kind of slave, that he could and should work to better conditions for the free men and women of color, but the mulatto resignedly counters that nothing can be done (pp. 254–256).

Mulatto Honoré's self-enslavement is heightened by comparison to Bras Coupé, the African prince who, although legally and physically a slave, refuses to accept bondage even though his refusal costs his life (p. 252). The story of Bras Coupé, although it had taken place years earlier, occurs in the narration just before Frowenfeld's conversation with Honoré, fmc, to point up the ironic contrast between the "free" man of color and the black "slave." Honoré, fmc, finally acts to kill Agricola (p. 421), but his action is a momentary flash of latent violence sparked by a slap from Agricola, rather than the fulfillment of a struggle for freedom. Closer to the true nature of Honoré, fmc, is the negative act of suicide, which he commits shortly after escaping to France (p. 437).

Agricola Grandissime, in having a dominant and aggressive personality, differs greatly from Honoré, fmc, but in one essential way they are alike. Agricola, no less than the mulatto, enslaves himself to the system of caste discrimination produced by the miscegenetic society and is, like Honoré, fmc, destroyed by it. Agricola epitomizes Creole blindness on race; he states at one point, "The non-mention of color always implies pure white; and whatever is not pure white is to all intents and purposes pure black" (p. 73). He dies with a defense of the system on his lips, although his self-enslavement to the system causes his death: Honoré, fmc, stabs Agricola when the old man slaps the mulatto for the affront of saving the white Grandissimes from bankruptcy.

White Honoré parallels Palmyre in that both reject the structure of the caste system and in so doing achieve freedom. Honoré accommodates the new American government, to the annoyance of his Creole family who wish no association with foreigners. He completes the break with tradition by accepting mulatto Honoré's offer of the business partnership which allows him to return Aurore's property without destroying his own family. Freed from the wrongs of the past, Honoré is able to seek and win Aurore's love. The implication seems to be that those like Honoré and Palmyre who reject the bondage of tradition and refuse to accept the caste system find freedom and reward; even Bras Coupé, who is killed in his attempt, whispers on his deathbed that he is going home to Africa (p. 252). But Agricola and Honoré, fmc, who accept the bondage of race and caste produced by a miscegenetic society, bind themselves as well to self-destruction.

The Grandissimes is significant in this study of miscegenation largely because it is one of the few novels of literary merit that incorporates the theme. Richard Chase calls it "a minor masterpiece," a novel of ideas which describes an intricate society full of ambiguities of class, caste, and race, comparable to Faulkner's work.[9] Cable escapes, like Mrs. Stowe in creating Cassy, from stereotypes of the mulatto and provides in Palmyre and Honoré, fmc, studies of complex human beings. Moreover, the situation of the free mulattoes in New Orleans of 1803 is used to symbolize the plight of the blacks after the Civil War, who are free but despised and without rights.[10] Rubin notes that a new, more liberal government is imposed on a tradition-dominated society and the central problem is race. He sees Agricola's furious pride and insistence on racial integrity as typical of the post-war South. Indeed, the name Agricola Fusilier—the planter/soldier—can be taken a symbolic of the

Southern ruling class.[11] Cable seems to imply that, while other accommodations between the old and the new can be achieved, the conflict of black and white, embodied in the figure of the mulatto, cannot be reconciled. The only resolution, despite the efforts of good men such as Honoré, comes in violence or, at best, in escape or deception, such as occurs in two other works by Cable on the theme of miscegenation—" 'Tite Poulette" and *Madame Delphine.*

In the short story " 'Tite Poulette" (1874), Cable's earliest direct treatment of the miscegenation theme, he simply avoids coming to grips with the problem by utilizing two standard evasions: there is no real proof that the girl has mixed blood, and the white man she marries is not an American but a foreigner. With *Madame Delphine* (1881),[12] however, Cable develops new insights into the theme which he had treated the previous year in *The Grandissimes.* Captain LeMaitre, a wealthy Creole, has taken up piracy after the War of 1812 but is inspired to abandon his career by a beautiful young woman aboard a ship he captures. LeMaitre establishes himself as a respectable banker and searches out the identity of the girl. She is Olive, the daughter of Madame Delphine, a quadroon. LeMaitre asks Olive to disregard her heritage and marry him, and the arrangements are made. LeMaitre's sister and her husband, Mr. Thompson, discover the truth and threaten to turn LeMaitre over to the authorities for piracy unless the match is called off. Madame Delphine goes to the Thompsons and solemnly swears to them and to Olive that the girl is not her child. For proof she presents matching photographs of Olive's father and a white woman to whom the girl bears a striking resemblance, and swears that the woman is Olive's dead mother. Her testimony accepted, the marriage takes place. In a later deathbed confession, Madame Delphine reveals to Père Jerome the truth. She is, in fact, Olive's mother. The woman in the photograph was her lover's half-sister, whose features Olive inherited.

Olive is basically a stereotypic mulatto. She is beautiful and evokes instant devotion from a white lover, but this may be only the love-at-first-sight reaction conventional to the nineteenth-century novel. Her character is simply not developed;

we know only that Olive is beautiful and that she is devoted to her mother (pp. 27, 75–76). Madame Delphine presents a stronger, more interesting character. She accepts her lot as a quadroon in New Orleans, but refuses to accept this as good enough for her beloved child. The situation involves racial problems but has broader implications. Butcher points out that Madame Delphine evokes real compassion as a woman suffering a denial of basic rights,[13] but the compassion is universalized because she suffers not for herself but as a mother for her child. When Père Jerome tries to explain to Madame Delphine that marital laws were made to keep the races separate, she sums up the tragic plight of the quadroon—not, however, as she has suffered from it but as it affects her child's welfare:

Separate! No—oo! They do not want to keep us separated; no, no! But they want to keep us despised!... But, very well! From which race do they want to keep my daughter separate? She is seven parts white! The law did not stop her from being that; and now, when she wants to be a white man's good and honest wife, shall the law stop her? (p. 62)

Madame Delphine accepts the agony of denying her motherhood and the damnation for her perjury as not too high a price to pay for a mother to insure her child's happiness.

In *Madame Delphine*, as in *The Grandissimes*, Cable seems to be suggesting that no open and honest solution to the problems caused by miscegenation is possible. LeMaitre and Olive attempt such a path but are headed for disaster until Madame Delphine saves them through deception. Cable seems to have gone beyond his vision in *The Grandissimes* that resolution of miscegenetic problems can come only in violence or in physical escape from the society creating them, to the idea of a third alternative—refusing to accept the rules of that society, not by challenging them but by evading them. Butcher says that there was adverse public reaction to *Madame Delphine* because the story strongly suggests that over the years many quadroons and octoroons had passed into white society and into the best of Creole families.[14] This idea is noticeably absent from *The Grandissimes*. *Madame Delphine* suggests the concept which

Mark Twain develops fully some dozen years later in *Pudd'n-head Wilson*, that race is nothing but a fiction of law and custom and that this truth can be seen most clearly embodied in the children of miscegenation.

Cable's last novel about miscegenation is *Gideon's Band: A Tale of the Mississippi* (1914).[15] The melodramatic, highly involved plotting in this romance of pre–Civil War riverboating seems to bear out Butcher's contention that late in his career Cable came to believe that the primary function of fiction was to entertain.[16] The interest of the novel lies in adventure and romance rather than in an absorbing study of a society (*The Grandissimes*) or of an individual (*Madame Delphine*). Briefly, the complicated plot involves the rivalry through three generations of two families owning riverboat lines and the Romeo and Juliet romance of the youngest members, Hugh Courtenay and Ramsey Hayle. Ramsey's hot-tempered brothers vehemently oppose the love affair, and innumerable complications ensue before the novel culminates with the marriage.

Miscegenation enters in the person of a mulatto, Phyllis, who, as Helena Smith observes, plays a minor role but whose existence affects to some degree the motivations and attitudes of other characters.[17] The novel seems to emphasize again that race distinctions are a fiction of society, because Phyllis is so nearly identical to Ramsey she is able to double undetected for the white girl in a dramatic production aboard one of the riverboats (p. 316). The surprisingly explicit recounting of the entangled relationships between black and white also argues the unreality of racial distinctions (pp. 96–102). The incestuous, miscegenetic relationships and the explanation are suggestive, in fact, of Faulkner's *The Bear*. Phyllis is the daughter of Ramsey Hayle's grandfather in his old age, and the mulatto girl's mother was the old man's daughter as well. When grown, Phyllis has an affair with her white half-brother Dan, Ramsey's uncle, by whom she has a child. Ramsey's slow coming-to-awareness of these facts leads her to the decision that she owes Phyllis the kind of loyalty that she feels for the rest of her family (p. 316), and finally leads Ramsey to dismiss "race consciousness" as "nonsense" (pp. 413–414).

Phyllis herself emphasizes the idea that race distinctions are not real. She is not a typical tragic octoroon, but rather a strong and vengeful woman like Mrs. Stowe's Cassy or Cable's own Palmyre. Placed as nursemaid to the infant Hugh Courtenay, for ten years Phyllis secretly tyrannizes him, subjecting the child to all the brutality and degradation of slavery while keeping him silent under the threat of death (pp. 209–210). The questions of race, slavery, appearance, and reality are played out on two levels as Phyllis servilely functions as slave to the Courtenay family, while the son and heir of the family secretly functions as her slave. All the rules of society proclaiming that whites are masters and blacks are slaves and that "one drop of nigrah blood makes a nigrah" (p. 282) are broken not by challenge but by guile. We see that guile is the only way when Phyllis is eventually freed, and a white man named California wishes to marry her (pp. 410–411). Despite the approval of the best elements of white society, represented by Hugh Courtenay and Ramsey Hayle, the open violation of social taboo does not take place because California is dissuaded from his plan by others (pp. 414–415). Throughout his works dealing with miscegenation, Cable consistently implies that race distinctions, at least in the case of mulattoes, are a social fiction and have force only when accepted by those involved. He also implies, however, that the social fiction is so strong that it cannot be challenged openly, but only subverted.

William Dean Howells was a realist, committed in the scientific spirit of the late nineteenth century to the careful observation of people and society in order to record the truth about human behavior. In *An Imperative Duty* (1892),[18] Howells debunks the romantic emotionalism surrounding miscegenation, presenting the subject as a problem like any other, equally subject to a reasonable solution. In doing so, he also ridicules the stereotypic characters and situations found in the earlier romantic fiction of the tragic mulatto.

Dr. Edward Olney, the main character in the novel, had encountered Mrs. Meredith and her niece Rhoda Aldgate while in Europe, and shortly after his return to Boston meets them again when Mrs. Meredith is taken ill in the hotel where he resides. Mrs. Meredith confides to Olney that her illness is caused by the burden of a great secret. Rhoda is the daughter of an octoroon, but her parents died when she was a child, and the girl, raised by the Merediths has no knowledge of her black heritage. Mrs. Meredith now feels an overwhelming obligation to tell Rhoda the truth because a young minister, Mr. Bloomingdale, has proposed. When the aunt finally informs her niece, Rhoda is distraught and becomes enraged with Mrs. Meredith for having told her. Later the old woman, overcome by guilt and grief, commits suicide. Olney intervenes to aid the bereaved Rhoda, and later proposes to her. Rhoda attempts a dramatic rejection of him by declaiming the "truth," but Olney laughs it off and convinces her to abandon plans for a life dedicated to selfless work among blacks. They marry and live in Europe, but Rhoda is never completely free from worry that someone will discover her secret.

The novel's plot depends on the mental conflict of each character with his or her sense of duty. Anne Amacher points out that Mrs. Meredith is a clear case of overgrown conscience, of Puritan dutiolatry,[19] and Thomas Ford notes that Rhoda is also torn by the question of "imperative duty" concerning the devotion of her life to the black cause.[20] Even Olney is somewhat embroiled in an interior struggle over his duty toward his rival, Bloomingdale (pp. 116–126). But the main conflicts are clearly Mrs. Meredith's and Rhoda's, and miscegenation provides their dilemmas. Mrs. Meredith has known the truth from the beginning but, out of fear of hurting Rhoda, never told her. Now the possibility of future miscegenation convulses her sense of duty into action, with a result so apparently disastrous that she commits suicide (pp. 70–82). When Rhoda learns of her miscegenetic heritage, she is driven to temporary despair and to hatred for the woman who had been a mother to her (pp. 80–87, 96). She briefly resolves her dilemma by theoretically deciding her duty should be a life committed to helping blacks and consecrates herself to that (pp. 88–95). Actually, Rhoda's resolution of conflict comes only at the close of the novel when she accepts reality, understands her sense of duty is false, and agrees to follow her heart and marry Olney instead (pp. 142–146).

Just as miscegenation forms the base of the plot, it also plays an important role in characterizing Rhoda. Amacher notes that

Howells deliberately rejects the romantic stereotype of the tragic octoroon and creates a complicated, realistic character.[21] Rhoda is credible, not selfless and noble. Before knowing about her heritage, Rhoda speaks well of blacks (p. 62), but after learning the truth she suddenly finds them horribly unattractive (p. 85). She vacillates between waves of self-assertive pride and self-loathing despair (pp. 86–87). She finds an old mulatto woman to take her to a black church. There Rhoda decides she can endure herself only if she can endure blacks, that she can endure them if she can love them, and that she will love them if she tries to help them (pp. 89–95). Unlike the dedication engendered in other mulatto characters who find happiness when they abandon a phony attempt to deny their blackness, Rhoda's dedication and attempt to affirm her blackness are phony. Her devotion to blacks is not an instinctive or emotional response for her, but a rationalization. The essential dishonesty of Rhoda's consecration to her "duty" can be seen in her confrontation with Olney. He asks her to marry him, and she springs to her feet, crying:

"Never!... I am a [N]egress!"
Something in her tragedy affected Olney comically; perhaps the belief that she had often rehearsed these words as answer to his demand. He smiled. "Well not a very black one. Besides, what of it, if I love you?"
"What of it?" she echoed. "But don't you know? You mustn't!"
The simpleness of the words made him laugh outright; these she had not rehearsed. She had dramatized his instant renunciation of her when he knew the fatal truth.
"Why not? I love you, whether I must or not!" As tragedy the whole affair had fallen to ruin (p. 139).

Although not a stereotypic tragic octoroon, Rhoda is familiar with the type and tries to play the role. Howells had used a romantic tragic-octoroon figure in an earlier narrative poem, "Pilot's Story." In *An Imperative Duty*, he not only rejects that figure but mocks it by having Rhoda act out the influence which the stereotype would have had on a romantic young woman exposed to the literature of her age.
The influence of miscegenation is, in a sense, once removed

from reality in the formation of Rhoda's character, nor is it at the center of the novel's thematic concern. Sterling Brown remarks on the sympathetic tone of the novel but attacks Howells because "there were graver, less romantic problems of Negro life that a novelist of Howells' scope and ability might have presented."[22] Brown apparently believes that the novel is concerned with miscegenation as a problem of Negro life, but actually there is little concern in the work for blacks or their problems. Ford notes that the only treatment of race as a social problem is the implication that it can be solved by the use of reason.[23] The reasonable path is clearly delineated by Olney when he tells Rhoda that "the only way to help is to improve the white race which is causing the problem" (p. 143). Amacher notes that blacks appear in the novel only in the opening pages, where they are seen primitivistically by Olney as healthy, colorful, and lively, while whites are sickly and degenerate; Olney thinks that society would be better if blacks ran it.[24] Amacher's idea suggests a contrast between this cultural primitivism and the kind of chronological primitivism employed during the same decade by Thomas Nelson Page in treating blacks. In Howells' view they are noble savages; future saviors of corrupt civilization; in Page's view they were acceptable only in their proper place during the golden age "befo' de wah."

The concern with primitivism leads to the real theme of the novel, which is Howells' customary attack on the foolishness and destructiveness of the Puritan conscience. It is not Rhoda's maternal race which has cursed her, but, as Amacher notes, her father's sick one.[25] Olney is first attracted by Rhoda's spontaneous joy and warmth, and she contrasts sharply with Mrs. Meredith, the victim of an overgrown conscience.[26] The only burden of suffering that Rhoda carries in the end, is, in fact, the vestigial traces of Puritan conscience which keep her from being fully happy despite her good life with Olney (p. 149). The problems created by miscegenation are not the theme of the novel; they are nothing more in this book than the romantic inventions of a young woman and are solved readily by the reasonable move to Europe. The real theme is the conflict between reason and dutiolatry. Miscegenation is just another human problem occasioning the rise of Puritan consciences and their destructive effects.

After noting the multi-level ironies in this satiric work, Judith Berzon concludes: "Considering the intellectual milieu in which Howells produced this 'small' work, and viewing *An Imperative Duty* in the context of the racist stereotypes and ideology of tragic mulatto fiction, his achievement in this work was indeed considerable."[27] Although there is no character in *An Imperative Duty* faintly resembling Joe Christmas, Howells still adumbrates the manner in which Faulkner uses miscegenation to explore the general human lot. Howells explores the burden of conscience in the nineteenth century, while Faulkner searches for meaning in the burden of alienation carried by the twentieth.

The rise of social realism in American fiction during the Gilded Age reflected, among other things, concern over the growing disparities in wealth and the social stratification thus created. A Williams College professor took up miscegenation as a dramatic way to illustrate the problems of judging people by extrinsic rather than intrinsic qualities.

Set in a New England factory town, Bliss Perry's *The Plated City* (1895),[28] treats miscegenation as a complex social taboo. Two characters are suspected of having mixed blood and even though the question is never actually resolved, the fact of the suspicion alone destroys the man and almost destroys his sister. Tom Beaulieu had been brought from the South to Bartonvale, Connecticut, by his mother, a dark-complexioned, mentally unbalanced woman whom people assumed to be a quadroon. In Bartonvale, she married a drunken French Canadian, Pete Beaulieu, who adopted Tom and fathered a daughter, Esther. Both parents died and the children were separated. Esther was taken to Canada and raised by her aunt, but Tom was left without relatives and made a ward of the town, which assigned him to a black foster home. When the novel opens at a point twenty years later, Tom has become an extremely talented baseball player, the star of the local team. Esther returns to Bartonvale to seek work after her aunt dies, and encounters prejudice for the first time. Tom leaves town to pass for white and play professional ball, feeling that his absence will give Esther a better chance for success, but she has difficulties obtaining or holding a job because of her suspected color.

Mr. Atwood, an elderly bachelor, owner of the town's largest silver-plate factory, finds Esther appealing and hires her to run his household, treating her as an equal. A young lawyer, Norman Lewis, slowly develops an interest in Esther. Discharged by the professional team when his background is discovered, Tom returns to Bartonvale just as a great fire breaks out and spreads through several mills. In his bitterness, Tom recklessly leads the fight, taunting white men to match his efforts, but he is injured and taken dying to the Atwood house. Mr. Atwood sees in the dead youth a remarkable resemblance to his younger brother, who had died fighting for the Confederacy. Atwood knew that his brother had married a woman whose heritage was "questionable," but had never attempted to find her. He now feels terrible guilt for having neglected his nephew and resolves to build a hospital in atonement. Norman Lewis has learned the full story and knows that the question of whether Esther's mother was quadroon cannot be resolved, but he decides to marry her, despite the ostracism which he knows will be inevitable. In an ironic twist, Lewis suddenly comes into a fortune and the novel ends with the leading social arbiter of Bartonvale looking forward to giving a dinner for "Mrs. Lewis" when the couple return from Europe.

Not solely concerned with color discrimination, the novel attacks artificial class distinctions and espouses general social reforms. Like Mrs. Atherton's *Senator North*, published five years later, *The Plated City* makes use of mulatto characters as extreme examples to illustrate problems of class, in Perry's case to denounce rather than defend class distinctions. The book attacks the presumption of superiority based on wealth rather than native worth of an individual, as is symbolized by the title, *The Plated City*, and illustrated ironically by Bartonvale's eager acceptance of Esther once she acquires money.

After making his decision to marry Esther, Norman Lewis visits his club, thinking of the gulf which will now separate him from his former acquaintances, and thinking also that if he were wealthy the town would accept anything he chose to claim about Esther (p. 380). He is relieved of any lingering doubts when he suddenly sees the members of Bartonvale society for the shallow, vain people they are and realizes that despite his relative poverty, Esther's "questionable" heritage, and their imminent ostracism, they are both superior as people to the self-proclaimed aristocrats (p. 384). His sudden fortune and the town's reaction simply confirm the artificiality of class distinctions. Atwood is the only person of wealth portrayed sympathetically, and he is presented thus because in his childless old age Atwood has learned that he has wasted his life pursuing money and social prestige, even to the point of abandoning his dead brother's family (p. 310). Atwood now devotes his wealth to social causes advocated by the author, such as building schools, a library, and the hospital.

The mulatto characters Tom and Esther highlight the artificiality and destructiveness of social barriers. Tom, neither particularly intelligent nor well-educated, is a superb athlete. He cannot play professional ball, however, because he is believed to be a mulatto. An old black who knew his mother tells him that she was white, and on the basis of this testimony, Norman Lewis arranges to obtain an affidavit declaring that Tom is not believed to be of black descent. Immediately Tom is accepted by a professional team in California (pp. 112–119). The affidavit, a piece of paper which may or may not be accurate, symbolizes the artificiality of the social barrier preventing Tom from obtaining what he has earned on the basis of natural ability. Later, after Tom has become the star of a major-league team in New York, his past surfaces, and despite his affidavit he is fired (pp. 225–232). Deeply embittered, Tom begins drinking heavily (p. 234). When he arrives in Bartonvale during the fire, his bitterness and reckless courage lead him to stand with a hose at the greatest point of danger after the others have fallen back. Shouting to them to join him, Tom yells, "You fellows aren't afraid of the color line, are you?" (p. 270), just before being struck and fatally injured by falling debris. Lewis suspects that Tom deliberately courted death to free Esther from the burden of having a brother widely believed to be black (p. 280). Tom's destruction is the fruit of a social attitude that denies him the chance to fulfill his personal potential.

Esther's situation shows the arbitrary nature of such social attitudes, because through the accident of sudden wealth she escapes her brother's fate, to which she initially seems doomed. Unlike Tom, Esther has the advantages of intelligence and education, but these do not help her overcome the racial barriers. She had no knowledge, before coming to Bartonvale to find her brother, that they might be of mixed blood. When Tom tells her, she grants little importance to the fact, having been raised in an atmosphere free of prejudice. She soon learns, in a modification of the tragic-octoroon motif, what it means. The beautiful young woman of education and culture is now denied a place to live except in the poor black section of town (pp. 58–59). She obtains the position of French teacher at the school because of her superior qualifications, but is fired two days later when it is learned that she is Tom's sister (pp. 61–62). She gets a job in Atwood's factory, but a foreman makes advances to her because she is mulatto (p. 46); when Tom later beats an apology from the foreman, she is fired (p. 71).

The symbol of white social superiority in Bartonvale is the Episcopal minister, Whitesyde Trellys (the name seems suggestive of his symbolic function), who attempts to deprive Esther of an outlet for fulfillment when he discovers her reading Voltaire and other authors in the original French (something he cannot do), and demands that the library ban these books (p. 82). The social distinction which destroyed Tom is working on Esther, but her differing fate reveals the essential artificiality of the barrier. Unlike Tom, she is protected by the accident of money—first Atwood's wealth when he takes her in, and then by the sudden fortune her husband inherits.

In addition to using his mulatto characters as metaphors for the whole range of class distinctions stemming essentially from differentiation in wealth, Perry develops some interesting ideas on the relationship of racial and personal identity. In the writings of black authors, it is almost *de rigueur* that a mulatto identify with the black race in order to achieve personal identity, but Perry, a white, seems to suggest, like Clemens in

Pudd'nhead Wilson, published a year earlier, that racial identity is a question of conditioning rather than genetics. In *The Plated City* there are two characters of the same racial heritage who attempt to switch racial identities in adulthood, just as the characters in *Pudd'nhead Wilson* must exchange racial roles as infants.

Esther is essentially unaffected by her brief change in role because she is white by conditioning and winds up being accepted as white again, while Tom Beaulieu is brought up believing he is mulatto and is totally subjected to the concomitant prejudice and limitation of goals. When the novel opens, Tom feels quite content with his life, despite his awareness that certain avenues are closed to him (pp. 9–11). Once he is informed, however, that his mother was possibly white, he decides that it is true and that he will be white from now on (pp. 55–57). No one in town, of course, accepts his self-proclaimed change in status; rather, they find it amusing. People treat him with "a patronizing tolerance which a keener witted man would have fiercely resented" (p. 67). Tom believes that his popularity, actually due to his winning ball games for the local team, is evidence of acceptance as white. By rejecting his identity as a black, but not being truly accepted as a white, Tom finds himself without any racial identity and, as a result, without a personal identity. This is the dilemma, stated over and over by black intellectuals from W. E. B. DuBois to Hoyt Fuller, faced by blacks who attempt to become white in a figurative way through integration/assimilation. When Tom leaves and plays professional ball while passing for white, the insecurity of his position manifests itself in the terrible game he plays the day he notices Bartonvale men in the stands (p. 226). These men, who he thought accepted him as white, are the ones who tell everyone he is a "nigger" (p. 225) and destroy his career. Having rejected his identity as a black, Tom cannot go back to it by accepting a job playing in a black league, nor can he return to face sneers in Bartonvale. He is reduced to hiding in a Boston hotel, drinking and brooding over ways to "prove" his mother white, twenty years after her death (pp. 233–235).

In the self-destructive agony of his identity crisis, Tom provides a sharp contrast to the stereotyped figures like Iola Leroy

who briefly attempt to pass, then make their commitment to the
black cause and experience instant dissipation of the shadows
surrounding their lives. Clarence Garie, in Frank Webb's *The
Garies and Their Friends*, is the precedent for mulatto characters who suffer the agonies of secret guilt for trying to pass,
but Tom Beaulieu discovers that abandoning the racial identity
in which he has been formed can leave a person with something
worse than guilt—a total loss of self. In his crisis of racial and
thus personal identity, Tom foreshadows a basic theme of most
twentieth-century black novelists; indeed, in his retreat into
the locked hotel room, he seems almost a prototype of the narrator in Ralph Ellison's *Invisible Man*.

In another adumbration of a contemporary concern, Ellen
Glasgow uses miscegenation metaphorically to illustrate the
oppression of women in a male-dominated society. In her later
works—*The Sheltered Life* (1932) and *In This Our Life* (1942)—
she explores miscegenation at length. But her first use of the
theme occurs briefly in a novel written before the outbreak of
World War I—*Virginia* (1913).[29]

Virginia Pendelton, the daughter of the Episcopal minister
in the small southern town of Dinwiddie, had been raised in
the nineteenth-century tradition of what a lady should be: an
ornamental but helpless creature totally lacking interest in or
understanding of anything outside the home. Virginia marries
Oliver Treadwell, the nephew of the town's wealthiest citizen,
Cyrus Treadwell. Over the years, Virginia devotes herself exclusively to her children, while the once idealistic Oliver grows
further apart from the family in pursuit of an increasingly
profitable career as a writer of successful Broadway fluff. Eventually Oliver leaves Virginia for an intelligent and energetic
actress in New York. The novel closes with Virginia sitting in
her mansion in Dinwiddie, abandoned by her husband and two
worldly daughters, having nothing to live for but an anticipated
visit by her son.

Miscegenation occurs only incidentally in this plot. At age
fifteen, a pretty mulatto housemaid in Cyrus Treadwell's home,
Mandy, became pregnant with his child and was turned out
before the boy, Jubal, was born (p. 173). Eighteen years later,
Mandy, now the Treadwell's laundress, tries to obtain a small

raise by reminding Cyrus: "She ... added, with a kind of savage coquetry, 'I 'us a mought likely gal, Marster. You ain't done furgit dat, is you?' " (p. 173). Cyrus is enraged and sends her away, storming, "I'll not give you a red cent more.... Get out of here!... It's a pretty pass things have come to when men have to protect themselves from Negro women" (p. 174). Glasgow is well aware of the ironies inherent in a miscegenetic situation. Mandy seeks the raise from Cyrus because she wants to do more for their son Jubal; as Cyrus angrily stalks off, he is on his way to find Oliver, the nephew whom he had recently thrown out of the house: " 'I'll look up Henry's son before supper,' he was thinking. 'Even if the boy's a fool, I'm not one to let those of my own blood come to want' " (p. 175). Another incident occurs a few years later when Jubal is arrested for killing a white policeman. Mandy, in desperation, appeals to Cyrus to save their son from hanging, but he again coldly refuses. This time, however, he gives her a fifty-dollar bill and tells her never to come near him again (pp. 365–368).

Hardly central to the plot, miscegenation functions to shed some light on the character of Virginia and on the theme of the novel by establishing a parallel between Virginia and Mandy; both are victims of the society that created them and of the men who controlled that society. Virginia's education suits her for nothing but dependence and devotion to family. Oliver in youth loves her for these qualities, but in middle age abandons her because of them. Similarly, when Mandy makes her first appeal to Cyrus and is rejected, the narrator describes her thus: "In the negress's face an expression of surprise wavered for a second and then disappeared. Her features resumed their usual passive and humble look—a look which said ... 'I don't understand, but I submit without understanding. Am I not what you have made me? Have I not been what you wanted? And yet you despise me for being the thing that you made.' " (p. 174) When years later, in a New York hotel room, Virginia passively accepts Oliver's decision to leave her, she begins packing for her return to Dinwiddie, mechanically stuffing the sleeves of a gown with tissue paper "as carefully as if the world had not crumpled around her," her consciousness is like that of "one who is partially under an anaesthetic" (p. 494). Mandy reacts in like manner when her world is crushed by Cyrus Treadwell's refusal to save Jubal: "Instinctively, as if in obedience to some reflex action, she reached out and took the money from his hand, and still instinctively, with the dazed look of one who performs in a delirium the customary movements of every day, she fell back, holding her apron deprecatingly aside while he brushed past her" (p. 368). Cyrus physically rejects the consequences of his sexual desire by denying any responsibility for Jubal; Oliver, another Treadwell—and the name seems suggestive—is also little more than biological father to his children because he resents them and rejects them emotionally. Both men reject the women they have used. The sexual exploitation and abandonment of mulatto women in the South becomes a strong metaphor for the essentially similar treatment of white ladies by the dominant men, who control their destinies also. For Mandy the reward for being what male society demands she be is an empty life and a fifty-dollar bill. For Virginia it is an empty life and the biggest house in Dinwiddie.

Ellen Glasgow, like Cable, Howells, and Perry, did not write a simple polemic on slavery or racism. Instead, these authors used miscegenation as a rhetorical device to focus attention on various problems for human fulfillment created by society's artificial barriers. But miscegenation was not handled so broadly by most novelists in the decades immediately before and after the turn of the century. The majority wielded the subject like a rapier in the literary duel that mirrored increasingly vicious social and political conflicts over race.

NOTES

1. George Washington Cable, *The Grandissimes: A Story of Creole Life* (1880; reprint, New York: Scribners, 1908). Hereafter cited parenthetically.

2. Arlin Turner, *George W. Cable: A Biography* (Durham, N.C.: Duke Univ. Press, 1956), pp. 90–91.

3. Richard Chase, "Cable and His Grandissimes," *Kenyon Review* 18 (1956):375.

4. Philip Butcher, *George W. Cable* (New York: Twayne, 1962), pp. 50–51.

5. Chase, p. 379.
6. Philip Butcher, *Cable*, p. 52.
7. William Bedford Clark, "Cable and the Theme of Miscegenation in *Old Creole Days* and *The Grandissimes*," *Mississippi Quarterly* 30 (1977):604.
8. Chase, p. 379.
9. Chase, pp. 373–374.
10. Arlin Turner, p. 90.
11. Louis D. Rubin, Jr., "Divisions of the Heart: Cable's *The Grandissimes*," *Southern Literary Journal* 1 (1969):33–36.
12. George Washington Cable, *Madame Delphine* (1881; reprint, in *Old Creole Days*, New York: Scribners, 1944). Hereafter cited parenthetically.
13. Philip Butcher, *Cable*, p. 57.
14. Philip Butcher, *Cable*, pp. 58–59. On February 2, 1885, the New Orleans *Times-Democrat* published a joint assault by nine Southern editors on Cable because of his "miscegenetic tendencies"; see Lawrence J. Friedman, *The White Savage* (Englewood Cliffs, N.J.: Prentice-Hall, 1970), p. 116.
15. George Washington Cable, *Gideon's Band: A Tale of the Mississippi* (New York: Scribners, 1914). Hereafter cited parenthetically.
16. Philip Butcher, *Cable*, p. 46.
17. Helena Smith, p. 21.
18. William Dean Howells, *An Imperative Duty* (New York: Harper, 1892) Hereafter cited parenthetically.
19. Ann Ward Amacher, "The Genteel Primitivist and the Semi-Tragic Octoroon," *New England Quarterly* 29 (1956):220.
20. Thomas W. Ford, "Howells and the American Negro," *Texas Studies in Language and Literature* 5 (1964):552.
21. Amacher, pp. 224–225.
22. Sterling Brown, *The Negro in American Fiction* (1937; reprint, Port Washington, N.Y.: Kennikat Press, 1968), p. 76.
23. Ford, "Howells," pp. 534–536.
24. Amacher, pp. 220–222.
25. Amacher, p. 227.
26. Amacher, pp. 220–222.
27. Berzon, p. 115.
28. Bliss Perry, *The Plated City* (New York: Scribners, 1895). Hereafter cited parenthetically.
29. Ellen Glasgow, *Virginia* (Toronto: Musson Book Company, Ltd., n.d.). Hereafter cited parenthetically.

6

The Rhetoric of Racism,
1891–1914

From the beginning, slavery in America had been linked to
race, but the clear concept of formal racism—a "scientifically"
based, rational ideology of black inferiority—emerged only in
the nineteenth century.[1] Eighteenth-century environmentalism, which generally held sway into the 1820s and 1830s, encouraged the concept of slavery as a social/economic problem
to be solved by African colonization. After the 1830s, abolitionists shifted the issue to moral grounds, seeing slavery as
individual sin by each slave owner. Under such moral attack,
slavery apologists had to find a moral justification. Belief in
the unchangeable inferiority of blacks provided the moral
ground for seeing slavery as a paternal institution.

Beginning with Dr. Samuel George Morton's *Crania Amer-
icana* (1839), a string of "scientific" arguments appeared suggesting how and why the inferiority of blacks came to be. In
the 1850s, Thomas Drew proposed that blacks were inherently
"savage" and needed slavery to domesticate them. Of course
as soon as slavery's restraints were removed, the "happy darky"
would revert to savage monster. In 1860, a Louisiana physician
named Samuel Cartwright argued that blacks were some of
the animals created before Adam and Eve, over which Adam
was given dominion. Jefferson Davis held a similar view, and
slavery apologist W. W. Wright contended that the strongly
felt prejudice against color was actually a natural aversion to
hybridizing, thus giving white antiamalgamation sentiment a
"scientific" ground. Finally, the arguments became that the

constitutional rights to freedom and equality, as well as all other human rights, applied only to whites because blacks were not human. Thus the racist who wished to be a democrat could attack class distinctions in Europe because all Europeans were white, but continue to segregate and oppress blacks at home. The flip side of the racist coin was its antislavery version that Frederickson labels "romantic racialism." Many abolitionists saw blacks as having fixed, racially unique features that were good, adding up to a kind of natural Christianity that made blacks innocent, good natured, and docile. Romantic racialists supported colonization because they feared that blacks' natural goodness would be corrupted by white society, a specific version of the common nineteenth-century belief in the noble savage.

Political and economic conditions after the Civil War ended the dream of colonization, and the country set about adjusting to a biracial reality. Various forms of accommodation lost out, first to the paternalistic racism of the 1880s that viewed blacks as children and later to the vicious racism of the 1890s. During this period, of course, the basic concept of an exploitable underclass made up of blacks and immigrants was bolstered by capitalist support for theories of social Darwinism. Common belief held that mulattoes—the word comes from the Spanish for "mule"—were genetically weakened hybrids that would sink into sterility and cease to exist within a generation or two; blacks generally would be eliminated before too long in the battle for survival of the fittest. And there should be no interference with evolutionary inevitabilities—Frederick L. Hoffman's *Race Traits and Tendencies of the American Negro* (1896) argued that blacks, doomed by innate weakness and vice, could never be uplifted by education or other means. Indeed, Dr. Paul B. Barringer of the University of Virginia stridently proclaimed the need not for education but for strong control of blacks to prevent their reversion to savagery. Such arguments, later spread to mass audiences by Thomas Dixon, Jr., fueled the explosion of segregationist legislation and justified the rash of lynchings in the 1890s.

Because Jim Crow succeeded in rigid isolation of blacks as a group, it led to the problem of control over them. Lynchings became a powerful and necessary weapon of outside white con-

trol over the segregated black community. The increasing brutality, the torturing and burning that became part of lynchings
after 1892, whites justified by crying rape, but even statistics
kept at the time by white apologists for racism showed that no
such crime or even charge of rape existed in the "overwhelming
majority of cases."[2] Nonetheless, the growing myth of the black
man as a genetic sexual monster fanned the Negrophobia of
the 1890s, a myth encouraged by novelists such as Thomas
Nelson Page and later trumpeted by Thomas Dixon, Jr.

According to Lawrence Friedman, the rigid strength of Jim
Crow by the turn of the century resulted from two principal
causes: first, the failure of what he calls "differential segregation," and, second, the "myth of Negro disease." Friedman
argues that the Civil War generated great fear among white
Southerners about freed slaves, black Federal troops, even
armed black Confederate troopers. Lee's request in early 1865
that blacks be recruited and trained, although granted by the
Confederate government, led to a great outcry. The sight of
armed Confederate blacks marching in Capital Square a week
before the fall of Richmond occasioned as much fear as the
arrival of the Union army a few days later.

After Reconstruction, the policy of differential segregation,
named the "Brownlow tradition" after the Governor of Tennessee, emerged. This solution provided that "good," docile
blacks could live and work among whites, but "bad," "uppity"
blacks would be rigidly segregated. This flexible, situational
segregation existed in the rural South for several years, but
had been abandoned by the turn of the century. The impossibility of identifying "good" and "bad" effectively, especially in
growing urban centers, and the growing belief that all blacks
carried contagious diseases made differential segregation impossible. Given the choice between giving up on segregation or
making it total, the white South chose rigid, universal segregation of blacks.[3]

At the same time, during the two decades from 1880–1900,
the North abandoned its interest in the welfare of blacks and
allowed Southern states to institutionalize open defiance of the
Fourteenth and Fifteenth Amendments.[4] Kenneth Stamp suggests that a number of historical and economic influences were

at work. He maintains that the spirit of reconciliation between North and South by the end of the century had come about partially because the North conceded that the South had fought bravely for a cause it believed in, and the South agreed that preservation of the Union had been in the best interest of all.

The South had been willing to accept as inevitable the Thirteenth Amendment, but was outraged by the Fourteenth and Fifteenth. It had been possible to pass these amendments in the flush of victory, but by the mid–1870s Northern popular support for black equality was almost completely gone, and even support among radical leaders had greatly waned. The South had originally expected the states to control the freedmen and had planned a caste system. When it became apparent that the North had reached a stage of indifference toward the fate of freed blacks, or even had adopted Southern racial attitudes, the caste system was established in defiance of law.

The change in Northern attitude developed from the great increase in industrialization following the war, which gave rise to a middle-class fear in Northern cities of economic competition with, and loss of political power to, immigrants. The situation provoked much Northern prejudice toward Irish, Italians, Slavs, and other ethnic groups. The Northern middle-class began to look with new understanding on the Southern attitude toward blacks. This attitude was given the blessing of that group of social scientists who advanced presumed evidence of innate, racial traits of inferiority. Finally, the rising spirit of nationalism stimulated the desire for sectional reconciliation, and part of the price was Federal abandonment of responsibility for the protection of black civil and political rights.[5]

According to Louis D. Rubin, the actual development of the Jim Crow laws, widespread discrimination, and steadily worsening conditions for blacks in the South emerged from the clash between the business interests in the "New South" era and the growing restlessness of the agrarian elements, expressed in the rise of Populism. The agrarians, despite their brief flirtation with the black vote in the early 1890s, had a strong antiblack attitude, and the business interests were led into something of a compromise, whereby they went along with open antiblack moves while the farmers eased their hostilities to business and commercial issues.[6]

Whatever the totality of causes, the resulting discrimination and oppression in the 1890s and later evoked a literary response almost equal to the battle of books over slavery, and that shared some important similarities with the earlier fray. The backgrounds for both situations had been a long series of plantation romances that ignored problems such as miscegenation. Eventually, however, interracial sex emerged as the central issue, just as it had for the abolitionists and the slavery apologists a half century before. Among whites, turn-of-the-century beliefs in the genetic racial inferiority and the hereditary disposition of blacks to disease, led inevitably to rabid fear of interracial sex.

The broad problems of discrimination and hereditary inferiority—North and South—underlie Gertrude Atherton's novel, *Senator North* (1900).[7] A Californian, the author had married a Massachusetts Atherton and moved to New England. Hers is not a plantation romance, but a political novel arguing for aristocratic dictatorship in the United States to save the country from the hands of rabble, agrarian Populists, blacks, immigrants, and petty bourgeoisie. The basic argument rehashes the Jefferson-Hamilton debate, with obvious affinity for the Federalist position. The title character seems partially modeled on Henry Cabot Lodge; Senator North is in his fifties, the dean of the New England Congressional delegation, and leader of the fight against Populism in any manifestation, especially free silver. He does, however, differ significantly from Lodge in attitude toward blacks and in opposing the Spanish-American War, which Lodge supported. The main plot of the novel involves the love affair of North and Betty Madison, the beautiful, twenty-seven-year-old daughter of a wealthy, distinguished Southern family.

When the story opens, the willful young Betty has determined to involve herself in politics and to attract the attention of Senator North, whom she considers the most interesting man in politics at that time. She succeeds in both endeavors, and the older, but still vigorous, North falls in love with her as she does with him. The situation is complicated by the presence of North's ailing wife and by Betty's constant fear that any scandal might ruin his career. She decides to prevent this by breaking off their relationship. Shortly thereafter, however, North's wife conveniently dies and the lovers are reunited. Finally, North has a vision of Alexander Hamilton, his ideal. The spirit advises North to run for President and once elected to save the country by seizing dictatorial powers and establishing a monarchy (pp. 345–349). Betty willingly agrees to be his helpmate in this great undertaking, and the novel ends.

While not involved in the main plot, miscegenation controls an important subplot about Betty Madison's mulatto half-sister, Harriet. The girl had been raised by a family friend in Virginia, and Betty first learns of Harriet's existence when this guardian dies. On Senator North's advice, Betty takes in the young woman—who easily passes for white—educates her further, and plans to settle her in Europe. Betty and North warn Harriet that if she ever wishes to marry she must tell the man first because their children might be "coal black" (p. 87). After several months, however, tragedy strikes; Betty learns that her Southern-gentleman cousin, Jack Emory, has secretly married Harriet. When Harriet tells Jack the truth, he commits suicide. After his funeral, Harriet drowns herself (pp. 245–253).

Harriet's story has much greater significance in the novel, however, than simply adding a pathetic tale of true love thwarted as counterpoint to the successful love affair of the main characters. The mulatto girl develops as the principal symbol of natural inferiority, an inferiority that cannot be altered and which exists not only in blacks but in all lower-class people. Structurally, Harriet provides the basis for the whole genetic argument of the novel. It is through her that natural inferiority is demonstrated, thus justifying the thesis that an aristocracy should seize control. The author substantiates Harriet's inferiority by giving her the opportunity to rise above her background, then showing her inherent inability to do so. Betty has a strong dislike for blacks and is revolted by the discovery that she has a half-sister who is, "light or dark, a negress" (p. 79), but Betty's aristocratic sense of duty leads her to care for Harriet. After meeting the girl, Betty feels sorry for her and sincerely intends to aid as best she can (pp. 92–93). Notwithstanding Betty's best efforts on her behalf, Harriet is simply unable to escape her heredity.

Despite a respectable education provided by her guardian, Harriet has relapses into stereotypic negritude, such as wanting to buy a bright yellow-and-red dress and giving in to a compulsion to sing spirituals. Betty fears that Harriet will betray herself—"A bandana gown and a voice like a cornfield darky's!" (pp. 112–115). North advises Betty that "how much of racial lying, and slothfulness, barbarism and general incapacity that black vein of hers contains will give you food for thought, for she certainly will reveal herself in the course of a year" (p. 123). Harriet's self-revelation of her inability to benefit from the advantages given her makes the novel's point about natural inferiority. By intensive education over a period of months, Harriet's speech, self-control, and taste are greatly improved (pp. 158–159). However, just as Betty is congratulating herself, she is horrified when Harriet smiles broadly and reveals the "fatuous grin of the Negro"; Betty has to order Harriet never to smile again (p. 161). Harriet almost reveals herself another time when she is frightened and "shrieks like a darky" (p. 226). When the secret marriage of Harriet and Jack is revealed, North points out that Harriet's deceiving some white man was inevitable because of the basic deceptiveness of her race and the desire to rise to the white level (p. 217).

Stronger evidence of Harriet's inherently flawed nature comes when she insists on attending a black camp meeting. North warns Betty of the danger, saying that if Harriet is exposed to the emotional state of the meeting she will revert to "barbarism" (p. 240). When Harriet returns, she has indeed reverted, and Betty controls her only by shouting orders at her; she "counted on striking the slavish cord" in Harriet and succeeds (p. 242). But Harriet, still "drunk with religion," blurts out her secret to Jack, who flees into the night and later kills himself. North expresses concern only for Betty during this ordeal, remarking that if Harriet survives it, "she will fall upon some other miseries incidental to her breed" (p. 247). Harriet's "barbarism" surfaces fully when they tell her of Jack's suicide. She rages against the "unjust and murderous white race," swearing that she will go out and degrade herself, destroy every white man she can, "to do evil, to square accounts" (p. 248). But she later confesses to Betty that she does not have the strength of will necessary to carry out her plan, and goes out to drown herself instead (pp. 250–253). Harriet is developed as a living symbol that a sow's ear is basically a sow's ear and that the silk-purse ladies and gentlemen ought to control things in the best interest of all.

That natural inferiority is not limited by race but extends generally throughout the lower classes is seen in some other minor characters and in the narrator's tone. The housekeeper, Mrs. Trumbull, has to be fired because she is a troublemaker, a nosy gossip, but even more so because she feels she is just as good as the Madisons and the Norths (pp. 151–152). Harriet and Mrs. Trumbull are instinctively friendly, and Betty has to warn Harriet against being familiar with a servant (pp. 159–160). Like Harriet, Mrs. Trumbull is given the opportunity to improve, but fails. She becomes the wife of a crude but wealthy congressman from the West; she arrives in Washington grossly misfitted to her role as a woman of society because she is attempting to rise above her natural station of servitude (p. 304). The narrator's attitude also emphasizes that the problem is wider than just color; the narrator frequently remarks on such "problems" as the "fifteen million Irish plebians [sic] with which this country is cursed" (p. 331). Unlike the call to racial unity which Page earlier implied and which Dixon clearly sounded a few years later, the call in *Senator North* is to class unity. The tragic fate of the beautiful mulatto who belongs neither to the black world nor to the white, the disastrous compounding of that tragedy when she attempts to move out of her proper sphere, and the clearly implied condemnation of miscegenation are all used as dramatic metaphors of the need for aristocratic rule.

W. J. Cash says that the flood of plantation novels after Reconstruction, including those advocating discrimination against blacks, stemmed from a patriotic desire to rebuild Southern pride.[8] Obviously, this would have been one basic motivation, but another motivation seems to lie in chronological primitivism, the attempt to recapture a mythical "Golden Age." The problems in the post-Reconstruction South were all too real, as were Northern problems exploding out of rapid industrialization. The desire to go back to a simpler time, to an agrarian and mythically elevated way of life, had great appeal for readers and authors both North and South. Moreover, there was the need to build the strongest possible taboos against equality for blacks in order to protect the elaborate, but largely illegal—and therefore fragile—system of institutionalized discrimination which had slowly developed since the end of Reconstruction.

Miscegenation can be viewed as the ultimate manifestation of equality, and with the strident voice of Thomas Dixon, miscegenation is openly acknowledged as the central taboo, the most basic reason for keeping the black man "in his place." Indeed, William L. Andrews cites Henry W. Grady, Thomas Nelson Page, and others to this effect that the real reason for denying integration and civil rights was to prevent miscegenation. He credits the novelists, both black and white, of the 1880s and after, for having first raised the question of how miscegenation affects the American social structure.[9]

The plantation novels before 1890 had largely been devoted to the Golden Age "befo' de wah," but in the last decade of the century they became increasingly concerned with defending the South's post-Reconstruction behavior. Certain of these novels portrayed villainous blacks or mulattoes collaborating with carpetbaggers and scalawags stirring up the more ignorant blacks, but generally these works avoided the issue of miscegenation, and if troublemakers happened to be mulatto, such as Cornelius Leggett in Joel Chandler Harris' *John March, Southerner* (1894), the fact of their racial mixture was not made significant. In Thomas Nelson Page's *Red Rock* (1898),[10] however, we have the first real use of miscegenation as an important, if not overt, theme in the defense of Southern racial discrimination.

The story of *Red Rock* is played out by a group of stock characters depicting the various elements in the Reconstruction South. The old aristocracy is represented by Jacquelin Grey, his cousin Steve Allen, Dr. Cary and his beautiful daughter, Blair. The incredibly cowardly and evil carpetbagger is aptly named Jonadab Leech, and he is aided by scalawag Hiram

Still and renegade-mulatto Moses. The good Yankees, those who come South and are converted to an understanding acceptance of Southern views, are Captain Middleton, Major Welch, his wife, and their daughter, Ruth. Significantly, the good Yankees are or were military officers, while both Leech and Still avoided service during the war. Page suggests that honorable men who fought against each other can now work together against the cowardly forces of evil.

Red Rock opens with a short section from prewar days and quickly shows that Elysium did exist in that happy time. As a boy, Jacquelin Grey defends a black child against an attack by "white trash," and is even depicted as being envious of his freer black playmates (pp. 3–4). The Yankees Welch and Middleton happen to be traveling in the area and are received with an incredible display of unselfish aid and generous hospitality (pp. 15–33). There are idealized pictures of whitewashed cabins, slaves' gardens, and frolicking, happy "darkies" (pp. 29–30). There is a scene in which Dr. Cary offers one of his slaves money and freedom, both of which are vociferously refused (p. 41). The narration then jumps quickly to the end of the war, and the scenes that follow are in sharp contrast to the preceding bliss.

Jacquelin Grey lies recuperating from a serious wound, while Steve Allen and Dr. Cary attempt to work for the best interests of all, black and white, in the face of defeat. Their noble efforts are frustrated by Leech, the Provost-Marshal and head of the Freedman's Bureau, who constantly harrasses the whites by unwarranted searches and seizures, while stirring up the blacks with lies and promises. Captain Middleton is the Union military commander of the area and for a while is able to prevent the worst excesses by Leech and his cohort Still. The situation degenerates when Middleton's company is transferred and is replaced by a company of blacks. Leech and Still dispossess both the Greys and the Carys, and the behavior of the black militia grows worse daily. Steve Allen organizes the Ku Klux Klan, which disarms the blacks and drives Leech away. There are further complications, but eventually Leech's power is completely broken, white law and order return, and rightful owners regain their property. The novel ends with the engagement of

Jacquelin Grey and Blair Cary, and with the marriage of Steve Allen and the Northern girl, Ruth Welch.

The dominant theme in this novel appears to be Cash's "Southern rape complex,"[11] which had appeared symbolically in Mrs. Flanders' *The Ebony Idol*, but which is much more openly developed in *Red Rock*. Throughout Page's story, Southern women are identified with the South itself and are elevated to such a degree that they embody in the present the highest element of the mythological antebellum South. When the story jumps to the end of the war, the first statement by the narrator is praise for the bravery of the women, calling every Southern woman "a garrison of the South, impregnable" (p. 50). When Dr. Cary returns from the horrors of battle, he expresses awe at how much more the women had suffered and "fought the war," declaring, "they did it all" (pp. 60–61). The women are unanimous in opposing any contact with the Yankees and insist on regarding them as bitter enemies no matter what the cost (p. 85). Even Virgy, the daughter of the scalawag Hiram Still, is crushed by her father's behavior because she is a Southern woman (pp. 224–225), and secretly loves Jacquelin Grey, the symbol of the aristocratic Old South. Jacquelin's attitude toward Blair Cary exemplifies the general attitude in the novel toward Southern women: "For Jacquelin, to him she was no longer mortal: he had robed her in radiance and lifted her among the stars" (p. 82). With this identification between Southern women and the South itself, any insult or attack on a woman symbolizes the "rape" of the South during Reconstruction. When Leech and some cohorts search the Cary and Grey houses for arms, they are rough and insulting to the women present. When the men return and discover what has occurred, Steve Allen leads a delegation to town and informs Captain Middleton, "before we will allow our women to be insulted, we will kill every one of you" (p. 128).

The question of miscegenation increases the complexity of the Southern rape complex. White women are not only identified with the South, according to Cash, but are also seen as the "perpetuator of white superiority in legitimate line."[12] The freeing of the blacks left open the possibility of breaking taboo, of corrupting the legitimate line, the basis for superiority.[13]

Since the sons of the South must be guaranteed the heritage of being white men, any black assertion toward a white woman carried a symbolic threat far greater than the economic exploitation of the South by carpetbaggers and Federal troops. The difference in degree is seen in *Red Rock* when the response to white Leech's mistreatment of women from the two best families is simply a warning, but when black militiamen similarly insult and mistreat one white woman from a low-class family, hundreds of white men engage the blacks in open battle, killing many of them and forcing the Army to withdraw the black troops from the area (pp. 191–194).

Page also uses miscegenation in a manner foreshadowing Thomas Dixon's primary argument that the conflict between Southern whites and blacks was not a regional aberration but a racial struggle, with the future of civilization riding on the outcome. Page's specific concern, as noted, is the rape of the South during Reconstruction, but there are indications of more general concern with the relationship of the races. The only overt statement of this interest comes in the preface where Page praises the people of the South and remarks that "they reconquered their section and *preserved the civilization of the Anglo-Saxon*" (p. viii, italics mine). This idea does not appear openly in the novel, but does seem to be implied by events surrounding Ruth Welch, the Northern girl who comes South with her family at the war's end.

Ruth and her mother had been abolitionists and are active in supporting Freedmen's programs (pp. 340–341). Interestingly, Ruth, not a Southern woman, is the one most closely threatened by miscegenetic rape. On her first day in the South, she is frightened by overhearing a black man bragging that he is just as good as white and saying, "I'm goin' to marry a white 'ooman" (p. 291). Later, the mulatto troublemaker, Moses, tricks Ruth into riding out alone. He then lies in wait for her in an isolated, wooded area and seizes her horse's bridle. As he tries to drag her from the saddle, she beats at him and screams, attracting the aid of Steve Allen who was following not far behind (pp. 354–358). It is not difficult to see symbolic implications in this incident. Steve was present to save Ruth from violent rape because he had followed her deliberately, knowing as she did not that it was unsafe for her to ride alone. The Northern woman is saved by the knowledge and fore-thought of the Southern man who is, significantly, the leader of the Ku Klux Klan and in the forefront of the battle to contain blacks, to "keep them in their place." By implication, Page is warning the North, pointing out that the Southern gentlemen of the Klan are fighting a battle for the survival of the white race and "Anglo-Saxon civilization," which has been endan-gered by the North's own blind stupidity in freeing the blacks and filling them with ideas of equality, as Ruth earlier sup-ported abolition and Freedmen's programs. The author of *Sub-dued Southern Nobility* had used the marriage of a Southern mulatto and a Northern white to symbolize a hoped-for national racial harmony. Page seems to use the marriage of Ruth and Steve Allen, which saves him from prosecution as the Klan leader because, as his wife, Ruth cannot be forced to testify against him, to symbolize the growing union of whites, North and South, against the common racial enemy.

In *Gabriel Tolliver* (1902),[14] Joel Chandler Harris expresses great sorrow that barriers are in fact being raised between whites and blacks. This story of Reconstruction begins with the narrator's reminiscences about the happy days of old when there was friendship between black and white, as seen in the close relationship which the slave girl Tasma Tid shares with the white children, Gabriel Tolliver and Nan (pp. 12–31). But the children grow up; the war comes, and in its aftermath the schemes of self-seeking carpetbaggers and scalawags bring about division and race hatred as they lead the ignorant blacks astray. The worst of the troublemakers, Gilbert Hotchkiss, comes to form the Union League. The main plot details the growing problems as the blacks are agitated by continual lies and distortions, until the white community is forced to protect itself by taking the offensive. The Knights of the White Ca-mellia are formed; Hotchkiss is killed and Gabriel Tolliver is arrested for the crime. Freed by the Knights, he stays in hiding until Federal troops are withdrawn and state government re-verts to white control. Tolliver is then cleared of the charges and returns a hero, advocating peace, moderation, and common sense in meeting the problems around them.

The theme of miscegenation by no means dominates the novel, but it does play a key role in the climax of the action. As the situation degenerates toward open racial conflict, the narrator insists that something must be done to halt this movement before the blacks, who are really not to blame, are wiped out (pp. 258–259). The white radicals like Hotchkiss actually intend to stir up the blacks to the point that they will foolishly attempt to slaughter the whites (pp. 242–245). The Knights are able to reduce tensions temporarily by simply frightening blacks, but the flame of armed conflict is sparked by the first incidents suggesting miscegenation. Gabe overhears a group of white men going to town for ammunition because a "big buck nigger" stopped at one man's farm and insulted his wife (p. 268). Moreover, miscegenation directly causes the first real violence, the murder of Hotchkiss. Hotchkiss had been flirting with the mulatto wife of black Ike Varner, and Varner shoots Hotchkiss when he catches the two together (p. 299). Whether or not Harris fully intended it this way, the breaking point is reached by both black and white forces over the question of miscegenation, the ultimate point of conflict between the races.

By covert, but real, concern with the problem of miscegenation, Page, Harris, and other romancers of the Old South prepared the way for the open and vicious racism of Thomas Dixon, Jr.[15] Born in the North Carolina Piedmont, educated at Wake Forest and Johns Hopkins, Dixon was a lawyer, state legislator, preacher, novelist, playwright, actor, lecturer, real estate speculator, and movie producer. Familiar of three presidents and of such notables as John D. Rockefeller, Sr., he made and lost millions, ending up after a cerebal hemorrhage in 1939 as an invalid court clerk in Raleigh, North Carolina. Dixon was a complex man, and his life up to 1900 provides little indication that he was to become the champion of white racism; he had long been popular as an energetic and outspoken young clergyman, and, during his successful New York pastorate from 1889 to 1900, he was aligned with the liberal reformers of the Social Gospel Movement, demanding justice for immigrants, slum-dwellers, the weak and the helpless generally.[16] In a work published in 1896, Dixon even stated that "democracy is the destiny of the [black] race, because all men are bound together in the bonds of fraternal equality with one common father above."[17] It seems, however, that Dixon was strongly influenced by the Spanish-American War, which he championed and which had restored a sense of complete national solidarity by demonstrating the loyalty of the South. With America suddenly vaulted into the role of a world power and feeling a call to join nations such as England in the practice of beneficent imperialism, a sense of racial superiority sprang up to meet the task.[18]

Dixon directed three of his several novels written before World War I at the problem of race in America. His first novel, *The Leopard's Spots* (1902),[19] a runaway best seller, brought him fame and fortune. The book establishes all the basic themes which appear in Dixon's later novels on race: (1) blacks are subhuman, animal; (2) the two races cannot coexist in the same country without miscegenation, which means the destruction of Anglo-Saxon "purity" and of its divine mission in leading (conquering) the world; (3) blacks must be totally segregated to prevent this disaster, first by denying them political equality (which leads to social equality) and ultimately by physically removing all blacks from the United States. In *The Leopard's Spots*, Rev. John Durham, a Baptist minister, appears to be Dixon's alter ego and spokesman for his basic ideas on race.

The novel divides roughly into two parts: the first concerned with events during Reconstruction and the second with events some twenty years after its end, when the Populist coalition of farmers and blacks temporarily wrests control from the Democratic Party in North Carolina. In both sections the essential conflict is racial, with both whites and blacks striving for supremacy. The heroes of the first section are Rev. Durham and Major Stuart Dameron, who organizes the Klan in his county to meet the ever increasing outrages of the black militia and the evil whites who manipulate them. Dameron and the Klan frighten the blacks away from the polls and overthrow the carpetbag/scalawag government. Dameron and the responsible members of the Klan then disband it and openly break with the few young hooligans led by Andy McLeod who insist on continuing the organization.

In the second section set a generation later, Charlie Gaston, a child during Reconstruction but now a young lawyer, has

taken upon himself the burden of fighting the attempt to rein-
state black political strength in the state. The leader of the
blacks is the former renegade-Klansman Andy McLeod, who
has defected to the Republicans. When the Populist coalition
succeeds and many blacks take office, blacks are encouraged
for the first time in twenty years to begin crimes once again
against whites. The corruption in state government soon leads
to a total breakdown in law and order, and whites once more
must organize and wrest control from blacks by force. At the
state Democratic convention, Gaston, coached by the now elderly Rev. Durham, makes a speech stating that the basic issue
is racial survival and that if elected he will disenfranchise
blacks. He succeeds in uniting the Democratic party on this
issue and is overwhelmingly elected governor. The novel ends
with his inauguration and marriage to Sallie Worth, daughter
of an old Confederate general who had helped Dameron handle
the crisis during Reconstruction.

In both periods represented, blacks are essentially the same,
unchanged in the later section by twenty years of freedom,
opportunity, and education. Bloomfield notes that Dixon simply
viewed blacks as animals, distinctly impaired in the ability to
form moral judgments or to develop character, those inner re-
sources which, in Dixon's view of evolution, were the measure
of human standing. Dixon believed miscegenation grew out of
the animal status of blacks, because he believed that the sex
impulse was an irrational, elemental, animal force.[20] Calvin
Hernton argues that whites generally think of blacks in sexual
and animal terms, projecting the white, Protestant, bestial concept of sex onto blacks. As a result, whites fear blacks in the
way whites fear their own sexuality—as something monstrous.[21]

From the opening of the novel, Dixon consistently presents
blacks as subhuman by using figures built on animal images.
The first reference to blacks describes the freedman as changed
from "a chattel . . . to a possible Beast to be feared and guarded"
(p. 5). Durham refers to the black school established by a wealthy
Northern woman as a "menagerie" (p. 50). When enfranchised
in 1867, blacks in the novel celebrate by looting and burning,
wasting the summer, and growing nothing because they do not
have the foresight to know that there will be nothing to eat

later (p. 101). When the Klan arises, the blacks are controlled overnight and led like herd animals back to the path of law and order (p. 152). Twenty years later, after Reconstruction, the bestial nature of blacks remains unchanged. Charlie Gaston participates in the search for Flora Camp, the daughter of an old friend, and she is found brutally raped and dying. In his despair, Tom Camp rails against God, asking where he was "when my poor little baby was screamin' for help while that damned black beast was tearin' her to pieces!" (p. 379) The link between animality and sexuality is important to Dixon because he believed black sexual aggression to be the reason why the two races cannot coexist.

The idea that racial coexistence would lead inevitably to miscegenation and the destruction of the Anglo-Saxon race is the main theme of the novel. Dixon uses a disjunctive proposition—an either/or argument—to advance this claim. Rev. Durham poses this question: *"Shall the future American be an Anglo-Saxon or a Mulatto?"* (p. 161, italics in the original), and the query recurs in italics a half dozen times throughout the novel. Durham repeats this question to a Bostonian one time, who asks about the miscegenation that has already occurred. Durham dismisses previous amalgamation as insignificant, explaining that "unless by gradual encroachments of time, culture, wealth and political exigencies the time comes when a Negro shall be allowed freely to choose a white woman for his wife, the racial integrity remains intact. The right to choose one's mate is the foundation of racial life and civilization. The South must guard with flaming sword every avenue of approach to this holy of holies" (p. 337). He explains further that if blacks are educated and admitted to economic and political equality, a race war will result unless they are granted equal social rights as well, but that "the Anglo-Saxon cannot do this without suicide. One drop of Negro blood makes a Negro" (p. 338). Durham broods over the fact that there is enough black blood to "make mulatto the whole Republic" and thus destroy the Anglo-Saxon race (p. 244). Blacks will inevitably attempt this "pollution" because they are driven by their animal, sexual aggressiveness.

This animal sexuality is first unleashed when the element

of human control, the white master, is removed by freeing the slaves. Immediately after the war, Tim Shelby, a black organizer with the Union League, talks of Othello and Desdemona: "Othello's day has come at last. If he has dared dream dreams in the past, his tongue dared not speak; the day is fast coming when he will put these dreams into deeds, not words" (p. 90). After the blacks are enfranchised and take over the state government, the last vestige of control is lost. During Reconstruction, Tom Camp loses his first daughter, Annie, to the forces of black sexuality when sixteen drunken, armed, black troopers break into Annie's wedding party and seize her. In the exchange of fire ensuing between blacks and whites, Annie is accidentally killed, but that is better in Tom's eyes than what could have happened to her (pp. 126–27). This accident foreshadows the tragedy which will befall Camp's second daughter twenty years later. As early proof of black sexual aggression, the black Reconstruction legislature passes a bill permitting miscegenation: "It apparently commanded intermarriage, and ordered the military to enforce the command at the point of the bayonet" (p. 147). Emboldened by this law, Tim Shelby demands that a white girl let him kiss her (p. 150), but this provides the spark for the spontaneous emergence of the Ku Klux Klan. In their first action, the Klansmen hang Shelby from the courthouse balcony. They cut open his lips and attach a card to them saying, "The answer of the Anglo-Saxon race to black lips that dare pollute with words the womanhood of the South. K.K.K." (p. 151) Just as in the novels by Page and Harris, miscegenation, not political or economic causes, inspired the formation of the Klan. Dixon suggests that during Reconstruction only the Klan prevented miscegenation; left alone, uncontrolled blacks would have created a mulatto America then.

    Twenty years after Reconstruction the sexual aggressiveness of blacks has grown worse. Towns have doubled in size because of the menace of the "roving criminal Negro" in the country: "The birth of a girl baby was sure to make a father restless, and when the baby looked up into his face one day with the soft light of a maiden he gave up his farm and moved to town" (p. 202). The horrible rape of Tom Camp's second daughter,

Flora, provides "proof," the example that illustrates the thesis. One day a black whistles at the girl and two days later she is missing. Dixon enhances the rhetorical effect by having the narrator present at the discovery of the victim. After a night-long search by one thousand whites, she is found dying, "her clothes torn to shreds and stained with blood.... Her skull had been crushed.... It was too plain, the terrible crime that had been committed" (p. 375). At last Dixon has openly declared the issue; the black is a "damned black beast" who will rape and kill and destroy Anglo-Saxon racial purity. Once the "human control" provided by whites is taken away, the result is inevitable: "Such crimes as Dick had committed ... were unknown absolutely under slavery.... Now, scarcely a day passed in the South without the record of such an atrocity, swiftly followed by a lynching" (p. 385). In making his point about black sexual aggression, Dixon also takes advantage of the opportunity to justify the wave of lynchings in the 1890s.

By careful control of arrangement, Dixon extends his argument to suggest that even education and money will not change the animal-like, sexual aggressiveness of blacks, that miscegenation remains the basic end, even in a black educated and refined beyond the stage of brutal rape. Immediately after Flora's attacker is burned alive (p. 384), the scene shifts to the Boston home of Everett Lowell, a wealthy politician and philanthropist who has long championed the cause of freedmen's rights. Lowell's protegé is a black, George Harris, the Harvard educated son of Eliza Harris (Dixon uses several characters from *Uncle Tom's Cabin*, including Simon Legree). After listening to another of Lowell's impassioned speeches on equality, George decides to ask for Lowell's daughter Helen in marriage (p. 391). George declares his love for Helen to Everett Lowell, who explodes. Throwing George out of the house, Lowell screams that he would rather kill his daughter than see her marry Harris. Helen of course feels the same way (p. 398). Deprived of Lowell's white influence, Harris drifts for a while and then takes up a life of crime (p. 407). Dixon's point seems clear: blacks, like animals, are incapable of controlling sexual impulses, and they are driven to seek relations with white women. If the black man is ignorant and brutal, he will rape unless physically prevented. If educated and granted social equality, he will seek to marry a white woman. In either case, coexistence of blacks and whites in this country leads to the same thing—miscegenation. Miscegenation must be prevented at all costs because "amalgamation simply means Africanization" (p. 386), the destruction of Dixon's precious Anglo-Saxon race.

Dixon's solution to the threat of miscegenation forms the third basic proposition of the novel—that blacks must be physically removed from the country. As a first step, blacks must be deprived of all political rights, because political equality leads to economic equality, and hence to social equality and miscegenation. When blacks gained power during Reconstruction, the Klan rose and physically took away that power. Once this was accomplished, the Klan rightfully disbanded and white political leaders took its place. When political power is lost to blacks thirty years later in part two of *The Leopard's Spots*, it is again necessary to raise a white liberation army, this time called "Red Shirts" (p. 450), and to seize physical control of the state. Charlie Gaston is the political leader who replaces this armed force, but to prevent any possible recurrence of black political strength he vows to disenfranchise blacks completely so they can never again organize and vote themselves into political office. From Dixon's point of view Gaston's action is the first step in the right direction but is still shortsighted, representing the Southerners who accepted the Booker T. Washington approach. Gaston intends to allow disenfranchised blacks to be educated as farmers and industrial laborers. Rev. Durham, Dixon's spokesman, argues strongly against Gaston's plan, insisting that the only way to preserve the race is to banish blacks from the continent (pp. 463–464).

If Gaston has not progressed far enough in his thinking, at least he has come to grips with what Dixon sees as the basic reality and has brought it out into the open. At the Democratic state convention Gaston introduces as the total party platform the single resolution that the two races cannot coexist, "the future North Carolinian must be an Anglo-Saxon or a Mulatto" and therefore "the hour has now come in our history to eliminate the black from our life and to reestablish for all time the government of our fathers" (p. 437). Gaston speaks also of the potential of the Anglo-Saxon race to conquer the world "as God's annointed" (p. 439), and points to the unity of the Anglo-Saxon race now that the passions dividing North and South have subsided (pp. 444–445). Earlier, the narrator had said of the Spanish-American War that "most marvelous of all, this hundred days of war had reunited the Anglo-Saxon race" (p. 413). Gaston's speech laying bare the basic idea of an epic race struggle centered on miscegenation, with the future of civilization at stake, creates pandemonium in the novel and results in Gaston's overwhelming election victory (p. 447). The publication of Dixon's novel expressing these ideas had approximately the same impact, creating pandemonium among the public and reviewers, while catapulting Dixon to international fame and establishing Doubleday, Page and Company overnight as a major publishing house.[22]

The storm that broke over the appearance of Dixon's next novel on the race problem, *The Clansman* (1905),[23] later immortalized as the D. W. Griffith film *Birth of a Nation*, was even greater.[24] *The Clansman* divides into four sections and covers the chaotic years from 1865 to 1870. In the first part, a young Confederate colonel, Ben Cameron, lies wounded in a Washington hospital where he is visited by his family. Their discussions portray Lincoln sympathetically but as being surrounded by evil men, such as Austin Stoneman, a character obviously based on Thaddeus Stevens. The second section relates the events following the assassination of Lincoln: the battle between President Johnson and Congress; Stoneman's success in pushing through legislation enfranchising blacks; the setting up by Stoneman's Congress of the machinery to crush the South. In the third part, the scene shifts to the Cameron's hometown in South Carolina where Stoneman, with his son and daughter, now lives. This section depicts terrible sufferings for Southern whites under Reconstruction and growing outrages by blacks, culminating in the rape of a young girl, Marion Lenoir, who then commits suicide along with her mother. The final section shows the organization and development of the Klan as the only answer to the conditions prevailing. Ben Cameron, as head of the Klan, is arrested and almost executed by Stoneman, but Stoneman's children turn against their father to help Cameron escape. That night the Klan defeats the black troops stationed in the area. The terrorized blacks fail to vote and a new, white government gains control of the state.

The Clansman enlarges upon two of Dixon's basic propositions laid down in *The Leopard's Spots*: first, that blacks are animals, and, second, that miscegenation and destruction of racial purity are inevitable in a mixed society. These themes are linked to a further warning that the North must realize that by emancipating the blacks it has unleashed an epic racial conflict, with the future of civilization at stake.

Dixon establishes the basic animality of blacks by using animal imagery, particularly with regard to the two most important black characters, Lydia Brown, the mulatto mistress of Austin Stoneman, and Gus, a black rapist. Lydia is first referred to as "a woman of extraordinary animal beauty" (p. 57), and later as "the tawny leopardess who keeps his house" (p. 163). Stoneman himself calls her a "yellow vampire" and says that he was drawn down with her "into the black abyss of animalism" (p. 371). When Gus and three companions break into the Lenoir home, they are described as "brutes" who "leap" into the room (p. 304). Gus has "yellow teeth grinning through thick lips" and "bead-eyes wide apart gleaming ape-like." When he attacks the girl it is "a single tiger spring, and the black claws of the beast sank into the soft white throat." Later, a footprint is found and identified as having been made by a black because it is entirely different from the print of a white foot (p. 310). Finally, when Dr. Cameron (Ben's father) examines the eyes of the dead woman with a microscope, he finds burned on Marion's retinas "the bestial figure of a negro . . . huge black hand . . . massive jaws and lips" (pp. 313–314).

Gus and Lydia Brown are also used to develop the important second claim, that black animality leads to sexual aggression and "pollution" of the Anglo-Saxon race. Gus obviously corresponds to the rapist in *The Leopard's Spots*, but in *The Clansman* Dixon escalates the rhetorical effect of brutal sexual aggression by depicting the rape scene itself, rather than just the aftermath. This time we hear the horrible laughter of the brute rapist and the "cry, long, tremulous, heart-rending, piteous" of his victim (p. 304). The effect is further heightened by repeating the scene when Gus has been captured by the Klan, and Dr. Cameron hypnotizes him to obtain the truth. Under hypnosis, Gus rehearses the crime in gruesome detail, even to the act of rape, at which point the Klansmen are driven mad and force him to stop (pp. 323–324).

The "pollution" of Anglo-Saxon racial purity has taken place, and only one catharsis is possible. Marion cleans the house, burns her clothes, bathes, puts on a dress of "spotless white" and goes with her mother to the cliff's edge. When her mother momentarily hesitates, the sixteen-year-old Marion quietly reassures her, "This shame I can never forget, nor will the world forget. Death is the only way." As dawn breaks, they step hand-in-hand into the gulf, plunging to the river below, perhaps suggesting baptism and rebirth. Marion's desecration obviously exemplifies Cash's "Southern rape complex," a symbol of the rape of the South during Reconstruction. Lydia Brown functions in roughly the same capacity as George Harris did in *The Leopard's Spots*. She is, like Harris, no rapist, but has by beauty and education attached herself to her white superior. Unlike Harris, she succeeds in dragging her white supporter down into her "black abyss of animalism."

Dixon uses Lydia to further his argument about black sexual aggression because through her he has extended it to include black women as well as men. Lydia plays an important role in showing the power of blacks to "corrupt" and "destroy" Anglo-Saxon purity. At the end of the novel, Stoneman brags to Dr. Cameron that he alone is responsible for the totality of Reconstruction in the South: "My will alone forged the chains of black rule" (p. 371). But he also states that he was "ruled" in doing this by three forces—"party success, a vicious woman, and the quenchless desire for personal vengeance" (p. 371). Actually, the book reveals that he cared only about his personal power, not about his party, and that the motive for his personal vengeance was the burning of his iron mills in Pennsylvania by Lee's army (p. 372), hardly sufficient to drive a man to Stoneman's fanatic state. The real cause of the attempt to crush the South is none other than Lydia, the "yellow vampire" who had dragged Stoneman down to her level of animalism through her sexual domination of him. Early in the novel, the narrator describes the house where Stoneman lives alone with Lydia, separated from his children. His house has become the center of all national politics and Lydia presides over his table, where decisions are made. The narrator tells us, "No more curious or sinister figure ever cast a shadow across the history of a great nation than did this mulatto woman in the most corrupt hour of American life" (p. 94).

The mulatto woman is presented as real cause of the rape of the South, of which the brutal Gus is merely a symbol. Traditionally, of course, mulatto women were considered victims in American literature. The stereotyped figure of the tragic mulatto had been a favorite in abolitionist novels. But Dixon reverses the image; victim is now seen as tyrant. The reversal is crucial to Dixon's ideology, because to see black women as sexually exploited by whites would destroy his thesis that all miscegenation results from the aggressive, animal sexuality of blacks.

Finally, *The Clansman* argues that the North has no one to blame but itself for the near victory of blacks in the epic racial struggle. Stoneman says, "When I first fell a victim to the wiles of the yellow vampire who kept my house, I dreamed of lifting her to my level" (p. 371), but the reverse occurred, just as the North's idealistic dream of raising blacks to a white level can only lead to the opposite—the fall and destruction of the Anglo-Saxon race. Salvation lies in the example of Stoneman's children, Elsie and Phil, who reverse the attitude of the previous Northern generation by going South, learning to despise blacks, and marrying the Klan leader and his sister. Their union is Dixon's lesson—the need for racial unity, North and South, against the common enemy seeking to destroy the Anglo-Saxon race by miscegenetic conquest.

Originally written in 1909 as a play, *The Sins of the Fathers* (1912),[25] again develops Dixon's three basic racial themes, with particular emphasis on the final warning given by Rev. Durham in *The Leopard's Spots*—that controlling blacks is not enough; they must be removed from contact with whites. The book argues that simple contact will inevitably lead to miscegenation and Anglo-Saxon racial suicide. Miscegenation is inevitable because whites are helpless in the face of black animal sexuality, particularly when this bestial drive is linked to the cunning, derived from their white heritage, found in mulattoes.

The mulatto, especially the mulatto woman, emerges from this novel as the greatest threat to white racial purity. In *The Leopard's Spots*, the mulatto George Harris is ineffective and overshadowed by the black rapist; in *The Clansman*, the mulatto Lydia is seen as the basic force behind the rape of the South, but the threat she represents is blurred by the graphic brutality of black Gus. In *The Sins of the Fathers*, the mulatto Cleo stands alone, not outweighed or counter-balanced by a black rapist, as representative of the primary threat to the Anglo-Saxon race. The novel attempts to absolve whites from all responsibility for any miscegenation, even under slavery, by placing the blame on the sexual aggressiveness of female mulattoes. Naturally, the book ignores the chicken/egg question of whence came the first mulatto. *The Sins of the Fathers* almost seems an apology for Austin Stoneman in *The Clansman*, because it takes a fine, strong white man, Major Norton, and shows that he is blameless for falling under the sexual domination of a mulatto woman, Cleo. The difference between Norton and Stoneman is that Norton, a Southerner, shakes off the woman's control and uses his experience as a well of strength to fight for banishment of blacks. Norton, like the rape victim Marion Lenoir in *The Clansman*, is guiltless, but still must undergo the catharsis of suicide to expunge the "pollution" which has occurred.

The Sins of the Fathers opens near the end of the Reconstruction period. Major Norton, twenty-four years old and a leader of the K.K.K., aids Bob Peeler, who has recently married his quadroon housekeeper, by whom he has a beautiful octoroon daughter, Cleo. The Klan has threatened Peeler, and Norton acts to break up the unauthorized raid on the old man. When Norton saves Peeler and his family, the beautiful Cleo throws herself at his feet in gratitude. Cleo then volunteers to work in Norton's office, and while he is temporarily in jail for Klan activities, she goes to work in his home, aiding his invalid wife with their son. Despite his best efforts, Norton succumbs to the girl's charms and they have a brief affair. During the same period, Norton is instrumental in disarming the black militia and reestablishing a white government, but shortly afterwards his wife dies and he leaves the South. While in New York, he receives a telegram from Cleo in Baltimore saying she has had their baby. The infant daughter is left in the care of a convent to be raised as white, and Cleo returns south with Norton as nurse to his small son. Norton never resumes his affair with Cleo, and over the next twenty years devotes himself to the cause of removing blacks from this country.

After the Spanish-American War, Norton feels that the North and South are at last reunited, and it is the golden chance to lead an all-out effort to disenfranchise blacks and deport them. He throws himself into an upcoming election campaign, making race the sole issue. Seeking revenge, Cleo invites her daughter Helen to visit while Norton is off campaigning, having left his grown son Tom to manage affairs at home. Tom falls in love with the beautiful Helen, but Norton returns and demands that he give her up. Tom refuses, even after Norton tells them both that Helen is part black. When Norton learns they are already secretly married, he takes Tom into his study and tells him the whole truth, that Helen is his half-sister. They agree to commit suicide; Norton shoots Tom and kills himself. But Tom is only wounded, and when he recovers he learns that Helen is not really Cleo's daughter. The baby she had in Baltimore died, and she secretly adopted a white infant before Norton arrived in order to retain some hold on him. Tom banishes the woman from his house and takes up his father's crusade.

Most basically, the novel argues that in the face of Cleo's cunning animality, Norton is biologically helpless. By exonerating Norton of any guilt, the novel implies that the white men who had practiced miscegenation during slavery and who continued the practice after the war are also guiltless. They are all helpless victims of biology, and the only protection for the Anglo-Saxon race is total exclusion of any possibility of contact with blacks, to be achieved by removing them from the land.

In *The Clansman*, the "tawny leopardess," Lydia, is seen only in the background, throwing her shadow over great events. In

The Sins of the Fathers, Dixon has taken the idea of this character and developed it, again emphasizing animality and this
time showing the cunning predator at work. The first night
Major Norton encounters Cleo, he is shocked by the "over-
powering" physical reaction he has to her (p. 25). When she
comes to his office the next day, he cannot take his eyes off her
slightest movements, which are all "sinuous" and "rhythmic"
(p. 35). The narrator comments that while Norton had successfully smashed the scalawag governor's black army, "he was
at the same time proving himself defenseless against the silent
and deadly purpose that had already shaped itself in the soul
of this sleek, sensuous young animal" (p. 37). When Norton
finally realizes that Cleo is in love with him, he is angry and
tries to dismiss her, but she charms him out of it and arouses
a corresponding animality in him that he calls "the Beast." He
tries to fight back by dismissing her the next day, but she only
touches him and laughs as she leaves, knowing now that he is
afraid of her (pp. 43–45). While he is in jail, Cleo cleverly
ingratiates herself with his wife and makes herself indispens-
able as nurse to their son, so that Norton cannot fire her without
explaining why to his wife. Cleo has thus managed to move
into his house. Norton is angry and fights her, but it is a lost
cause. One night she slips into his room dressed in a "revealing
silk kimono," to plead with him not to fire her. He agrees not
to, but after she leaves the room, "through every hour of the
long night, maddened by the consciousness of her physical near-
ness—he imagined at times he could hear her breathing in the
next room—he lay awake and fought the Beast for the mastery
of life" (p. 97). When we next see Norton the battle has been
lost, but he has risen again from defeat, having broken off the
affair some two months previously.

The first part of the novel shows the animal seductiveness
of Cleo, and Norton's struggle to escape. In the next section,
the author presents an elaborate exoneration of Norton for
what has happened. In an attempt to win Norton back, Cleo
tells his wife of the affair, hoping that the shock will kill her,
which it nearly does. Norton tries to explain his actions to the
old family doctor attending his wife, but the doctor interrupts,
"No, you needn't. It's an old story. The more powerful the man

the easier his conquest when once the female animal of Cleo's race has her chance" (p. 121). Norton tells of his struggles and the doctor replies, "Yes, I know, my boy, with that young animal playing at your feet, in physical touch with your soul and body in the intimacies of your home, you never had a chance" (p. 123). When Norton's wife refuses to see him, he goes to his mother-in-law for help. She is most understanding and agrees to see her daughter on his behalf. She tells her daughter that Cleo's mother was fathered by the former governor, a dear friend of theirs—and that her own husband, Mrs. Norton's father, died in the cabin of a mulatto slave girl. She also tells her daughter that this is the heritage of slavery and is why the white women of the South would have abolished it eventually—the mulatto women were corrupting the best men (pp. 135–137). Mrs. Norton forgives her husband and they grow closer than ever during her final illness. He attempts to explain himself to her in a lengthy discourse, showing that his actions were the results of biological determinism based on "animal magnetism" (p. 153). She exonerates him from any blame, and, asking only that he raise their son free from the "curse," she dies peacefully (p. 162). Cleo follows him north, deceives him about the baby and works her way back into his household by playing on the affection that the motherless boy has for his old nurse. But all of her wiles are to no avail, and over the next twenty years Norton comes to see her no longer as a woman but as "the thing he hated—the mongrel breed of a degraded nation" (p. 196).

Dixon has met head-on the problem of the mulatto and resolved it to his own satisfaction. Many authors resolve the dilemma which the mulattoes represent by following the general American attitude of simply considering them black. Others show the mulatto attempting to pass for white and resolve the dilemma in that way, even though it is often not a permanent resolution. Dixon deals with mulattoes as mulattoes— neither blacks nor whites, evolving through his treatments of George Harris and Lydia Brown to Cleo Peeler, progressively insistent that the mulatto is more evil than the pure black.

To Dixon, mulattoes are not tragic figures caught between the two races; they are creatures who inherit the worst elements from both heritages and combine them to become living symbols of evil and race destruction. Everett Carter comments on motivation for Dixon's treatment of mulattoes, suggesting that the deep moral convictions of the Protestant South would lead to viewing the living evidence of lust as evil in itself. He also believes that the mulatto serves as a reminder of the burden of guilt that whites must bear in the record of sexual aggression against blacks, and that Dixon discharges this guilt by making the mulatto the evil force.[26]

Whatever his motivation, Dixon has come to one of the two logical extremes possible in the dilemma first posed in the American novel by Cooper—that is, the conflict between white attraction to the mulatto and white revulsion at miscegenation. In one resolution, the white man decides that his distaste for miscegenation is a base feeling and allows his natural attraction to the beauty of the mulatto full play, as exemplified in novels such as Mayne Reid's *The Quadroon* or John T. Trowbridge's *Neighbor Jackwood*. Dixon's answer is the other, to fight the attraction felt for the mulatto by building the distaste for miscegenation into an epic racial conflict and to triumph over "the Beast" within by banishing completely "the beautiful animal" that appeals to it. Among the many novels between 1891 and 1914 that advocated racial discrimination, Dixon's works stand alone in their open, direct and compulsive insistence that miscegenation is the only issue at stake. Page and Harris, for example, were attempting to romanticize the South and to act as apologists for discrimination against blacks, so that the North would understand and accept a Southern point of view. They were concerned with healing sectional conflict and reuniting the nation, with the South fully accepted and accorded its due. Dixon, writing after the Spanish-American War, assumed national unity and argued simply that because the nation is reunited it must now look to the only threat facing the Anglo-Saxon mission of divinely inspired world leadership—the potential for racial suicide if blacks are allowed to coexist on this continent.

Dixon's impassioned commitment to conservative racial and religious values led him always to seek the grandest pulpit from which to preach his views. He abandoned a successful

Baptist ministry in New York City for a larger nondenomi-
national church. He abandoned the ministry altogether for the
national audience he could reach as a lecturer and, after the
success of *The Leopard's Spots*, as a novelist and playwright.
As partner with D. W. Griffith in the movie *Birth of a Nation*,
Dixon believed he had found the ideal medium to educate the
masses, to bring them to political and religious salvation. While
his work is seldom read today, both in his conservative social
themes and as a politicized preacher seeking a national congregation through mass media, Thomas Dixon clearly fore-
shadowed the political television evangelists of the modern
South.

NOTES

1. See Frederickson. The next several paragraphs summarize
Frederickson's argument.
2. Frederickson, p. 275.
3. See Friedman for the full argument I summarize here.
4. Rayford W. Logan, ed., *The Negro in American Life and Thought:
The Nadir, 1877–1901* (New York: Dial Press, 1954).
5. Kenneth Stamp, *The Era of Reconstruction, 1865–1877* (New
York: Knopf, 1965), pp. 13–21.
6. Louis D. Rubin, Jr., *The Faraway Country: Writers of the Modern South* (Univ. of Washington Press, 1963), pp. 26–27.
7. Gertrude Atherton, *Senator North* (1900; reprint, Ridgewood,
N.J.: Gregg Press, 1967). Hereafter cited parenthetically.
8. Cash, p. 153.
9. William L. Andrews, "Miscegenation in the Late Nineteenth-
Century Novel," *Southern Humanities Review* 13 (1979):14–15.
10. Thomas Nelson Page, *Red Rock* (1898; reprint, Ridgewood, N.J.:
Gregg Press, 1967). Hereafter cited parenthetically.
11. Cash, p. 118.
12. Cash, p. 87.
13. Cash, p. 119.
14. Joel Chandler Harris, *Gabriel Tolliver: A Story of Reconstruction* (1902; reprint, Ridgewood, N.J.: Gregg Press, 1967). Hereafter
cited parenthetically.
15. Theodore Gross, "The Negro in Literature of Reconstruction,"
in *Images of the Negro in American Literature*, ed. by Gross and Hardy,
p. 78.

16. Maxwell Bloomfield, "Dixon's *The Leopard's Spots*: A Study in Popular Racism," *American Quarterly*, 16 (1964):390.

17. Thomas Dixon, quoted by Raymond A. Cook, *Fire from the Flint: The Amazing Careers of Thomas Dixon* (Winston-Salem: John F. Blair, 1968), p. 119.

18. Bloomfield, p. 398.

19. Thomas Dixon, Jr., *The Leopard's Spots* (1902; reprint, Ridgewood, N.J.: Gregg Press, 1967). Hereafter cited parenthetically.

20. Bloomfield, pp. 396–397.

21. Calvin Hernton, *Sex and Racism in America* (Garden City, N.Y.: Doubleday and Company, 1965), pp. 42, 96–97.

22. Cook, p. 112.

23. Thomas Dixon, Jr., *The Clansman* (1905; reprint, Ridgewood, N.J.: Gregg Press, 1967). Hereafter cited parenthetically.

24. Cook, p. 126.

25. Thomas Dixon, *The Sins of the Fathers: A Romance of the South* (New York: D. Appleton and Co., 1912). Hereafter cited parenthetically.

26. Everett Carter, "Cultural History Written with Lightning: The Significance of *Birth of a Nation*," *American Quarterly* 12 (1960):353.

7
Black Voices, 1891–1914

Despite the tremendous popularity of Thomas Dixon's work, in a basic way he ran counter to the current of his time. The period from 1891 to 1914 was essentially one of reform and social progress. The foundations appeared during the 1880s with such legislation as the Pendleton Act (1883) and the Interstate Commerce Act (1887). The Sherman Anti-Trust Act (1890) and the reform measures urged by the Populists in the 1892 election were further signs of movement. Reform governments soon appeared in cities, such as Toledo, Ohio, and spread finally to state levels. By 1900 Robert LaFollette had been elected governor of Wisconsin and had instituted a wide program of reform. In the following year Theodore Roosevelt became President of the United States and reform programs became national. The times between 1900 and World War I were dominated by the need to adapt social attitudes and institutions from a basically agricultural society to a newly industrialized one. The necessary reform movements were spurred on by such things as the development of the reform-oriented social sciences, the pragmatism of William James and John Dewey—which encouraged change—and the advent of the muckrakers after 1902. Blacks were one of the few groups which did not benefit from the reform feelings of the era.

While social/political progress advanced on many fronts, the situation of blacks in the United States was degenerating. In the South, disenfranchisement by deception had been practiced since the end of Reconstruction, but in 1890, beginning with

Mississippi, "legalized" subversion of the Fifteenth Amendment began, leading to the first "grandfather clause" in Louisiana in 1898 and culminating in "legal" disenfranchisement of blacks in eight states by 1910. In 1896, the Supreme Court in *Plessy v. Ferguson* upheld the doctrine of "separate but equal," and segregation became legally entrenched throughout the South. Blacks were largely excluded from the industrial boom by white refusal to employ or to work with them. Booker T. Washington was the most prominent spokesman for blacks until his death in 1915, and in 1895 at the Atlanta Cotton Exposition he agreed that blacks should accept a position of political and social inferiority. Given these anti-black realities, it is not surprising that, even in the midst of a reform era, white literature continued to present blacks in the most unfavorable stereotypes, culminating in the bestial characters of Thomas Dixon.

From 1891 to 1914, conditions for blacks were atrocious; lynchings were at an all-time high. Blacks were without the energetic support of reform-minded whites, such as they had received in the abolition controversy and during the early period of Reconstruction, and were forced to defend themselves. They had tried since Emancipation to improve their lot by education, and though little improvement had come, increasing numbers were well-educated; by 1900 more than 2000 blacks had graduated from college and more than 1,500,000 black children were in school. These educated men and women, many led by W. E. B. DuBois in the Niagara Movement, were the vanguard in the blacks' struggle to defend themselves and change the condition of black people in America. After a number of race riots, especially the 1908 one in Springfield, Illinois, many white Americans were shocked into an awareness of the mistreatment suffered by blacks, and a group of prominent whites joined with DuBois and his followers to form the NAACP in 1910. Slow progress, first seen in the overthrow by the Supreme Court in 1915 of the "grandfather clause" in Oklahoma's Constitution, was made toward alleviating the conditions which had grown steadily worse since 1890. But before 1910, blacks had been largely on their own in the struggle against oppression. One means of defense they had taken up had been writing novels that attacked discrimination.

Robert Bone believes that the cultural history of American blacks originates in folk art and becomes literary in the full sense about 1890.[1] By this date, a full generation after the end of slavery and forced illiteracy, the educational efforts mentioned above had produced the first sizable body of literate blacks. Given this base in literacy, adopting fiction as a means of social reform came naturally. Henry Steele Commager calls the decade of the nineties "the watershed of American history,"[2] and Fred Lewis Pattee says that 1890 marks the beginning of both a new era in America and a new American literature.[3] For novels in which blacks appear, 1890 certainly inaugurates an era of change, of increasing stridency in the argument over racism. The decade of the 1880s had been one of solid triumph for new romancers of the Plantation Tradition, sweeping dissenters like Tourgée from the field in despair.[4] But in the following decade a number of new writers, mostly black, were to pick up the pen dropped by Tourgée in 1890 and continue the literary battle for their rights with mounting intensity until the outbreak of World War I. The very worsening of conditions which drove Tourgée, tired of the fray, to abandon it, drove fresher men and women to launch a new offensive against oppression.

The first antidiscrimination novel of the decade in which miscegenation plays a role was by a black author, Frances E. W. Harper, who had been a well-known writer of abolitionist verse before the war and a leading black feminist.[5] *Iola Leroy; or Shadows Uplifted* (1892)[6] does much to establish the precedent in black novels of developing exceptional, educated black characters to counter the stereotypes of the plantation tradition.[7] The story follows the fortunes of Iola Leroy, a fair-skinned mulatto, during the Civil War and for several years after. By means of a flashback, her childhood before the war is also brought in. The novel opens with a group of slaves in North Carolina rejoicing that the Yankees are near and they will soon be freed. Iola is liberated by the soldiers and becomes a nurse; she meets white Doctor Gresham, who falls in love with her and proposes.

The flashback interposes here, giving Iola's background. She refuses Gresham and explains her heritage, but he says it makes no difference. Meanwhile, Iola's brother Harry had been serving in the Union army and was wounded in the South. After the war, Iola returns to the South to look for her mother and discovers her with Harry in Georgia, where he is teaching. Iola has also encountered her uncle and grandmother in her search and is able to reunite her mother's family. Iola goes back to the North and has great difficulty obtaining or keeping work once it is discovered that she is part black. She re-encounters Dr. Gresham, who is still in love with her, but she again refuses his proposal. She meets a light mulatto, Dr. Latimer, who has turned down a fortune by refusing to pass for white, and they marry. Iola's brother Harry, who could also pass easily, instead marries a pure African, Miss Delaney, and the four return to the South to work for their race, Iola and Dr. Latimer in medicine, Harry and his wife in education.

The novel is highly melodramatic and filled with improbable coincidences, but two principal themes are developed throughout. The work creates an image of blacks that destroys the Plantation Tradition stereotypes, and it answers the question of where the mulatto belongs. The author develops the first theme by presenting, in various situations, educated and accomplished blacks and mulattoes such as Iola, her brother Harry, the beautiful Miss Delaney, who manages a large school, and Dr. Latimer. Harper also attacks stereotypes through emphasis at the beginning of the story on dissimulation, a common theme in much black literature, which explains the origins of white stereotyped ideas about blacks. The slaves all seem to be very light-hearted and careless (p. 8), but they are actively engaging in secret self-education, plotting to escape, and deceiving their masters to gain information on the progress of the war and the proximity of the Union forces (pp. 8–17). One slave, for example, commiserates at length with his mistress's sorrow at a Confederate reverse, but begins doing somersaults for joy when she leaves the room (p. 11). In other words, stereotyped concepts of blacks originated in roles assumed by slaves in their own self-interest.[8]

Miscegenation and the question of passing dominate much

of the action. While waiting for the Yankees to arrive, slaves discuss their situation, and miscegenation is a common subject. They talk of a neighboring mistress who had hated her slaves and would probably turn in her grave if she knew that her sons had fathered ten mulatto children (p. 27). Uncle Ben talks about his greatest sorrow when his beautiful mulatto wife, Miranda, ran off with a white slave trader because "he gave her a chance to live easy, to wear fine clothes, an' be waited on like a lady" (p. 30). Ben himself was the son of a white man (p. 31).

The first real action comes when the Union soldiers arrive and save Iola from her master's attempts to rape her (pp. 38–39); she tells them that he had even attempted to force her submission by whipping (p. 42). Miscegenation is used, as it had been in the abolitionist novels, as a shocking example of the evils present under slavery. In the flashback presenting Iola's background and the story of her mother, Marie, miscegenation centers an indictment of slavery under even the best of masters.

Iola's father, Eugene Leroy, is a wealthy planter who falls in love with her quadroon mother, Marie. Eugene frees, educates, and finally marries Marie, bringing upon himself social ostracism. He comments bitterly that he could live with her and sell his own children without condemnation, but to marry her is a crime (p. 66). Marie and the children are subjected to insult, and she fears greatly what might happen if Eugene should die (p. 80). Iola and Harry are sent north to school, where they pass for white, unaware of their black heritage (pp. 83–85). Eugene does die; Marie and her youngest child are seized by his evil cousin, who also plots to enslave Iola and Harry. The thesis that even a good master is helpless to protect his slaves from the system is presented ironically. Iola is defending slavery to her Northern classmates by arguing that her father treats slaves well at the very moment that her mother and baby sister are being seized (p. 97). Tricked into returning home, Iola is also enslaved (p. 105). Basically, the subplot presented in the flashback reruns the old abolitionist motif of the tragic octoroon condemned to slavery.

The more important concern with miscegenation in the novel

involves the problem of the freed mulatto in the postwar years. Iola, Harry, and Dr. Latimer all face the dilemma of a mulatto light enough to pass, and all determine to align themselves with their maternal race, despite the personal loss which this means for each. Iola first has the opportunity to cross into the white world through Dr. Gresham's proposal, which she refuses in spite of her love for him (p. 117). She sacrifices both her love and the social position which Gresham can offer; she tells him she will not marry him but will instead go south to look for her mother. This action seems symbolic of the mulatto's search for racial identity.

Harry rejects life as a white when he enlists in a black regiment, much to the shock of the recruiter, who thinks him white (pp. 126–127). After the war, Harry brings home the pure African Miss Delaney and announces that he has "linked my fortunes to the race" (p. 203). The emphasis on Miss Delaney's Africanism appears to make Harry's aligning himself with her also a symbol of search for racial identity.

Iola faces the dilemma again when she first returns to the North after the war. She passes for white by simple omission rather than denial, but each time she admits to being mulatto she is fired or refused employment (pp. 205–209). She encounters Dr. Gresham again and is given a final chance by his second proposal (p. 230), but she again refuses, telling him that she has decided that her destiny is to work among her people in the South (p. 234).[9] Once this choice is finally made the "shadows" are "uplifted" from her life and all goes well for her. Her uncle had earlier said that it would be "treason" to masquerade as white (p. 203), and this lesson is emphasized by the introduction of Dr. Latimer near the end of the story. Young, brilliant, and totally white in appearance, he has been offered a fortune by his father's family if he will pass, but Latimer "has nobly refused to forsake his mother's people" for wealth and fame (p. 238). This use of superior characters, who by education, culture and appearance are equal to any white and who choose to be black, becomes a basic device for black writers defending their people against the stereotypes of Thomas Dixon and the latter-day plantation romancers.

Besides the counter-stereotype, Harper adds another significant dimension to the fictional treatment of miscegenation. In
her novel, interracial sex is treated not as an awesome taboo,
but as a common fact of life, with black characters casually
joking about the subject among themselves (p. 27). For blacks
raised in slavery, miscegenation was a commonplace occurrence,[10] and the treatment of it as such by this black writer
indicates realism amid her otherwise often idealized elements
of plot and character. On the other hand, white writers, whether
condemning or defending miscegenation, treat the subject as
immensely charged, as filled with socially and morally explo-
sive implications, reflecting the white culture's oft noted need
to deny the reality of miscegenation in the United States. If
one pretends that something just doesn't exist, then any admitted instance necessarily carries the potential to disrupt the
whole order built on the denial.

Finally, while Marian Musgrave is generally correct that
white writers before the 1960s stuck to portraying only the
relationship between a white man and a black woman, her
corollary that "when the black writer deals with the interracial
affair, he does so in terms of the black man with the white
woman"[11] seems more true for black writers after World War
I. At the turn of the century, black writers—as Frances Harper
does here—continued to see the sexually exploited black woman,
before and after slavery, as an appealing rhetorical device in
their battle against racism. As Sutton Griggs was to proclaim
shortly, "The world at large has heard that the problem of the
South is the protection of the white woman. There is another
woman in the South." What we do find in some black novels
of this period is the addition of the black male/white female
relationship to its long-present opposite.

J. McHenry Jones belongs with Frances Harper and other
black authors who relied on a basic counter-stereotype to combat the image of blacks presented by the plantation romances.
Born 1859 in Ohio, Jones was an educator and editor. In 1898,
he became the first president of the West Virginia Colored
Institute. His novel, *Hearts of Gold* (1896),[12] presents a number
of exceptional mulatto and black characters in a biting attack

on racism, particularly on the specific results of institutionalized discrimination such as lynchings and the Convict Lease
System.

Two mulattoes, Lotus Stone, a medical student, and Clement
St. John, crusading editor of a black newspaper, are boyhood
friends from New England who meet at the annual convention
of the Knights of the Red Cross in Mt. Clare, Canada. Stone
meets Regina Underwood, who appears white but is of mixed
blood. He rescues her from a boat accident in superheroic fashion, and they promise to write each other after he leaves Mt.
Clare. Clement St. John marries a black girl, Lucille, and en-
ergetically pursues the cause of "Afro-Americans," as blacks
are called in the novel. Lotus Stone completes medical school
and goes south to work among the blacks. Regina Underwood
is defrauded of her inheritance by a white cousin, Dr. Frank
Leighton, who is attracted to her but will not stoop to marry
her because of the "taint." Regina goes south to teach, choosing
the same town as Lotus Stone. Leighton shows up and, out of
jealousy, frames Stone on a malpractice charge, which sends
Lotus to the convict mines. Regina notifies Clement St. John,
who comes south and works with her to obtain Stone's release.
They are eventually successful, and all return north. St. John
and Stone go to Mt. Clare, where they uncover the true will
left by Regina's mother, and she is awarded her inheritance.
Leighton attempts to murder Stone, but is himself killed instead. The novel ends with a reunion of the two couples, now
both married and the parents of children, at the annual convention of the Knights in Mt. Clare once again.

The characters in the novel are all persons of incredible morality, devotion to the cause, and general virtue. Even the style
of speech they normally employ is so refined and inflated that
it almost becomes unintentional burlesque. But there are some
powerful scenes in the novel, particularly the lynching of Stone's
cellmate (pp. 221–227), the horrors of the prison mines, and
the sentencing of blacks to ten and fifteen years for minor
offenses in order to meet the labor needs of the Convict Lease
System (pp. 235–284). Miscegenation is important in the plot
because it provides motivation for Frank Leighton, who initi-
ates most of the action. Leighton also desires Regina's inher-

itance but his pursuit of her south and his attempts to destroy
Stone stem from Leighton's lust for Regina and jealousy of the
mulatto doctor. Leighton's feelings toward Regina are described as alternating "between desperate love and blind hatred"
(p. 58). At times he feels he wants to marry her, but when he
thinks of his social position and the pride of his relations, he
rejects her (p. 58). When he succeeds in defrauding her, Leighton feels he will now be able to accomplish all his intentions.
He had wanted to marry to obtain her money, but since he no
longer need marry her for that, he decides to make her his
mistress (pp. 140–141). Regina flees south to escape him, but he
follows her and attempts to regain her goodwill (pp. 177–178).
When she starts seeing Stone, Leighton is pushed by jealousy
into his schemes to destroy the mulatto doctor and even attempts, unsuccessfully, to kill Regina (pp. 217–219). Leighton's
death, caused when he is struck by a train, evolves from miscegenetic jealousy, because he had been fleeing from an unsuccessful attempt to murder Stone (pp. 295–296).

Of special interest is the briefly recounted story (pp. 33–38)
of Regina's mother, one of the few instances in the literature
of miscegenation in which a white woman marries a black man.
Regina's grandparents, Judge and Mrs. Underwood, lived in
the United States before the war and operated a station on the
Underground Railroad. Their daughter, Ethel, as a young child
helped aid a fugitive mulatto named George Stewart, who stayed
on with the family for several years as a servant. When she
reached eighteen, Ethel announced that she was in love with
George, greatly upsetting her parents. They determined to separate the two by sending Ethel to boarding school and George
to Canada, but Ethel ran away from school and found George
in Canada, where they married. George died before long, however, and Ethel gave birth to Regina.

Ethel attempted to contact her parents, who were in Europe
and did not discover her plight until they returned. They went
to Canada immediately, but Ethel had already died. Judge and
Mrs. Underwood then settled in Mt. Clare to raise their granddaughter. There are two things of interest about this little
episode. Just as in Mrs. Wilson's *Our Nig*, it is a black author
who depicts a white woman willingly marrying a black man.

It seems the one taboo which white authors dealing with the subject could not break is the idea that a white woman would desire sexual relations or marriage with a black man. Unlike the situation in *Our Nig*, however, where the marriage involves a white woman of the lowest class—and there is much historical evidence that such unions were common—the marriage in *Hearts of Gold* involves a white woman of the upper class. Jones is apparently the first novelist before World War I openly to defy the ultimate taboo—that is, to maintain that a wealthy, educated, upper-class American white woman might freely choose to marry a black man.

A significantly stronger writer than Jones, Charles Waddell Chesnutt was born in Cleveland of free mulatto parents, and raised in North Carolina. He returned to Cleveland where he became a court stenographer and later a successful attorney. In his first novel, Chesnutt relies on the old Cooper dilemma, a white man attracted by the beauty of a mulatto woman, but repulsed by the idea of miscegenation, to develop a sensitive story of tragically thwarted love, *The House Behind the Cedars* (1900).[13] Although imbued throughout with defense of blacks and attacks on discrimination against them, the novel is far less a mere polemic than most of the racist and antiracist works contemporary with it. Despite Arlene Elder's characterization of it as a "thin" book,[14] in many ways *The House Behind the Cedars* is the first artistically mature novel by a black American. Robert Hemenway even argues that Chesnutt's social realism can be compared favorably to Faulkner's obscurity and impressionism. He describes Chesnutt's characters as "distinct, memorable, and individual. . . . not universal in the empty modern sense. . . . They are real social beings tied to a particular social fabric."[15]

The story centers on John Warwick and his sister Rena, the children of an octoroon mother, Molly, and her white protector. A few years after the war, John returns to his home in North Carolina following an absence of ten years. During this time he had moved to South Carolina, passed as white and married a planter's daughter who inherited the estate. His wife had died after giving birth to their son, and John wants Rena to come with him to raise the child. Rena agrees, and after a year's preparation at a boarding school, she appears as his sister and mistress of the house. After a while she is courted by George Tyron, a young gentleman with whom she falls in love. Tyron appears very liberal and broadminded, but Rena and John decide it is best not to confide in him. Two weeks before Rena and George are to be married, George accidentally discovers her secret and totally breaks off the relationship. Crushed and embittered, Rena finally takes a job away from home as a teacher in a black school and devotes herself to work. George Tyron is unable to forget her and tries to see her, but she wishes to avoid him. She is also trying to avoid the attentions of a corrupt mulatto, Mr. Wain, who is pursuing her. One day, on her way home, she is trapped between the two men and flees off the path into a swamp. Hours later she is found quite ill, and in her delirium she wanders away again. Discovered by the young black man Frank, who had been devoted to Rena for years, she is taken back to her hometown and her mother. George Tyron learns this fact and rides to Patesville with the intention of marrying Rena immediately, but he discovers upon arrival that she has just died.

The theme of miscegenation in the novel provides George Tyron with a conflict between love and deep-seated prejudice. By the time he is able to resolve the dilemma in favor of love, it is too late to avert tragedy, and love is thus thwarted by social convention. There are also other ways in which the subject appears, particularly intertwined with the question of where the mulatto belongs. As a black novelist, Chesnutt introduces a new twist on the theme of color prejudice among blacks and its relation to the mulatto's often anomalous situation. In earlier works by white writers, such as *The Slave* or *Uncle Tom's Cabin*, there had been expression of resentment by the darker field hands toward light-skinned slaves such as Archy or Cassy who held easier positions, but there is little indication in these novels that the mulattoes felt themselves superior on the basis of their color alone. After the war, however, this feeling of superiority did exist among the "mulatto elite,"[16] and Chesnutt explores it in *The House Behind the Cedars*. Because she is a quadroon and had been the freed mistress of a white man, Molly exhibits a consistent prejudice toward blacks. She will not allow

Rena to ride in a cart with Frank, the young black who loves Rena with a private and hopeless passion, but thinks it appropriate for Rena to ride in a carriage with a black driver (p. 40). Molly always patronizes Frank's family and feels infinitely superior to them (p. 175). Rena has learned from her mother to despise darker people because they are not as white as she and had been slaves; it is only after her tragic rejection that Rena feels at all close to other members of her race and feels any desire to help them (pp. 193–194). The extent to which the color prejudice exists comes clear when Molly has a party and the narrator comments ironically on the attitudes of the guests, who are all mulattoes (pp. 209–210). The irony is highlighted by Frank, who has not been invited because he is too dark, but is allowed to sit outside on the back porch and observe the dancing and music through the window (p. 216).

Because of this feeling of superiority to and alienation from blacks, Molly and her children are all faced with the problem of where they belong. Molly avoids the question by attempting to exist in the never-never land of the past, living in seclusion in the little house behind the cedar trees that her lover had bought for her, and dreaming of what things had been like while he was alive. She attends the white church in town and sits in the colored balcony looking over the congregation:

She was not white, alas! She was shut out from this seeming paradise; but she liked to see the distant glow of the celestial city, and to recall the days when she had basked in its radiance. She did not sympathize greatly with the new era opened up for the emancipated slaves; she had no ideal love of liberty; she was no broader and no more altruistic than the white people around her, to whom she had always looked up; and she sighed for the old days, because they had been the good days (pp. 159–160).

Both John and Rena attempt to answer the question of where they belong by passing, and the different effects they experience suggest it is not true that a mulatto must feel guilt and fear about denying his race and keeping his secret. The characters in other novels who react to passing with guilt and fear are being stereotyped, just as the "tragic mulatto" of aboli-

tionist fiction had been a stereotype. Chesnutt develops John
and Rena as human beings who happen to be mulatto, but who
differ quite significantly from each other.

John passes successfully and acquires what he desires, wealth
and social standing, but he succeeds because he is aggressive,
selfish, and self-controlled. John comments that he has forced
himself to live by reason, not sentiment, and is always con-
scious of the danger in letting down even for a second (p. 30).
As a child he read extensively in the library which his father
left and became discontented with his lot (p. 163). He decided
to study law and pass for white because it was the only way
to achieve what he felt he had a right to. By age eighteen he
had prepared himself and left (pp. 165–173). John's self-interest
keeps him away from any contact with his mother and sister
for ten years; it is only when he has need of Rena that he comes
for her. Molly is distraught at the possibility of losing her
daughter, but John cleverly plays on her love for Rena, obtaining her consent by convincing Molly that the move is in
Rena's best interest (pp. 24–28). We later learn that John would
never have asked Rena to join him if she had not met the
standards of beauty and intelligence necessary for her to be an
advantage to him (p. 65). After the disastrous end of Rena's
engagement, John suggests the very practical idea that she go
out West with him and try again; he is not only concerned with
her welfare but has decided that too many people now know
his secret, and he may have to relocate anyway (pp. 182–184).
There is no destructive, mysterious, racial guilt eating at John;
he is an aggressive, self-centered, goal-oriented person who has
obtained what he set out to get and has no deeper concerns
than preserving his position.

Rena, who fails at passing and turns to work among blacks,
would seem to fit the stereotype of the guilt-ridden mulatto
better, but in many ways she differs significantly from the
mold. Most importantly, she is not a failure because of racial
guilt; she does not begin to feel any racial allegiance to blacks
until after her failure to pass (p. 194). Rena's inability to live
comfortably as white is due to personality, not genetics. Unlike
John, she is timid, insecure, openly emotional and closely tied
to her mother. She is not driven by the need to escape her lot

as John had been, and only moves into the white world passively when a ready-made opportunity presents itself. Rena weeps over leaving her mother during the whole train journey to the boarding school (p. 41). Even after a year's experience at passing, Rena feels insecure. When she arrives at John's home and is accepted by all, she confides to him that she feels like "Cinderella before the clock has struck" (p. 62). John had never considered telling the woman whom he married his secret, but Rena worries about it constantly and devises elaborate tests of George's love to try to guess if the truth would matter to him (pp. 75–85). Rena's emotional reaction to news that her mother is ill leads directly to the revelation. When Rena receives the letter, she immediately packs and goes home to Patesville to care for Molly (p. 95). John, of course, does not and is very disturbed when he discovers that Rena has gone (p. 97). While in Patesville, Rena cares openly for her mother, going out for the doctor, medicines, and such, which leads to the revelation of her secret when she encounters George in Patesville on business, accompanied by a man who knows her identity (p. 141). Even her later "commitment" to the black cause is not a real one at first; it is an emotional reaction to her rejection by white George (pp. 179–181). If Chesnutt stereotypes these characters at all, it is along male/female lines rather than racial ones. John is stereotypically masculine, aggressive, ambitious and rational, while Rena is feminine, timid, passive, and emotional. In any event, the qualities that lead to failure at passing do not, contrary to the suggestions of most other black writers treating the theme, derive from the nature of being mulatto.[17]

While not condemning mulattoes who pass, Chesnutt does seem to imply a preference for alignment with the black struggle. Perhaps the ambiguity reflects what Donald Gibson calls Chesnutt's "paradoxical, multifaceted attitudes about his racial identity."[18] The narrator actively defends John's course at one point and praises the courage necessary for the deception (p. 128), but Rena's development as a truly committed worker for her people he portrays even more sympathetically. Her initial decision was based on bitter emotions, but as she works with the children of her school she develops real concern and finds meaning in her life (p. 246). Frank, the young black man who loves Rena, is also used to suggest that Rena was on the better path. Frank had saved her life as a child and was totally devoted to her. Each time she left, first to go to John's home and later away to teach, Frank followed her and stayed until he was sure that she was content (p. 127). He also tried to protect her from encountering Tyron in Patesville, but was unsuccessful (pp. 129–130). Frank discovers Rena wandering in a delirium because he had left home and gone looking for her when he learned her employer, Mr. Wain, was not trustworthy (pp. 286–291). The suggestion that alignment with blacks is the better course for mulattoes seems to lie in Rena's final recognition of Frank's loyalty and devotion. As she lies dying, Frank sits with her, holding her hand; Rena's last words are, "You loved me best of them all" (p. 293).

A year after *The House Behind the Cedars*, Chesnutt published his second novel, *The Marrow of Tradition* (1901),[19] a more openly rhetorical attack on racism. The novel was prompted by a particularly savage 1898 race riot in Wilmington, North Carolina, about which Chesnutt's friends and relatives were able to supply him detailed, first-hand information.[20] When Dixon's *The Leopard's Spots* exploded on the scene the following year, Chesnutt expressed the hope, regrettably unfulfilled, that *The Marrow of Tradition* might serve as a counter to it.[21] The novel attacks the increasing disenfranchisement, Jim Crow laws, and lynchings, and does not concern itself with the problems of mulattoes attempting to pass for white. The miscegenation theme occurs in an exploration of intrafamily tension between the black and white branches of a Southern family.

Major Carteret publishes the most influential newspaper in Wellington, North Carolina, and leads a new white-supremacy crusade. His wife, Livy, has a mulatto half-sister, Janet, who married a prosperous black physician, Dr. Miller. The main plot involves the machinations of Carteret and his cohorts to stir up racist feelings before the next election. In the preceding election, blacks, who make up two-thirds of Wellington's population, had managed to capture several minor positions, and Carteret is determined to prevent any further advances. His group manages to create state-wide support for disenfranchisement by restrictive voting requirements coupled with a "grandfather clause," but they also feel the need to eliminate certain white and black leaders in Wellington who have formed a coalition party capable of interfering with the proposed changes. Carteret and his co-conspirators, General Belmont and Captain McBane, organize a controlled riot to effect the removal of selected opposition leaders. The riot gets out of hand, however, and turns into an indiscriminate slaughter of blacks, including the small group who fight back under the leadership of Josh Green, who has been defying white authority ever since his father was murdered by K.K.K. raiders led by McBane. As the riot finally subsides, Carteret, unsuccessful in attempts to stop it, returns home to find his only child deathly ill. A white physician is not available, and the only man who can save his son is Dr. Miller. He goes to Miller and pleads for his aid, but Miller refuses, showing Carteret the body of his own son who was killed by a stray bullet in the riot Carteret organized. Stunned, Carteret returns home and tells his wife; Livy rushes to the Miller home to plead with her half-sister Janet, whom she has never before acknowledged. Livy reveals that she had destroyed papers proving that her father had legally married Janet's mulatto mother after his first wife's death and had bequeathed her ten thousand dollars. She offers Janet the money and calls her "sister" but Janet haughtily refuses all that Livy proffers. Having rejected Livy's attempts to buy aid, Janet then freely asks her husband to go save the child, which he does.

In this novel, Chesnutt elucidates a black perspective on the subject of miscegenation. As Robert Farnsworth points out in his introduction to the book, Chesnutt treats interracial sex as a normal social fact, not as a strong taboo the way Faulkner (and I believe other white writers) treat the subject.[22] What shocks Chesnutt, is the irrationality and extraordinary fear with which whites deny miscegenation. Blacks have lived openly with the fact of miscegenation throughout their history in this country, and black novelists accordingly seem to have no difficulty writing about it. They are the only writers before Faulkner to present white women in sexual relationships with black men, which does not appear from a black perspective to be any sort of ultimate taboo. Whites, however, have tended to deny the existence of miscegenation since the beginning of interracial contact in the United States during the colonial period. This heritage of denying a relatively common social reality is generally reflected in the tone of white novelists writing on the subject. The white author may be very sympathetic to blacks, may even advocate miscegenation, but the white attitude that miscegenation is somehow something special—a taboo to be observed or violated—is usually present. In *The Marrow of Tradition*, Chesnutt shows the difference between blacks and whites in attitude toward miscegenation by presenting the divergent feelings of Livy Carteret and Janet Miller toward their relationship.

The two women had lived together as children until separated after their father's death, and they look enough alike to be twins. There is no question of the relationship's being a secret from the town (pp. 8–9). Livy, however, does everything possible to avoid even seeing Janet, who is deeply hurt by her white half-sister's refusal to acknowledge her (p. 66). While Janet is simply hurt by rejection and does not concern herself further with the matter, Livy is obsessed with denying the relationship which everyone knows exists. The mere sight of Janet can make Livy ill (p. 3), or cause her to drop her child (p. 105). A specialist called in to operate on the Carterets' son asks that Miller, a well-trained physician, assist him. Livy will not allow it, not because Miller is black, but because she wants no connection whatsoever with Janet (p. 74). When Livy hears the news that her old aunt has been killed and robbed,[23] her only concern is to get certain papers that her aunt held (pp. 177–178). Livy destroys the certificate of her father's marriage to Janet's mother and his will, which Livy needs to protect her own inheritance, because both documents are links to Janet. She also gives $10,000 to charity because the money is legally Janet's, and Livy wants nothing connected with her (pp. 257–272). At the end of the novel, Livy tries to buy Janet's aid by admitting their relationship and is shocked to discover that Janet attaches no great significance to this act (pp. 326–329).

The contrasting white and black perspectives on miscegenation, the former considering it a monumentous taboo, the latter considering it a normal fact of life, are highlighted by the incident which Carteret uses to set off the riot. Some months earlier, a black newspaper editorially protested lynchings, pointing out that the supposed rape of white women was in many cases voluntary, that the women were simply living with black men whom the law forbid them to marry (p. 85). This newspaper had no white circulation; thus the editorial did not come to the attention of whites. Carteret, however, obtained a copy of it which he saved (p. 88), and later reprinted in his own paper. The public statement by a black that miscegenation might be a normal occurrence sparks the bloody riot (pp. 248–249). Chesnutt wrote *The Marrow of Tradition* to protest lynchings and riots, and he seems to imply that a basic motive for both is an irrational need on the part of whites to deny the existence of miscegenation.

Another black author who attacked vicious racism was Chesnutt's contemporary, Sutton E. Griggs. Born in Chatfield, Texas, in 1872, Griggs was the son of a Baptist minister. After graduating from Bishop College in Marshall, Texas, he completed his education in Virginia at the Richmond Theological Seminary and became a minister himself. During his time as a Baptist preacher in Nashville, Tennessee, Griggs managed the Orion Publishing Company where he published all but the first of his books.[24] Hugh Gloster calls him "the most vocal and didactic" of all the black novelists challenging discrimination and extolling the virtues of their race in the period before World War I.[25] Of Griggs' five polemical novels, four concern themselves to some degree with the theme of miscegenation.

Imperium in Imperio (1899)[26] details the machinations of an unworthy black leader, Bernard Belgrade, who heads a secret society of educated, angry blacks, the *Imperium*. Belgrade, a mulatto, wants to start a race war against whites but is opposed by a conciliatory figure, Belton Piedmont. A tangential concern with miscegenation arises when the pure African Viola Martin commits suicide rather than marry Belgrade, the mulatto man she loves. Viola has read and accepted the racist genetics of the time, now believing that to "marry light" will mean the destruction of the black race through an unhealthy hybridizing that leads to racial weakness, sterility, and death.

Overshadowed (1901)[27] presents the thesis that the shadows of a slave past and the unscrupulousness of whites who control society make survival and advance almost impossible for blacks, particularly if they accept the Booker T. Washington approach. In the novel, Erma Wysong is the illegitimate, mulatto daughter of the ex-governor of Virginia. The ex-governor's legitimate son, John Lawson, does not know that Erma is his half-sister and attempts to make her his mistress, but the girl's aunt, Dolly, frustrates his plan by publicly revealing the whole story. Erma's grief is heightened by the death of her brother, whom she had advised to follow Booker T. Washington's lead, and the tragic mulatto girl finally dies from sorrow. Miscegenation is treated as a symbol of the burdensome legacies of slavery against which blacks must struggle with little hope of success. Griggs' last novel, *Pointing the Way* (1908),[28] is concerned with miscegenation in the form of color prejudice among blacks and the bad effects of this attitude on racial unity and advancement. Letitia Gilbreath, a mulatto, strongly opposes light-skinned people's marrying dark and insists that her niece Clotille marry a light mulatto, Baug Peppers, instead of the darker Conroe Driscoll, whom Clotille loves. Clotille invites a beautiful Spanish-Indian girl, Eina Rapona, to her home for the purpose of distracting Peppers' attention. Eina decides to cast her lot with blacks in the South, working for enfranchisement and better government. She marries Peppers, but Clotille's love for Driscoll is thwarted when he dies fighting a fire before they can be married. Her aunt's intervention led to the tragedy, which symbolizes the evil effects of intraracial color prejudice. The marriage of Eina, who came from the North, to the crusading Southern mulatto, Peppers, seems to suggest the need for Northern cooperation with the aspirations of Southern blacks.

Griggs most fully explores the theme of miscegenation in *The Hindered Hand* (1905),[29] a polemical work that openly attacks Thomas Dixon and his views expressed in *The Leopard's Spots*. *The Hindered Hand* has a complex and confusing plot. Mr. and Mrs. Seabright arrive in the Southern town of Almaville with their beautiful daughter Eunice. Although accepted as white, the Seabrights are actually mulatto. They also have a son passing as a white minister under the name of Percy

Marshall and another daughter, Tiara Marlow. Tiara is much darker than the rest of the family and lives apart as a black. There are three young mulatto men in town who are all Spanish-American War veterans and advocates of civil rights. Ensal Ellwood, a minister and a moderate in his approach to race problems, is in love with Tiara. Earl Bluefield, almost white in appearance, is the illegitimate son of a prominent politician, H. G. Volrees. Earl is interested in Eunice Seabright and is much more radical than Ensal about the race situation. The third young man, Gus Martin, is the most radical; he is deeply embittered by the problems of blacks. They are all friends of a young black girl, Foresta Crump, and her fiancé, Bud Harper.

In a confusing series of actions, Foresta's little brother is killed by a mob, her father dies of shock, and her mother becomes indebted to an evil white, Arthur Daleman. Daleman compels Foresta to become a servant in his home and intends to make her his mistress. Foresta and Bud elope, but that night Daleman's sister sleeps in Foresta's room and is accidentally murdered by Bud's brother, who believed Foresta was having an affair with Daleman. Bud and Foresta flee to Mississippi, where they are brutally murdered for killing a white man in self-defense.

Meanwhile, Mrs. Seabright is attempting to put into effect a plan to help blacks. Her son has become a minister who preaches better race relations to his white congregation, and she wants Eunice to marry the politician Volrees and influence him to work politically for better conditions. Eunice marries him, but runs away before the marriage is consummated and disappears for years. No one knows that Percy Marshall and Tiara Marlow are brother and sister or that they are the Seabright's children. After Gus Martin sees Tiara kissing Percy, he kills Marshall because Martin thinks Tiara is deceiving Ensal with a white man. After telling Ensal what he saw, Martin in turn is killed by a mob. Ensal believes that Tiara has deceived him and leaves for Africa.

Some years later Eunice Seabright Volrees is discovered living as "Mrs. Johnson" with a husband and son in another town. She is brought back to Almaville for trial as a bigamist, and Tiara is put on the stand. Under oath, Tiara tells the whole truth and reveals that Eunice is her sister. "Mr. Johnson" is Earl Bluefield, the illegitimate son of Volrees. Eunice viciously rejects Tiara's testimony, screaming that she is white, but the jury does not believe her and refuses to convict her of bigamy, because as a mulatto she could not have legally married Volrees. Driven mad by the revelation of her race, Eunice is taken to an institution. Ensal learns of the trial and returns from Africa to marry Tiara now that he knows her true relationship with Percy Marshall. Earl Bluefield commits himself to active political work for the betterment of conditions for blacks in the United States, while Ensal and Tiara return to Africa to prepare for the great influx there if the situation in the United States fails to improve.

In *The Hindered Hand*, Griggs uses miscegenation in multiple ways as a symbol of the many evil legacies of slavery militating against black progress. White oppression, particularly in the form of lynching, presents a particularly difficult obstacle for blacks, and this oppression is often justified on the fallacious grounds of rape. Five black characters meet violent deaths at the hands of white mobs in the novel, but none have committed rape. One is an innocent eleven-year-old boy (p. 61). Bud Harper's brother is lynched for the murder of Alene Daleman, but the whites know that he did not rape her (p. 104); Gus Martin is shot by a mob, despite assurances of safety if he surrenders, for his killing of Percy Marshall (p. 190); Bud Harper and Foresta suffer the most gruesome fate of all, simply for self-defense. Bud was fired on twice by a white, hired to kill him and his wife, before he returns the fire, killing his attacker (p. 126). When they are captured for this "crime," Bud and Foresta are tied to stakes and subjected to horrible mutilation and torture, described in detail, for three hours (suggestive of Christ's time on the cross) before being burned alive (pp. 133–134). A Northerner arrives just after the slaughter and is shocked to learn that a woman had been killed, because he thought lynching was only for the "one crime." He is laughingly reassured by one of the white men that those stories are pure propaganda to make whites appear justified in killing blacks: "That's all rot about one crime. We lynch niggers down here for anything. We lynch them for being sassy and sometimes we lynch them on general principles. The truth of the matter is the real 'one crime' that paves the way for a lynching whenever we have the notion, is the crime of being black" (p. 136). Griggs contends that the accusation of rape is a convenient fiction and lays the blame for its acceptance on Thomas Dixon's *The Leopard's Spots*. In a lengthy set-piece discussion of Dixon's novel, Ensal Ellwood rejects point by point that author's accusations, disclaiming any desire of blacks to marry white women and denouncing Frederick Douglass's marriage to a white woman as having separated him from his race (pp. 206–213).

According to Griggs, the true relationship of miscegenation to the problems faced by blacks is not their desire to rape, but the sexual aggressiveness of white men toward black women, another legacy of slavery. When Tiara Marlow first arrives in Almaville, she is approached by a man who runs a black whorehouse for whites. This motif of white prostitution of black women runs through the novel. After Daleman succeeds in compelling Foresta to come to work for him, he tells her:

"Be a good girl and you won't have a better friend than I am," said he, in a significant tone, trying to awaken Foresta to the real situation.

If she understood it her impassive countenance did not reveal the fact.

The world at large has heard that the problem of the South is the protection of the white woman. There is another woman in the South (p. 71).

White sexual aggression toward that other woman causes both of the actual crimes committed by blacks in the novel. Dave Harper kills Alene Daleman because she is in Foresta's room at Daleman's' house, and he had seen Daleman in the room with her. Dave committed the murder to punish what he believed to be unfaithfulness with a white man by his brother's fiancée (p. 121). Gus Martin kills Percy Marshall for essentially the same reasons. Martin believes that Marshall has forced Tiara's submission despite her engagement to Ensal and kills Marshall to punish him (p. 200). The lynchings related to miscegenation are not because black men raped white women, but because black men killed in an attempt to punish the presumed despoilers of their women. White sexual aggression leads to black retaliation and more tragic oppression. Linked to this is the arbitrariness of the oppression. Eunice Seabright has all her life been treated with respect as a lady, but the minute she steps outside the courthouse after being revealed as a mulatto, she is subjected to crude, suggestive remarks by white men (p. 247).

Besides white oppression, there are intraracial problems which cause the hindering of black hands, and miscegenation is linked in the novel to some of these problems. For example, color discrimination among blacks impedes racial advance, and this problem is symbolized in the novel by Eunice's denunciation and rejection of her dark sister Tiara (p. 245); the disruption caused in one individual family represents the disruption within the racial family. Griggs' concern with the burdensome legacies of slavery surfaces in the light mulattoes produced by generations of miscegenation before emancipation. These alienated people—like Eunice and like Earl Bluefield, who considers himself Anglo-Saxon but since he is not accepted as such feels himself an outcast (p. 52)—are living representatives of the problems left by slavery. In attempting to escape those problems by passing for white, they destroy themselves: Eunice goes insane, Percy is murdered, Mrs. Seabright commits suicide. Earl finds salvation only because he does not continue to pass, but returns to live as a black and work openly for the betterment of the race. The advances which must come for survival will be achieved only if blacks work for them, but blacks cannot work effectively as long as they are held back by pre-emancipation legacies of white oppression and intraracial strife. For Sutton Griggs, blacks must, like the mulatto who is a living legacy of slavery, shake off the temptation to hide and move out openly to work for their own best interests.

James Weldon Johnson's *The Autobiography of an Ex-Colored Man* (1912)[30] is the story of a mulatto who gives up the battle and hides, sacrificing his potential to make a contribution to his race for personal security in the white world. Johnson's father was born a free mulatto in Richmond, Virginia, and became a successful headwaiter at luxury hotels in New York, Nassau, and Jacksonville, Florida, where James William (later changed to Weldon) was born in 1871. His mother taught at a prominent black school that James attended before going to Atlanta University. When he graduated in 1894, he returned to Jacksonville to be principal of his old school. Over the years, Johnson achieved success in many different fields— as a lawyer, Broadway show-tune writer, journalist, novelist, poet, diplomat, and civil rights leader—he served as executive secretary of the NAACP from 1920 to 1930.

Written during his three years (1906–09) as United States Consul at Puerto Cabello, Venezuela, *The Autobiography of an Ex-Colored Man* was quietly published in 1912.[31] The novel opens with a statement by the unnamed narrator that he is seeking relief from a feeling of regret, almost of remorse, by putting down the story of his life and its great secret. He begins with childhood recollections of a home in Georgia a few years after the Civil War. He remembers a big man who gave him a ten-dollar gold piece the day he left with his mother to go to Connecticut, where he grew up. By the time the narrator graduates from high school he has learned that despite his appearance he is actually colored, and he knows the story of his parents' affair. During this time, the boy becomes an accomplished pianist, is visited by his father once and experiences the death of his beloved mother. He has a small sum of money, enough to begin college, and he chooses Atlanta University because of curiosity about his Georgian heritage. He arrives in Atlanta, but, before he can enroll, he is robbed of all his money and decides to give up the idea of college. Instead he sneaks a ride to Jacksonville, Florida, where he becomes expert at cigar making, a very lucrative profession. For the first time, he is living and socializing as a black.

After three years, he goes to New York, where he has a fling at being a professional gambler, but winds up as a piano player of the new ragtime music, which had migrated from New Orleans by way of Memphis, St. Louis, and Chicago. He becomes a retainer of an eccentric white millionaire, who takes him to Europe. After a year or so in Europe, the narrator decides that he wants to return to the United States and develop his music seriously, to live in the deep South and gather all the heritage of the slave songs and spirituals. He does this with great enthusiasm and dedication for quite some time, but after seeing a black man burned alive in a small Southern town, he returns embittered to New York. There he changes his name, passes for white and makes a great deal of money in business. He is engaged to a white woman whom he loves dearly, but she rejects him when he reveals his secret. Later, however, she admits that she still loves him and they marry. They have two children before she dies, and the narrator's life is now devoted to caring for his children and to protecting them from the stigma of being black.

Johnson moves away from the strident propaganda of Griggs. Writing in the first-person tradition of the slave narrative, he looks both backward to the realism and artistry of Chesnutt and forward to the cosmopolitan concerns of the Harlem Renaissance writers. The novel is, to be sure, filled with polemic discussions by the narrator of the race problem, but his pronouncements are more rational and free from bitterness than those of Griggs. The theme of dissimulation is important in the novel. Johnson explains that blacks conceal a secret side of their lives from whites, and reveals much of that hidden side, presenting a range of black characters and situations far wider than earlier black novels that adhere to stereotyped figures in the rural or smalltown South. Two additional themes help bind the discursive work together, the "function of color prejudice in bolstering the white man's ego" and "the development of a positive racial identity among blacks."[32]

Johnson, like Chesnutt, reveals a different black perspective on interracial sex from Griggs' passionate denunciation of the practice. Miscegenation is accepted by the narrator and other black characters in the novel as an ordinary part of life. His mother discusses her affair with his father very openly and tells how she still worships the man. The narrator's observation on her behavior is simply, "Perhaps she was right. Who knows?" (p. 43) In Jacksonville and New York, most of the people with whom he associates are mulattoes, indicating to some degree the extent of miscegenation. In the New York club where he becomes a celebrity by virtue of his piano playing, many wealthy and attractive white women have a sexual interest in him. He has a passing affair with one white woman known as the "Widow" because she constantly changes her black gigolos. Johnson provides a very simple explanation for the tendency of blacks to marry whites or lighter mulattoes: economic necessity, since society places a premium on a lack of color for finding good jobs (p. 155).

Johnson openly ridicules the white Southern phobia about miscegenation in a scene between a Texan and a Northern man on a train. The Northerner has been defending blacks, and the Texan asks if he would "want his daughter to marry one." The man replies, "If you Southerners have one boast that is stronger than another, it is your women; you put them on a pinnacle of purity and virtue and bow down in a chivalric worship before them; yet you talk and act as though, should you treat a black fairly and take the anti-intermarriage laws off the books, these same women would rush into the arms of black lovers and husbands" (pp. 163–164). The narrator and his white wife share a normal and happy life until her untimely death (pp. 209–210). The fact of miscegenation is simply unimportant.

The narrator's feelings about his black heritage and his allegiance to it do not make his mixed blood become an overwhelming, dominating factor in his life. He is not driven to despair and death by guilt and fear. Rather he lives a basically well-adjusted life, but is troubled that he had had a chance, in collecting and transcribing the black heritage of slave music, to contribute greatly to the image of his mother's race. The novel ends with the narrator's bittersweet summation:

My love for my children makes me glad that I am what I am and keeps me from desiring to be otherwise; and yet, when I sometimes open a little box in which I still keep my fast yellowing manuscripts, the only tangible remnants of a vanished dream, a dead ambition, a sacrificed talent, I cannot repress the thought that, after all, I have chosen the lesser part, that I have sold my birthright for a mess of pottage (p. 211).

Like Johnson's exploration of the cosmopolitan urban life of blacks, Oscar Micheaux breaks new ground in his novel of a black pioneer in South Dakota, *The Conquest* (1913)[33] our final work by the group of black authors between 1891 and 1914 who used the theme of miscegenation rhetorically to protest racism. Micheaux's story is highly autobiographical (the first-person narrator's name is Oscar Devereaux) and presents a modified view of Booker T. Washington's philosophy. The novel details Micheaux's own success story up to about 1908. After his third novel, *The Homesteader*, was published in 1917, Micheaux decided to produce it as a film, which appeared in 1919—the first full length, all black American movie. Over the next thirty years, Micheaux produced thirty-three movie films, often with miscegenation as the basis of the plot.

In a couple of didactic chapters, the narrator of *The Conquest* claims that blacks have failed because they are too ready to use slavery and prejudice as excuses for lack of ambition. He argues that they should follow his example of being aggressive and doing as immigrant groups do. Rather than staying in the South or going to Northern cities, blacks should homestead unsettled plains areas and achieve success in agriculture by hard work. Devereaux leaves home in the South at eighteen and goes to Chicago. After a succession of jobs, he manages to become a Pullman porter by dint of his aggressiveness. Several years on the railroads familiarize him with the country and enable him to save enough money to buy a farm. He shrewdly investigates various areas and decides that he can do best in relatively unsettled South Dakota. He is inexperienced and has great difficulty at first, but by persevering he is able to develop and add to his holdings over a period of years. At one point, out of loneliness, Devereaux has a brief affair with a white girl, but he decides against continuing the relationship. He marries a black girl from Chicago, but the marriage is destroyed by her domineering father, an opinionated clergyman who ruins his daughter's life to satisfy his own ego.

The novel, aside from the marital problems of the narrator which parallel Micheaux's own difficulties with his father-in-law,[34] is a sort of exemplum for black success. The approach to miscegenation taken in the book is consistent with the generally pragmatic approach to other problems faced by the narrator. The subject does not play a dominant role in the novel;

rather, it appears as an incident which creates difficulty for the narrator, much the same as a blizzard or a drought. The point is that any black who follows the narrator's advice and migrates to South Dakota will encounter the problem of loneliness and the desire to marry complicated by the total lack of available black females, leading to the possibility of miscegenation. Micheaux discusses the best way to face this problem.

Devereaux's romance with a Scottish girl from a neighboring farm is not fully developed. Only one page is devoted to the affair, in which he meets the girl; their relationship grows to the stage of kissing while reading *Othello* together, and they fall in love (p. 154). The concern is not with the relationship itself; the girl is never even given a name. Micheaux's interest lies in how to deal with the problem such a relationship presents. To help resolve the dilemma, he brings in the story of the Woodring family. Devereaux notices a handsome young man on the street, and a friend tells him that the youth is Frank Woodring from Nebraska. Devereaux knows that a few blacks had settled in the territory twenty or thirty years before and had married whites. The Woodrings are one of those families. Devereaux ruminates about them:

What worried me most, however, even frightened me, was, that after marriage and when their children had grown to manhood and womanhood, they, like the Woodring family, had a terror of their race; disavowing and denying the blood that coursed through their veins.... They looked on me with fear, sometimes contempt.... The question uppermost in my mind became "Would not I become like that, would I too, deny my race?" (p. 162)

The need for racial identity argues against miscegenation, and there also exists the practical concern with the immediate consequences of such a marriage. The narrator considers carefully that he has maintained the goodwill of the community but feels sure that it would be lost if he married white. The plains farmer needs the goodwill of neighbors to survive, and Devereaux decides he will not marry the white girl (p. 168). She disappears from the novel and is never mentioned again. Proof of the practical correctness of his decision comes later when he goes to Chicago to bring back a black wife, and some sixty of his white neighbors give the couple a friendly charivari upon their return (p. 241). Miscegenation is seen, then, as a possible solution to the loneliness of the black pioneer, but a solution that must be avoided. Two practical considerations, possible damage to the sense of identity necessary for positive action and probable loss of vital community goodwill, argue that miscegenation must be rejected.

In this period from 1891 to 1914, when a large number of black novelists are first writing about miscegenation, the general difference between black and white attitudes on the subject first emerges. Joel Chandler Harris and Thomas Nelson Page are so imbued with the genteel, plantation tradition that they do not deal at all openly with miscegenation; their reticence doubtless shows the strong taboo which they associate with the subject. Thomas Dixon enunciates the great white fear of miscegenation, making this horror his primary theme. The first black apologists, Mrs. Harper and Mr. J. McHenry Jones, are closely tied to the abolitionist tradition and rely on creating counter-stereotypes of virtuous blacks, who identify with their mother's race and deny white allegations that blacks seek miscegenation. Sutton Griggs relies on a similar formula, but he is more vehement and bitter. A number of other black novelists at least mention miscegenation and treat it in essentially the way represented by Mrs. Harper, Jones, and Griggs. Pauline E. Hopkins' *Contending Forces* (1900), J. W. Grant's *Out of the Darkness* (1909) and W. E. B. DuBois' *The Quest of the Silver Fleece* (1911) all contain mention of miscegenation, but in ways both incidental and better illustrated by the novels selected for discussion. A general black perspective emerges that miscegenation, desirable or not, is less a taboo than a common fact of life. This attitude, quite contrary to the white view, finds its clearest expression in the works of Chesnutt and Johnson. Finally, black authors far more than white explore the interrelated themes of "passing" and "marrying light," two miscegenation-related facts of life for black people in America.

NOTES

1. Robert Bone, *The Negro Novel in America*, rev. ed. (1958; reprint, New Haven: Yale Univ. Press, 1965), p. 11.

2. Henry Steele Commager, *The American Mind: An Interpretation of American Thought and Character Since the 1880's* (New Haven: Yale Univ. Press, 1950), p. 41.

3. Fred Lewis Pattee, *The New American Literature, 1890–1930* (New York: Century Co., 1930), p. 4.

4. Cash, p. 128; Davis, p. 117; Gaines, *Southern Plantation*, pp. 17, 37; Theodore L. Gross, "The Negro," p. 77; Robert A. Lively, *Fiction Fights the Civil War* (Chapel Hill: Univ. of North Carolina Press, 1957), p. 48.

5. Barbara Christian, *Black Women Novelists* (Westport, Ct.: Greenwood Press, 1980), pp. 5–6, 25.

6. Mrs. Frances E. W. Harper, *Iola Leroy: or Shadows Uplifted* (1892; reprint, College Park, Md.: McGrath Publishing Co., 1969). Hereafter cited parenthetically.

7. Hugh M. Gloster, *Negro Voices in American Fiction* (Chapel Hill: Univ. of North Carolina Press, 1948), p. 31. See also Arlene A. Elder, *The Hindered Hand* (Westport, CT: Greenwood Press, 1978), pp. 10–19, on the development of black counter-stereotypes out of nineteenth-century stock sentimental heroes and heroines.

8. See, for example, John W. Blassingame, *The Slave Community*, p. 312.

9. See Herbert G. Gutman, *The Black Family* pp. 320–21. Gutman insists on the overwhelming importance among slaves of family and kin networks, arguing that after the war ex-slaves felt powerful kin obligations as do the characters here.

10. Genovese, pp. 413–20.

11. Marian E. Musgrave, "Triangles in Black and White: Interracial Sex and Hostility in Black Literature," *College Language Association Journal*, 14 (1971):445.

12. J. McHenry Jones, *Hearts of Gold: A Novel* (1896; reprint, College Park, Md.: McGrath Publishers, 1969). Hereafter cited parenthetically.

13. Charles Waddell Chesnutt, *The House Behind the Cedars* (1900; reprint, Ridgewood, N.J.: Gregg Press, 1968). Hereafter cited parenthetically.

14. Elder, p. 177.

15. Robert Hemenway, ed., *The Black Novelist* (Columbus, Ohio: Charles E. Merrilll Publishing Co., 1970), pp. 30–32.

16. Williamson, pp. 82–87.

17. Nor does the novel seem to support Elder's statement that it shows mulattoes who attempt to pass "will, inevitably, be branded and forced back" (p. 176).

18. Donald Gibson, *The Politics of Literary Expression* (Westport, Ct.: Greenwood Press, 1981), pp. 126–27.

19. Charles Waddell Chesnutt, *The Marrow of Tradition* (1901; reprint with introduction by Robert M. Farnsworth, Ann Arbor: Univ. of Michigan Press, 1969). Hereafter cited parenthetically.

20. Robert Farnsworth, "Introduction," in Chesnutt, *The Marrow of Tradition*, p. viii.

21. Farnsworth, p. xiv.

22. Farnsworth, p. xiii.

23. Given that Chesnutt admired Samuel Clemens, even attended a dinner in his honor at Delmonico's in New York, December 5, 1905 (Elder, p. 195), an interesting possibility exists that the character of Tom Delamere in *The Marrow of Tradition* (1901) derives from Clemens' Tom Driscoll in *Pudd'nhead Wilson* (1894). Clemens' Tom, dressed in blackface murders his uncle for money to pay gambling debts. Chesnutt's Tom also disguises himself in blackface when he robs and kills his aunt for money to pay gambling debts. In both cases, the killers temporarily succeed in shifting the blame for their crimes to an innocent party.

24. Elder, p. 70.

25. Gloster, p. 57.

26. Sutton E. Griggs, *Imperium in Imperio* (1899; reprint, New York *Times* and Arno Press: New York, 1969).

27. Sutton E. Griggs, *Overshadowed* (Nashville: Orion Publishing Co., 1901).

28. Sutton E. Griggs, *Pointing the Way* (Nashville: Orion Publishing Co., 1908).

29. Sutton E. Griggs, *The Hindered Hand* (1905; reprint, Miami: Mnemosyne Publishing Co., 1969). Hereafter cited parenthetically.

30. James Weldon Johnson, *The Autobiography of an Ex-Colored Man* (1912; reprint with introduction by Carl Van Vechten, New York: Knopf, 1951). Hereafter cited parenthetically.

31. Eugene Levy, *James Weldon Johnson* (Chicago: Univ. of Chicago Press, 1973), p. 124.

32. Levy, p. 137.

33. Oscar Micheaux, *The Conquest: The Story of a Negro Pioneer* (1913; reprint, College Park, Md.: McGrath Publishing Co., 1969). Hereafter cited parenthetically.

34. Gloster, pp. 84–85; 263.

8
Nurture Not Nature: *Pudd'nhead Wilson*

At the height of Negrophobic belief in inherited, identifiable, and unalterable racial characteristics—long before the social science pendulum swung back to belief in environmentalism during the 1940s—Samuel Clemens wrote perhaps the most interesting of all the American novels before World War I about miscegenation, *Pudd'nhead Wilson* (1894).[1] Rather than confront racism directly, as the black authors just discussed were shortly to do, Clemens uses mocking irony to undermine and explode the racists' cherished myths. The main character, Roxy, a slave girl one-sixteenth black, gives birth to a son, Valet de Chambre, on the same day that her master's son, Thomas à Becket Driscoll, is born. When Thomas' mother dies in childbirth, Roxy is entrusted with the care of both babies. A short time later, fearing her master's threats to sell his slaves down the river, Roxy switches clothes on the infants and passes her son off as "Tom." But before the switch was made, David "Pudd'nhead" Wilson, an eccentric failure in the eyes of the town, had fingerprinted the two infants for his records.

During the ensuing years, "Tom," as the pampered son of a wealthy, slaveholding family, grows into a cruel and tyrannical young man, while the real Thomas à Becket Driscoll, known as "Chambers," is degraded by his treatment as a slave and molded into the forms of ignorance and servility. Roxy is torn between loving "Tom" because he is her son and despising him for his cruelty to her. When her master dies, Roxy is freed and leaves for eight years to work as a maid on a riverboat. "Tom"

becomes the ward and heir of Dawson's Landing's most prominent citizen, his "uncle" Judge York Leicester Driscoll. When
Roxy returns in need, she appeals to "Tom" for aid, but he
cruelly rebuffs her. Out of vengeance, she reveals the truth of
his parentage to "Tom," who is horrified at first. Very shortly,
however, he realizes it makes no difference as long as no one
else knows.

"Tom," a wastrel given to drunkenness and gambling, has
constant money troubles. At one point Roxy, who will still do
anything for her child, offers to let him sell her to get the money
he owes, with the understanding that he will buy her back
within a year. "Tom" sees an opportunity to rid himself forever
of the threat Roxy poses and betrays her by selling her down
the river. Roxy later escapes, returns and threatens to reveal
all to Judge Driscoll if "Tom" does not purchase her freedom.
"Tom" decides to obtain the money by robbing the judge.

Disguised in blackface and armed with a dagger he had previously stolen from Count Luigi, an Italian living in Dawson's
Landing with his twin brother, "Tom" murders the judge during the robbery and leaves the knife behind. Luigi is blamed
for the crime, but Pudd'nhead Wilson discovers from finger-
prints on the knife that "Tom" is the killer. In checking his
records, Wilson also discovers the truth about the infant-
switching years before, and all is revealed at the trial. "Chambers," now elevated to his rightful place as Thomas à Becket
Driscoll, is left miserably and hopelessly unsuited for his new
position in society, while "Tom" is sentenced to life imprisonment. In the culminating irony of this highly ironic work, certain creditors against the Driscoll estate claim a financial
interest in "Tom":

Everybody granted that there was reason in this. Everybody granted
that if "Tom" were white and free it would be unquestionably right
to punish him—it would be no loss to anybody; but to shut up a
valuable slave for life—that was quite another matter.
    As soon as the governor understood the case, he pardoned Tom at
once, and the creditors sold him down the river (p. 214).

Roxy's original fear is finally realized.
    Critical estimates of Roxy as a character range from Leslie

Fiedler's exorbitant praise of her as one of the few well-developed female characters in American literature,[2] to Philip Butcher's superficial dismissal of her as a mass of contradictions and not at all a real woman.[3] In any event, miscegenation plays an important role in the development of Roxy's character. As Florence Leaver notes, Roxy is a product and continuing agent of miscegenation, and all the ironies of her situation stem from this reality.[4]

Roxy's characterization does not depend upon miscegenation for a ready stereotype as a tragic mulatto, but like Cassy, Palmyre and Phyllis, she is a strong woman capable of vigorous action to determine her own destiny. Unlike these others, however, who feel accidentally trapped in slavery and fiercely resentful of it, Roxy seems closer to a realistic pre–Civil War attitude when we see her as a young girl unquestioningly accepting slave status as simply in the nature of things. As Roxy grows older and experiences freedom, we find her expressing more pride and a sense of equality with the "best" whites because of her descent from those lines (p. 99). In fact, Roxy distinguishes herself from other fictional mulattoes in accepting both her status as a slave and her sexual exploitation with equanimity, if not with actual pride in the latter. She is equally distinct from the stereotyped mulattoes, such as Iola Leroy, who bind themselves in service to their race, because Roxy takes no pride in her black heritage.

Barbara Chellis, in an interesting essay on the novel, makes this point very clearly.[5] She notes Roxy's blaming of "Tom's" cowardice on his drop of black blood and explains that Roxy does so because Roxy herself is white, not only in color but, more importantly, in attitude. Like the whites, Roxy is captivated by the idea of aristocratic status; her story of her own heritage is a confused jumble of John Smith, Pocahontas, and "Nigger Kings." She is indoctrinated by white Southern obsessions; she cares only about Kings, Queens, and the First Families of Virginia. Genovese notes that slaves were often committed this way to the "aristocratic ethos" of their masters.[6] As Chellis points out, Roxy shows a truly white attitude by deriding "Tom" for being a "nigger" only when he fails. We will return to this important point later. Roxy also derives a significant part of her character from her black heritage. As James Cox says, Roxy is legally black and is imbued with passion denied the Southern white woman. In her dual role as mother to the white man's illegitimate children and mammy to his legitimate ones, Roxy becomes a primary force in the world she serves.[7]

Miscegenation plays an equally important role in the characterization of Roxy's son, "Tom." Cox sees "Tom's" dual heritage as serving an important symbolic role in the novel. FFV society is built on the concept of family honor, but that honor is stained. Whites cannot see the stain because it is invisible, as symbolized by "Tom's" invisible blackness. The color line is a legal fiction created to define slavery, but the masters are willing to cross it constantly. "Tom" crosses the line in a white disguise that the whites themselves have given him. He is an agent bearing the guilt of slavery back home; when he kills the judge, the symbol of white society and law, "Tom" is, appropriately, disguised as a black.[8]

Critical evaluations of *Pudd'nhead Wilson* produce many, sometimes quite varied, comments on the significance and meaning of the novel. Jack Wysong's essay, at best sophistic and at worst deliberate misreading, considers the work a failure and Clemens a subconscious racist.[9] At the other extreme, F. R. Leavis sees the novel falling in "the great tradition of English literature, upholding the values of Christian civilization and the code of the gentleman."[10]

More realistically, John Freimarck sees in *Pudd'nhead Wilson* the tragedy of our racially divided society. On his first day in Dawson's Landing, David Wilson became a "pudd'nhead" in the eyes of the town by joking that he would like to kill one half of a barking dog. "Tom" and "Chambers" are the two halves of Pudd'nhead's divided dog, and are contrasted to the Italian twins who escaped from slavery together and work in harmony even though one is a little fairer than the other. Freimarck notes that Luigi had stabbed a man to save his brother, but "Tom" stabs and kills to deny his "brother," and in so doing destroys himself.[11] Marvin Fisher and Michael Elliott agree that the divided dog constitutes the central symbol, suggesting the fragmentation and divisive distinctions of property, race, and class in America.[12]

Arthur Pettit sees the white South divided by the denial of miscegenation, the lie at the heart of its social structure: "From blood consciousness springs the stultifying pride of those who believe they are pure and the paralyzing fear of those who believe they are not. Southern pride in blood and Southern fear of miscegenation are two sides of the same sword and the sword cuts black and white alike.... *The Tragedy of Pudd'nhead Wilson* implies that the greater tragedy of the South is not miscegenation but the curse that white Southerners have placed upon it; and, therefore, upon themselves."[13]

More recently, poststructuralist concerns have entered the discussions of *Pudd'nhead Wilson*. For example, in a reader response approach detailing the dual nature of implied audiences, Peter Rabinowitz uses this text by way of illustration. He suggests that Clemens achieves his effect on us at the end by undercutting the "authorial" audience's basic assumption that a great change in fortune would allow us to escape our environmental conditioning.[14]

Over the years, the question of environmental versus genetic determinism has been central to discussions of this novel, at least since Henry Nash Smith proposed it in 1962.[15] According to Smith, Clemens' overriding concern with training, especially with the negative effect of society's role in shaping the individual, forms the novel's theme, and that slavery serves as a powerful metaphor for it. Following Smith's line of thought, Berzon poses the "crucial question" about the novel: "If Twain wanted to come down clearly on the side of training in the controversy surrounding the importance of nature versus nurture, why did he present 'Tom' in such a negative light and 'Chambers' in such a positive light?"[16] Berzon finds the answer only outside the novel in earlier drafts and in letters by Clemens in which he declares his intention to blame environment, the "brutalizing effects" of slavery on the white owners, for "Tom's" depravity.[17]

But the question of "Tom's" bad character still troubles. Is it possible to derive Clemens' rhetorical intention from the novel itself?

To begin, we should look at the genetic heritage of both "Tom" and "Chambers." Except for the 1/32 "black blood" in "Tom," they both spring from similar aristocratic stock—the

First Families of Virginia. "Tom" was fathered by Cecil Burleigh Essex, and Roxy, his mother, boasts of her aristocratic white lineage. Despite his pure genetic heritage, the cruel training and debased environment of "Chambers" shape his ignorance and social crudity—the slave environment makes a shuffling slave out of anyone, even a highborn white gentleman. But where does "Tom's" negative character come from? His 1/32 black blood? Or his environment?

"Tom" lives alone with his "father," Percy Driscoll, from infancy through all his formative years. Clemens attributes his infant ill-temper to Roxy's spoiling, but "Tom" also practices cruelty toward "Chambers" and Roxy from an early age, behavior that he has learned—not inherited—from Driscoll. As "Tom's" role model, his "father" behaves cruelly and treats slaves badly. The book opens with Percy's serious intention to sell all his slaves down the river—"equivalent to damning them to hell"—over the theft of two dollars. When the "criminals" confess the crime, he carries out a lesser punishment—selling them locally—"and that night he set the incident down in his diary, so that his son might read it in after years, and be thereby moved to deeds of gentleness and humanity himself." While the boys are still young, Percy brutally beats "Chambers" with a cane on several occasions. "Tom's" physical cruelty toward "Chambers" and his later mistreatment of Roxy are, arguably, behaviors learned from his "father's" example. Genovese notes that in reality black and white children did not all play happily together until a certain age before assuming their roles as masters and slaves. Rather, young white children often behaved brutally toward slave children, especially in cases when a parent presented such a model.[18] And Clemens knew firsthand the cruelty of white youth toward slaves that resulted from society's example.[19] Taken together, these elements suggest a strong environmental bias behind the cruel shape "Tom's" character takes.

"Tom's" other great character flaw, one that leads to his fall into theft and murder, is his inability to resist gambling. Here we should remember that his "father," Percy, engages in constant land speculation—a form of gambling—that he cannot give up, eventually losing his whole estate. In short, "Tom" who has no genetic relationship to Percy, but who is raised by him, develops that man's flaws of cruelty and compulsive gambling. "Chambers," Percy's actual son, develops neither. Clemens' intention to blame nurture—not nature—seems clear. The answer to charges, such as Wysong's,[20] that Clemens subconsciously attributes inherent character weaknesses to blacks by making the partially black "Tom" a thief and a coward can be found by comparing Roxy with her son. Clemens carefully points out that Roxy is one-sixteenth black and her son is one-thirty-second, so she has twice as much "black blood" in her as "Tom" (p. 43). Yet Roxy is not a thief; with good justification and in great temptation on at least one occasion she declines to steal from her master (pp. 45–46). It is the "whiter" "Tom" who, with no moral justification, steals repeatedly. Likewise, "Tom" displays cowardice before the whole town by refusing to duel with Count Luigi, and Roxy berates him, blaming it on the "nigger" in him (p. 142). In keeping with the consistently ironic tone of the novel, Roxy is twice as much "nigger" as "Tom" but not a coward. When the shootout takes place between Judge Driscoll and Count Luigi, Roxy impudently stands at a window in the line of fire to observe better, getting her nose skinned by a ricochet, unbudging as other bullets splat into the wood just below her (p. 145). To point up this irony, Clemens makes rhetorically effective use of arrangement by juxtaposing Roxy's speech denouncing "Tom's" cowardice for avoiding the duel with the scenes of her own bravery during it.

But why does Clemens have Roxy assert so roundly the responsibility of "Tom's" black drop for his miserable character? This overblown assertion goes unchallenged by the author because we are supposed to see the irony of having Roxy—the best character in the novel, the only match for Wilson in intelligence, and "Tom's" self-sacrificing mother—be the one to offer the obvious racial explanation in such an exaggerated manner. Here, as elsewhere, Clemens uses exaggeration as a rhetorical clue to an intended irony. In many ways this scene parallels the one in *Huckleberry Finn* when Huck—an unreliable narrator—says "All right, then, I'll go to hell" for helping Jim. We must see the distance between Huck's statement and the implied author's belief or we miss the irony and the meaning of the novel. In *Pudd'nhead Wilson*, Roxy is a "disguised narrator"[21]—like Huck an unreliable one—and we must see the same distance between her statement and the implied author's belief. In addition, by having Roxy, Wilson, and everyone else in the novel accept racist stereotypes, Clemens shows the total effect social conditioning has on everyone in a community.

"Tom," a product of miscegenation, embodies the central proposition of the novel, which is that except for physical appearances, distinctions between black and white are "a fiction of law and custom" (p. 43). Roxy glimpses this truth when she switches the babies, but her inability to reject completely society's view of race is seen when she blames "Tom's" failures on the "nigger" in him. "Tom" temporarily holds society's view of race, but discovers that it is false.

When first told his heritage by Roxy, "Tom" is appalled and begins feeling and acting inferior, as, for example, in stepping aside for the lowest whites (p. 101). As the shock wears off, however, so does his negative self-assessment; he quickly reverts to his old attitudes and ways (p. 103). He soon ceases to have any concern for the physical reality that he is part black, and realizes fully that the only thing that makes a difference between black and white is society's fiction that a difference exists. He need not change his view of himself; he need merely protect himself from exposure which he does by selling Roxy down the river (p. 161). "Tom" is the only character to learn the truth. The others, including Roxy and Pudd'nhead Wilson, persist in the "fiction of law and custom." At the end, when "Tom" is sold down the river, we see that society, both in Dawson's Landing and in the larger world represented by the governor, stands firm in blind acceptance of its self-created fiction. There is final irony in realizing that "Tom" alone knows the truth, and the truth makes him a slave.

In its irony and complexity, *Pudd'nhead Wilson* stands apart from most nineteenth-century American novels about miscegenation. Abandoning stereotype and sentiment, Clemens slashes away at "scientific racism" and "the one-drop rule," arguing that society, not biology or miscegenation, makes "niggers." In many ways, *Pudd'nhead Wilson* is, as Cox says, "a prevision of the world of William Faulkner, Robert Penn Warren, and Ralph Ellison."[22] We should add, of Ellen Glasgow, Zora Neale Hurston, and Lillian Smith as well. Harriet Beecher Stowe, Frank Webb, and George Washington Cable are major points on a line stretching into twentieth century treatments of miscegenation. Clemens, who explored a lot of new territory in his day, broadened that line into the path followed by many of the novelists who later approached the tangled wilderness of miscegenation in American society.

NOTES

1. Samuel L. Clemens, *Pudd'nhead Wilson, A Tale* (1894; reprint with introduction by F. R. Leavis, New York: Grove Press, 1955). Hereafter cited parenthetically.

2. Leslie Fiedler, "As Free as Any Creetur...," *New Republic* 133 (22 August, 1955):17.

3. Philip Butcher, "Mark Twain Sells Roxy Down the River," *College Language Association Journal* 8 (1965):225–233.

4. Leaver, p. 16.

5. Barbara A. Chellis, "Those Extraordinary Twins: Negroes and Whites," *American Quarterly* 21 (1969):102–08.

6. Genovese, p. 115.

7. James M. Cox, "*Pudd'nhead Wilson*: The End of Mark Twain's American Dream," *South Atlantic Quarterly* 58 (1959):354–355.

8. Cox, pp. 353–57.

9. Jack P. Wysong, "Samuel Clemens' Attitude Toward the Negro as Demonstrated in *Pudd'nhead Wilson* and *A Connecticut Yankee in King Arthur's Court*," *Xavier University Studies* 7 (1968):44.

10. F. R. Leavis, "Introduction," in Clemens, pp. 9–31.

11. John Freimarck, "*Pudd'nhead Wilson*: A Tale of Blood and Brotherhood," *University Review* 34 (1968):305–06.

12. Marvin Fisher and Michael Elliott, "*Pudd'nhead Wilson*: Half a Dog is Worse than None," *Southern Review* 8 (1972):533–47.

13. Arthur G. Pettit, "The Black and White Curse: *Pudd'nhead Wilson* and Miscegenation," in Samuel L. Clemens, *Pudd'nhead Wilson and Those Extraordinary Twins*, ed. by Sidney E. Berger (New York: W. W. Norton, 1980), p. 360.

14. Rabinowitz, pp. 408–19.

15. Henry Nash Smith, "*Pudd'nhead Wilson* and After," *Massachusetts Review* 3 (1962):235–37.

16. Berzon, p. 44.
17. Berzon, pp. 44–46.
18. Genovese, p. 517.
19. Berzon, p. 45.
20. Wysong, p. 44.
21. Booth, p. 152.
22. Cox, p. 362.

9
Conclusion

From the beginning, American slavery was tied to race, and the racial conflicts that have followed slavery result from the American commitment to racism, that is, to a defined ideology of racial superiority and inferiority. Miscegenation lies at the core of racism because of the belief in genetic transmission of race-specific intelligence and behaviors.[1] As we have seen, miscegenation has been a useful literary symbol for the many problems associated with slavery and racism in America.

In studying the novels here, I have focused on how the concept of miscegenation was handled by those novelists who wrote of it. On one level, I have examined how the idea of miscegenation affected the structure and development of the individual novels, often what rhetorical role it played in the "argument" of each novel. On a broader plane, I have viewed the general pattern of novelistic arguments using miscegenation, and, in a general way, related this pattern to the social/political ambiance along the time line represented here. These two approaches lead to a number of conclusions.

To begin, miscegenation generally appears embodied in stereotyped characters and stereotyped situations. The tragic octoroon is the most common character and her condition of being suddenly cast into slavery where she encounters evil owners and overseers is the most common situation. The historicity of much of the stereotyping seems doubtful, however; for example, we can be sure that not every mulatto possessed extra-ordinary physical beauty, and we know that the Klan arose from a multiplicity of causes; it did not always and everywhere spring spontaneously into existence solely because of the threat of miscegenation. But many historically accurate situations are repeated in the novels, such as the sudden breakup of estates and the sale of slaves following the plantation owner's death, sometimes including the sale of his children.

The treatment of miscegenation was overwhelmingly influenced by the ambient social and political situation. From the beginning of the American novel, the subject was tied to the controversy over slavery. Following the war, miscegenation appeared almost exclusively in novels dealing with the problems of discrimination and of social inequality for blacks. It is difficult to think of another subject in our literature that has been so dominated by conflict over the same political and social issues for so long a time. Perhaps the theory of evolution and the place it held in the protracted nineteenth- and twentieth-century conflict between science and religion and in the social agenda of the religious right today would provide some parallel. Unlike evolution, however, miscegenation had few champions.

Before the Civil War, those novelists opposed to slavery made much greater use of miscegenation than did those defending the South's "peculiar institution." Northern abolition writers like Hildreth and Stowe saw clearly the rhetorical value of miscegenation for attacking slavery, frequently linking it with incest to increase the shock value and to further disparage slave owners. Southern writers like Kennedy and Carruthers, also seeing the South's vulnerability, avoided the issue, hiding interracial sex behind the whitewashed cabins. Following Emancipation and Reconstruction, however, Southern apologists like Harris, Page, and Dixon took up miscegenation to justify the South's discriminatory racial policies. The other writers who continued with the theme were mostly blacks like Sutton Griggs and Charles Waddell Chesnutt, who wished to put the lie to Dixon's accusations that all blacks were miscegenetic maniacs.

In the years from 1830 to the end of the Civil War, the South developed through repetition to belief its cultural myth of the happy darky, while the North focused on miscegenation to develop a different cultural myth, that of the tragic mulatto.[2] These conflicting cultural myths marked the divergence between

the pre-war North and South. In a similar fashion, miscegenation plays a role in the literary expressions of a longed-for
reconciliation of sectional and racial divisions after the war.
Former abolitionists like Tourgée used the marriage of white
Southerners to black ex-slaves as a hopeful symbol of racial
unity and the end of racism; white Southern apologists for
racism such as Dixon and Page used the sexual union of whites,
North and South, to symbolize white racial and sectional unity
against all blacks.

For these neo-plantation novelists, the black rapist became
a powerful symbol not only of the economic rape of the South
during Reconstruction, but also of racial division and conflict.
For Southern writers, the pre-lapsarian Eden ended with
Emancipation and defeat; after the war the phallic snake, the
black rapist, was loosed in the garden. "Protecting white womanhood" became a mystification used to create group identity
among whites of all classes and regions. As Kenneth Burke
has shown us, much such rhetoric is unconscious and aimed at
persuasion of the divided self.[3] Ironically, these postwar apologists for racism tried to convert the rape victim into the rapist,
to reverse reality in order to justify past and present inhumanity. In reality, given the absolute power of whites over
blacks, all miscegenation under slavery could be considered
rape. As Susan Brownmiller has made so clear, rape is a political act of subjugation and exploitation carried out through
violence or the power inherent in an authoritarian structure.[4]
In reality, no more perfect metaphor for whites' exploiting the
bodies of all blacks under slavery could be found than the rape
of black women.

The switch of this subject from being the grounds for condemning slavery to being the grounds for justifying racism
shows how much the literary view of miscegenation depended
on ambient social and political values. Perhaps a parallel switch
influenced by changing values can be seen in what happened to
the theme of the frontier in American literature during the
social and political upheavals of the late 1960s. From the days
of Hugh Henry Brackenridge and James Fenimore Cooper, the
frontier, the rugged individual matched against the elements,
always moving the edge of civilization forward, had been the

proud justification of the Euro-American experience. But beginning in the 1960s, Native American and other writers have seen in the theme of the advancing frontier a story of ruthless exploitation and genocide, exemplified by Dee Brown's 1971 revisionist history, *Bury My Heart at Wounded Knee.*

In addition to symbolizing the evils of slavery generally, miscegenation also produced the mulatto light enought to pass. The sufferings of these characters, "blacks" trying to live in a white world, become symbolic of the suffering of all American blacks, because in America all blacks are trying to live in a white world. And, on some universal level, the predicament of the mulatto becomes a symbol of general human alienation. The primary thematic concern with miscegenation has been the question of where mulattoes "belong." The essential question seems to lie in the very concept of race in America. Can a person who appears white be black? The significant feature of the American problem with race is the whites' unwillingness to make any distinctions between the various degrees of racial mixture and pure blacks,[5] which forces a choice between absolutes. This obsession with dividing into absolutes of black and white dominates much of the fiction. White authors who defend slavery and racism argue that race distinctions are real, that blacks are genetically inferior and that miscegenation means genetic weakening of a superior race. Therefore, anyone with "one drop" of "Negro blood" must be kept from sexual relations with whites. The white novelists who oppose slavery and discrimination insist on the common humanity of blacks, and generally imply that race distinctions, other than appearance, are not genetic but social, an attitude most clearly expressed by Clemens.

Black writers tend to agree, however, not with their supporters but with their enemies, that racial distinctions are more than social fictions. They too generally argue that miscegenation should be avoided, and that mulattoes "belong" in the black race, just as their detractors insist, but for a far different reason. The black attitude is basically that which W. E. B. DuBois expresses in the opening section of *Souls of Black Folk*, that blacks wish to maintain their racial integrity and identity while being accorded the fullness of freedom, equality, and dignity shared by their fellow Americans.[6]

The alienated mulattoes presented fit Stonequist's description of the "marginal man." Each mulatto character is "one who is poised in psychological uncertainty between two (or more) social worlds; reflecting in his soul the discords and harmonies, repulsions and attractions of these worlds."[7] There emerges from the novels no clear, generally accepted resolution to this central conflict. In this lack of resolution, the theme of miscegenation shares something with the great themes of Western literature generally and of American novels specifically. The theme of the quest, from the *Odyssey* to *Moby Dick* or of initiation, from Saint Augustine to Hemingway, or of the absurd, from Kierkegaard and Camus to Thomas Pynchon and Joseph Heller, are all similarly unresolved and unresolvable. Perhaps most closely of all, the theme of miscegenation is linked to the theme of alienation, from "The Wanderer" and "The Seafarer" to *The Scarlet Letter*, *The Great Gatsby* and *Light in August*, in which novel the two themes merge.

The novels studied here act, in M.H. Abrams' phrase, as both mirror and lamp. Some of what these novels tell us about miscegenation must be seen as expressionism, the outward manifestation of an author's—even a people's—strongest feelings, no matter how harshly those emotions and desires clash with reality. Houston Baker has applied the term "conative discourse" to black social and literary criticism that "substitute[s] will for reason, volition for analysis, and desire for systematic observation" in an attempt to "restructure the world on the basis of volition alone."[8] Many of these novels, black and white, when viewed as rhetorical works, are also examples of such conative discourse. Ironically, it is more often the white, proslavery romancers such as John Pendleton Kennedy, Thomas Nelson Page, and Thomas Dixon, Jr., whose books defy reality to express a vision of race relations that never had nor ever could exist. Black novelists from Martin Delaney, to Harriet E. Wilson, to James Weldon Johnson—despite romantic idealization and hyperbole—more often reflect the practice of miscegenation in America.

The tone in novels by black authors and white authors parallels the historically divided perspective of black people and white people on interracial sex in America. For white Americans, especially in the nineteenth century and early twentieth-century South, the taboos were against sex between black men and white women, and against admitting the existence of other miscegenation. These taboos were self-imposed and very powerful. The practice of miscegenation between white men and black women, however, remained irrelevant as long as the fact of it could be denied. The importance of this denial to the integrity of the whole social fabric meant that any mention of miscegenation could rend society. As a result, white authors—with the exception of Clemens who wanted to tear the mask of social hypocrisy anyway—invariably treat the subject (whether accepting miscegenation or damning it) as taboo, as laden with frightening potential. Blacks, however, lived with forced miscegenation as a fact of life under slavery, and after Emancipation with the white man's attitude that any black woman was still available should he want her. Blacks knew and did not deny their mixed heritage, no matter how much some of them might despise it. Accordingly, black authors invested miscegenation with less symbolic power during this period. Later twentieth-century black authors—Richard Wright, James Baldwin, Ralph Ellison, John Williams—use the relationship of black men to white women in a number of symbolic ways, but for the writers discussed here, the tone is more factual or angry about actual miscegenation than it is pregnant with symbolic implications. While certain authors, particularly Clemens and Chesnutt, appreciate the ironies involved in miscegenation, both black and white authors treat the subject seriously. There are no clearly humorous interpretations. Perhaps for whites the subject was too scary, perhaps for blacks it was too enraging.

Finally, we should note the absence of miscegenation in the works of the preeminent novelists of the period other than Clemens: Nathaniel Hawthorne, Herman Melville, and Henry James. James apparently ignores the subject completely in his novels, and Hawthorne only toys with the idea. In *The Marble Faun*, the narrator discusses a number of stories circulating about Miriam's mysterious past, and one story, which is not true, has her the daughter of a Southern planter and a mulatto mistress. Melville comes closer to dealing with miscegenation. A mulatto character, Lavender, appears in *Redburn*, and the relationship of the narrator in *Typee* with Fayaway may well have been sexual, although there is nothing overt in the novel to indicate a sexual affair. Harry Levin points out the culminating, marriage-like convergence of Ishmael and Queequeg,[9] but this theme of brotherhood, despite its sexual overtones, does not rightly fall within a study of miscegenation. It is impossible to say why these major authors avoided such a potentially rich and symbolically fruitful subject. Perhaps for Hawthorne and Melville it was too closely linked in their minds to the abolitionists and their sentimental novels, "the damned mob of scribbling women," as Hawthorne once referred to some of them. Perhaps James' curiosity about the problems of clashing cultures was more amply satisfied in his favored union of American and European. In any event, the "best" novels of the period were not about miscegenation.

Robert Lively studied some five hundred historical novels in preparing *Fiction Fights the Civil War*, a work which he calls his "extended sampling from the bargain basements of the literary market place."[10] The present study of miscegenation has required similar rooting among the picked-over leavings on the library shelves. In many way these sentimental novels filled with stock characters and situations resemble the soap operas of today. The novels appealed to the equivalent audience of a hundred years ago and provided the same sort of opportunity to eavesdrop on, and suffer vicariously with, the domestic problems of others. In a further parallel, soap operas today have as regular fare such subjects as miscegenation, incest, adultery, and abortion, delighting in their titillation value, and many television series rhetorically promote one argument or another on contemporary social issues—following, as did the novels discussed here, the Horatian injunction to teach and to please. To study this didactic fiction, largely forgotten novels of forgotten people who wrote them and who wept over them, leads to agreement with Lively about such works:

Literary historians seem, on the whole, to be snobs—or at any rate to be tediously repetitive in their dependence on a very few samples from our literature.... They skip along the tops of the pyramids of taste.... Pyramids of taste have very broad bases in a culture so variously served as ours. At these bases lie the unrefined emotions and conventional banalities by which a whole people reveals its definition of truth, of beauty, of human purpose.[11]

The novels discussed herein are filled with "unrefined emotions" and "conventional banalities," but they are also filled with the intellectual and moral struggle of nineteenth-century Americans over the emotionally charged issue of miscegenation—the ultimate point of contact and conflict between races. Some novels reveal distressing ignorance, hatred, and brutality; others make miscegenation the compassionate symbol of racial harmony dreamed of by the best of men and women for their land long torn by racial strife. But amalgamation, the meld of black and white, was not to be. As large-scale miscegenation passed with the end of the nineteenth century, interracial sex became less a social reality with symbolic possibilities for literature and more a symbolic fiction apart from social reality.

NOTES

1. While sociobiologists have rekindled belief in certain genetically determined human (not racial) behavior, other persons at the opposite pole—some contemporary feminists, for example—still argue that even sexual differences (other than the physiological) are culturally determined. Perhaps the most accepted stance today on nature versus nurture is an interactive view, recognizing the possibility of genetic behavioral tendencies that may then be culturally reinforced in a culture given certain inclinations by its genetic heritage.

2. See Richard Slotkin, *Regeneration Through Violence* (Middletown, Ct.: Wesleyan Univ. Press, 1973), pp. 20–21, on the origin and development of American cultural myths as opposed to universal myths.

3. Kenneth Burke, *A Rhetoric of Motives* (Berkeley: Univ. of California Press, 1969), pp. 37–45.

4. Brownmiller, p. 256.

5. Everett V. Stonequist, *The Marginal Man: A Study in Personality and Culture Conflict* (New York: Scribners, 1937), p. 24.

6. W. E. B. DuBois, *The Souls of Black Folk: Essays and Sketches* (1903; reprint, New York: Johnson Reprint Corp., 1968), pp. 3–4.

7. Stonequist, p. 8.
8. Baker, pp. 136–37.
9. Harry Levin, *The Power of Blackness: Hawthorne, Poe, Melville* (New York: Knopf, 1958), p. 177.
10. Lively, p. 191.
11. Lively, p. 192.

Chronology of American Novels of Miscegenation, 1792–1914

First editions are listed here. Actual editions cited are identified in chapter notes.

1792

Hugh Henry Brackenridge. *Modern Chivalry: Containing the Adventures of Captain John Farrago, and Teague O'Regan, His Servant.* Vol. II. Philadelphia: John McCulloch.

1826

James Fenimore Cooper. *The Last of the Mohicans: A Narrative of 1757.* Philadelphia: H. C. Carey and I. Lea.

1835

Oliver Bolokitten [pseud]. *A Sojourn in the City of Amalgamation in the Year of Our Lord, 19—.* New York: the author.

1836

Richard Hildreth. *The Slave; or, Memoirs of Archy Moore.* 2 vols. Boston: John H. Eastburn, printer.

1841

Joseph Holt Ingraham. *The Quadroone: or, St. Michael's Day.* 2 vols. New York: Harper.

William Gilmore Simms. "Caloya; or, The Loves of the Driver." In *The Magnolia*, 3 (May, June, July), 222–229, 264–273, 317–324.

1842

William Gilmore Simms. *Beauchampe; or, The Kentucky Tragedy. A Tale of Passion.* 2 vols. Philadelphia: Lea and Blanchard.

Walt Whitman. *Franklin Evans; or, The Inebriate. A Tale of the Times.* New York: in *New World.*

1846

[Howard Meeks]. *The Fanatic; or, The Perils of Peter Pliant, the Poor Pedagogue.* Philadelphia: American Citizen.

1849

Mrs. E. D. E. N. Southworth. *Retribution; or, The Vale of Shadows. A Tale of Passion.* New York: Harper.

1852

Harriet Beecher Stowe. *Uncle Tom's Cabin; or, Life Among the Lowly.* 2 vols. Boston: John P. Jewett and Co.

1853

William Wells Brown. *Clotel; or, the President's Daughter; A Narrative of Slave Life in The United States.* London: Partridge and Oakey.
Emily C. Pearson. *Cousin Franck's Household; or, Scenes in the Old Dominion.* Boston: Upham, Ford and Olmstead.

1856

James S. Peacocke. *The Creole Orphans; or, Lights and Shadows of Southern Life. A Tale of Louisiana.* New York: Derby and Jackson.
Mayne Reid. *The Quadroon; or, A Lover's Adventures in Louisiana.* New York: Robert M. DeWitt.
Harriet Beecher Stowe. *Dred: A Tale of the Great Dismal Swamp.* 2 vols. Boston: Phillips, Sampson and Co.

1857

Paul Creyton [John Townsend Trowbridge]. *Neighbor Jackwood.* Boston: Phillips, Sampson and Co.
Frank J. Webb. *The Garies and Their Friends.* London: G. Routledge and Co.

1858

Frances H. McDougall. *Shamah in Pursuit of Freedom; or, The Branded Hand.* New York: Thatcher and Hutchinson.

1859

Martin R. Delaney. *Blake; or, The Huts of America.* New York: in *The Anglo-African Magazine* (January-July).

Mrs. H. E. Wilson. *Our Nig; or, Sketches from the Life of a Free Black in a Two-Story White House, North. Showing That Slavery's Shadows Fall Even There.* Boston: George C. Rand and Avery.

1860

Mrs. G. M. Flanders. *The Ebony Idol.* New York: D. Appleton and Co.
H. Lord Hosmer. *Adela, The Octoroon.* Columbus, Ohio: Follett, Foster and Co.

1861

Mrs. Metta Victoria Victor. *Maum Guinea, and Her Plantation "Children"; or, Holiday-Week on a Louisiana Estate: A Slave Romance.* New York: Beadle and Co.

1862

Edmund Kirk [James R. Gilmore]. *Among the Pines; or, South in Secession-Time.* New York: G. P. Putnam.

1863

Edmund Kirk [James R. Gilmore]. *My Southern Friends.* New York: Carleton.

1864

Edmund Kirk [James R. Gilmore]. *Down in Tennessee, and Back by Way of Richmond.* New York: Carleton.
Epes Sargent. *Peculiar: A Tale of the Great Transition.* New York: Carleton.

1865

Elizabeth Stoddard. *Two Men.* New York: Bunce and Huntington.

1867

Rebecca H. Davis. *Waiting for the Verdict.* New York: Sheldon & Co.

1868

Anna E. Dickinson. *What Answer?* Boston: Ticknor and Fields.

1874

Henry Churton [Albion W. Tourgée]. *Toinette: A Novel* New York: J. B. Ford and Co. Also published as:
Albion W. Tourgée. *A Royal Gentleman.* New York: Fords, Howard and Hulbert, 1881.

1880

George Washington Cable. *The Grandissimes: A Story of Creole Life.* New York: Scribners.

1881

George Washington Cable. *Madame Delphine.* New York: Scribners.

1882

Subdued Southern Nobility: A Southern Ideal. New York: Sharps Publishing Co.

1883

Albion W. Tourgée. *Hot Plowshares: A Novel.* New York: Fords, Howard and Hulbert.

1886

Margaret Holmes Bates. *The Chamber Over The Gate.* Indianapolis: Charles A. Bates.

1890

Albion W. Tourgée. *Pactolus Prime.* New York: Cassell Publishing Co.

1892

Mrs. Frances E. W. Harper. *Iola Leroy; or, Shadows Uplifted.* Philadelphia: Garrigues Bros.
William Dean Howells. *An Imperative Duty.* New York: Harper.

1894

Mark Twain [Samuel L. Clemens]. *Pudd'nhead Wilson. A Tale.* London: Chatto and Windus.

1895

Bliss Perry. *The Plated City.* New York: Scribners.

1896

J. McHenry Jones. *Hearts of Gold: A Novel.* Wheeling: Daily Intelligencer Steam Job Press.

1898

Thomas Nelson Page. *Red Rock.* New York: Scribners.

1899

Sutton E. Griggs. *Imperium in Imperio*. Cincinnati: The Editor Publishing Co.

1900

Gertrude Atherton. *Senator North*. New York: John Lane.

Charles Waddell Chesnutt. *The House Behind the Cedars*. Boston: Houghton, Mifflin.

Pauline E. Hopkins. *Contending Forces: A Romance Illustrative of Negro Life North and South*. Boston: The Colored Co-operative Publishing Co.

1901

Charles Waddell Chesnutt. *The Marrow of Tradition*. Boston: Houghton, Mifflin.

Sutton E. Griggs. *Overshadowed*. Nashville: Orion Publishing Co.

1902

Thomas Dixon. *The Leopard's Spots: A Romance of the White Man's Burden - 1865–1900*. New York: Doubleday, Page & Co.

Joel Chandler Harris. *Gabriel Tolliver: A Story of Reconstruction*. New York: McClure, Philips. and Co.

1905

Thomas Dixon. *The Clansman*. New York: Doubleday, Page & Co.

Sutton E. Griggs. *The Hindered Hand; or, The Reign of the Repressionist*. Nashville: Orion Publishing Co.

1908

Sutton E. Griggs. *Pointing the Way*. Nashville: Orion Publishing Co.

1909

J. W. Grant. *Out of Darkness; or: Diabolism and Destiny*. Nashville: Baptist Publishing Board.

1911

W. E. B. DuBois. *The Quest of the Silver Fleece*. New York: A. C. McClung & Co.

1912

Thomas Dixon. *The Sins of the Fathers: A Romance of the South*. New York: D. Appleton and Co.

James Weldon Johnson. *The Autobiography of an Ex-Colored Man.*
    Boston: Sherman, French and Co.

1913

Ellen Glasgow. *Virginia.* Toronto: Musson Book Co., Ltd.
Oscar Micheaux. *The Conquest: The Story of a Negro Pioneer.* Lincoln:
    Woodruff Press.

1914

George Washington Cable. *Gideon's Band: A Tale of the Mississippi.*
    New York: Scribners.

Bibliography

Amacher, Anne Ward. "The Genteel Primitivist and the Semi-tragic Octoroon." *New England Quarterly* 29 (1956):216–227.

Andrews, William L. "Miscegenation in the Late Nineteenth Century Novel." *Southern Humanities Review* 13 (1979):13–24.

Baker, Houston A., Jr. *The Journey Back: Issues in Black Literature and Criticism.* Chicago: Univ. of Chicago Press, 1980.

Bennett, Lerone, Jr. "Miscegenation in America." In *Marriage Across the Color Line*, ed. by Cloyte M. Larson, 5–28. Chicago: Johnson Publishing Co., 1965.

Berry, Brewton. *Almost White.* New York: Macmillan, 1963.

Berzon, Judith R. *Neither White nor Black: The Mulatto Character in American Fiction.* New York: New York Univ. Press, 1978.

Blassingame, John W. *Black New Orleans, 1860–1880.* Chicago: Univ. of Chicago Press, 1973.

————. *The Slave Community: Plantation Life in the Antebellum South.* Rev. and enl. ed. New York: Oxford Univ. Press, 1979.

Bloomfield, Maxwell. "Dixon's *The Leopard's Spots*: A Study in Popular Racism." *American Quarterly* 16 (1964):387–401.

Bone, Robert. *The Negro Novel in America.* Rev. ed. 1958. Reprint. New Haven: Yale Univ. Press, 1965.

Booth, Wayne C. *The Rhetoric of Fiction.* Chicago: Univ. of Chicago Press, 1961.

Brown, Herbert R. *The Sentimental Novel in America, 1789–1860.* Durham: Duke Univ. Press, 1940.

Brown, Sterling. "Negro Character as Seen by White Authors." *Journal of Negro Education* 2 (1933):179–203.

————. *The Negro in American Fiction.* 1937. Reprint. Port Washington: Kennikat Press, 1968.

242   Bibliography

Brownmiller, Susan. *Against Our Will: Men, Women and Rape.* New York: Simon and Schuster, 1975.

Bullock, Penelope. "The Mulatto in American Fiction," *Phylon* (1945) 6:78–82.

———. "The Treatment of the Mulatto in American Fiction from 1826–1902." M.A. Thesis. Atlanta Univ., 1944.

Burke, Kenneth. *A Rhetoric of Motives.* 1950. Reprint. Berkeley: Univ. of California Press, 1969.

Butcher, Margaret. *The Negro in American Culture.* New York: Knopf, 1956.

Butcher, Philip. *George W. Cable.* New York: Twayne, 1962.

———. "Mark Twain Sells Roxy Down the River." *College Language Association Journal* 8 (1965):225–233.

Canaday, Nicholas, Jr. "The Anti-slavery Novel Prior to 1852 and Hildreth's *The Slave* (1836)." *College Language Association Journal* 17 (1973):175–91.

Carter, Everett. "Cultural History Written With Lightning: The Significance of Birth of a Nation." *American Quarterly* 12 (1960):347–357.

Cash, W. J. *The Mind of the South.* 1941. Reprint. New York: Vintage-Knopf, n.d.

Chase, Richard. "Cable and His Grandissimes." *Kenyon Review* 18 (1956):373–383.

Chellis, Barbara A. "Those Extraordinary Twins: Negroes and Whites." *American Quarterly* 21 (1969):100–12.

Christian, Barbara. *Black Women Novelists.* Contributions in Afro-American and African Studies, no. 52. Westport: Greenwood Press, 1980.

Clark, William Bedford. "Cable and the Theme of Miscegenation in *Old Days* and *The Grandissimes*." *Mississippi Quarterly* 30 (1977):597–609.

———. "The Serpent of Lust in the Southern Garden." *Southern Review* 10 (1974):805–22.

———. "The Serpent of Lust in the Southern Garden: The Theme of Miscegenation in Cable, Twain, Faulkner and Warren." Ph.D. Dissertation. Louisiana State Univ., 1974.

Clinton, Catherine. *The Plantation Mistress: Woman's World in the Old South.* New York: Pantheon Books, 1982.

Commager, Henry Steele. *The American Mind: An Interpretation of American Thought and Character Since The 1880's.* New Haven: Yale Univ. Press, 1950.

Cook, Raymond Allen. *Fire from the Flint: The Amazing Careers of Thomas Dixon.* Winston-Salem: John F. Blair, 1968.

Cox, James M. "*Pudd'nhead Wilson*: The End of Mark Twain's American Dream." *South Atlantic Quarterly* 58 (1959):351–363.

Croly, David Goodman. *Miscegenation: The Theory of the Blending of the Races, Applied to the American White Man and Negro.* New York: H. Dexter, Hamilton and Co, 1864.

Davis, Richard Beale. "Mrs. Stowe's Characters-in-Situations and a Southern Literary Tradition." In *Essays in Honor of Jay B. Hubbell*, ed. by Clarence Gohdes, 108–125. Durham: Duke Univ. Press, 1967.

Dollard, John. *Caste and Class in a Southern Town.* Garden City: Doubleday Anchor, 1957.

DuBois, W. E. B. *The Souls of Black Folk: Essays and Sketches.* 1903. Reprint. New York: Johnson Reprint Corp., 1968.

Duvall, Severn, "Uncle Tom's Cabin: The Sinister Side of the Patriarchy." *New England Quarterly* 36 (1963). Reprint in *Images of the Negro in American Literature*, ed. by Seymour L. Gross and John E. Hardy, 163–180. Chicago: Univ. of Chicago Press, 1966.

Elder, Arlene A. *"The Hindered Hand": Cultural Implications of Early African-American Literature.* Contributions in Afro-American and African Studies, no. 39. Westport: Greenwood Press, 1978.

Farrison, William E. *William Wells Brown, Author and Reformer.* Chicago: Univ. of Chicago Press, 1969.

Fiedler, Leslie. "As Free As Any Creetur ..." *New Republic* 133 (15, 22 Aug., 1955):17–18, 16–18.

Fisher, Marvin and Michael Elliott. "*Pudd'nhead Wilson*: Half a Dog is Worse than None." *Southern Review* 8 (1972):533–47.

Fogel, Robert William and Stanley L. Engerman. *Time on the Cross: The Economics of American Slavery.* Boston: Little, Brown, 1974.

Ford, Thomas W. "Howells and the American Negro." *Texas Studies in Language and Literature* 5 (1964):530–537.

———. "The Miscegenation Theme in *Pudd'nhead Wilson*." *Mark Twain Journal* 10 (1955):13–14.

Frederickson, George M. *The Black Image in the White Mind: The Debate on Afro-American Character and Destiny, 1817–1914.* New York: Harper and Row, 1971.

Friedman, Lawrence J. *The White Savage: Racial Fantasies in the Postbellum South.* Englewood Cliffs: Prentice-Hall, 1970.

Freimarck, John. "Pudd'nhead Wilson: A Tale of Blood and Brotherhood." *University Review* 34 (1968):303–306.

Gaines, Francis Pendleton, "The Racial Bar Sinister in American Romance." *South Atlantic Quarterly* 25 (1926):396–402.

———. *The Southern Plantation.* New York: Columbia Univ. Press, 1924.

Genovese, Eugene D. *Roll, Jordan, Roll: The World the Slaves Made.* New York: Pantheon Books, 1974.

Gibson, Donald B. *The Politics of Literary Expression: A Study of Major Black Writers.* Contributions in Afro-American and African Studies, no. 63. Westport: Greenwood Press, 1981.

Gloster, Hugh M. *Negro Voices in American Fiction.* Chapel Hill: Univ. of North Carolina Press, 1948.

Gross, Seymour L. "Introduction: Stereotype to Archetype: The Negro in American Literary Criticism." In *Images of the Negro in American Literature,* 1–28. Chicago: Univ. of Chicago Press, 1966.

———. and John E. Hardy, eds. *Images of the Negro in America Literature.* Chicago: Univ. of Chicago Press, 1966.

Gross, Theodore L. *Albion W. Tourgée.* New York: Twayne, 1963.

———. "The Negro in the Literature of Reconstruction." *Phylon* 22 (1961). Reprint in *Images of the Negro in American Literature,* ed. by Seymour L, Gross and John E. Hardy, 71–83. Chicago: Univ. of Chicago Press, 1966.

Gutman, Herbert G. *The Black Family in Slavery and Freedom, 1750–1925.* New York: Pantheon Books, 1976.

———. *Slavery and the Numbers Game: A Critique of "Time on the Cross."* Urbana: Univ. of Illinois Press, 1975.

Hemenway, Robert, ed. *The Black Novelist.* Columbus: Charles E. Merrill Publishing Co. 1970.

Hernton, Calvin C. *Sex and Racism in America.* 1965. Reprint. New York: Grove Press, 1966.

Hubbell, Jay B. *The South in American Literature, 1607–1900.* Durham: Duke Univ. Press, 1954.

Johnston, James Hugo. *Race Relations in Virginia and Miscegenation in the South, 1776–1860.* Amherst: Univ. of Massachusetts Press, 1970.

Jordan, Winthrop D. *White over Black: American Attitudes Toward the Negro, 1550–1812.* Chapel Hill: Univ. of North Carolina Press, 1968.

Justus, James H. "The Kentucky Tragedy in Simms and Warren: A Study in Changing Milieux." M.A. Thesis. Univ. of Tennessee, 1952.

Kovel, Joel. *White Racism: A Psychohistory.* New York: Pantheon Books, 1970.

Leaver, Florence B. "Mark Twain's *Pudd'nhead Wilson.*" *Mark Twain Journal* 10 (1956):14–20.

Levin, Harry. *The Power of Blackness.* New York: Knopf, 1967.

Levy, Eugene. *James Weldon Johnson: Black Leader, Black Voice.* Chicago: Univ. of Chicago Press, 1973.

Liedel, Donald E. "The Authorship of Two Anti-Slavery Novels of the 1840's: *The Fanatic* and *Winona*." *Papers of the Bibliographical Society of America* 67 (1973):447–49.

Litwack, Leon. *North of Slavery: The Negro in the Free States, 1790–1860*. Chicago: Univ. of Chicago Press, 1961.

Lively, Robert A. *Fiction Fights the Civil War*. Chapel Hill: Univ. of North Carolina Press, 1957.

Logan, Rayford W., ed. *The Negro in American Life and Thought: The Nadir, 1877–1901*. New York: Dial Press, 1954.

Mencke, John G. *Mulattoes and Race Mixture: American Attitudes and Images, 1865–1918*. Ann Arbor: UMI Research Press, 1979.

McDowell, Tremaine. "The Negro in the Southern Novel Prior to 1850." *Journal of English and Germanic Philology* 25 (1926). Reprint in *Images of the Negro in American Literature*, ed. by Seymour L. Gross and John E. Hardy, 54–70. Chicago: Univ. of Chicago Press, 1966.

Musgrave, Marian E. "Triangles in Black and White: Interracial Sex and Hostility in Black Literature." *College Language Association Journal* 14 (1971):444–51.

Myrdal, Gunnar. *An American Dilemma*. New York: Harper, 1944.

Nelson, John Herbert. *The Negro Character in American Literature*. 1926. Reprint. College Park: McGrath, 1968.

Papashvily, Helen W. *All the Happy Endings*. New York: Harper, 1956.

Parrington, Vernon L. *Main Currents in American Thought*. 3 vols. New York: Harcourt, 1930.

Patee, Fred Lewis. *The New American Literature, 1890–1930*. New York: Century Co., 1930.

Pettit, Arthur G. "The Black and White Curse: *Pudd'nhead Wilson* and Miscegenation." In Samuel L. Clemens. *Pudd'nhead Wilson and Those Extraordinary Twins*. Ed. by Sidney E. Berger, 346–60. New York: W. W. Norton, 1980.

Rabinowitz, Peter J. "Assertion and Assumption: Fictional Patterns and the External World." *PMLA* 96 (1981):408–19.

Reuter, Edward Byron. *The Mulatto in the United States: Including a Study of the Role of Mixed-Blood Races throughout the World*. Boston: Richard G. Badger, 1918.

———. *Race Mixture: Studies in Intermarriage and Miscegenation*. New York: Whittlesey House of McGraw-Hill Book Co., 1931.

Roy, Ratna. "The Marginal Man: A Study of the Mulatto Character in American Fiction." Ph.D. Dissertation. Univ. of Oregon, 1973.

Rubin, Louis D., Jr. "The Division of the Heart: Cable's *The Grandissimes*." *Southern Literary Journal* 1 (1969):27–47.

———. *The Faraway Country: Writers of the Modern South.* Seattle: Univ. of Washington Press, 1963.

Scheick, William J. *The Half-blood: A Cultural Symbol in 19th Century American Fiction.* Lexington: Univ. of Kentucky Press, 1979.

Slotkin, Richard. *Regeneration Through Violence.* Middletown: Wesleyan Univ. Press, 1973.

Smith, Helena M. "No-Nation Bastards." *Studies in the Humanities* 1 (1969):18–28.

Smith, Henry Nash. "*Pudd'nhead Wilson* and After." *Massachusetts Review,* 3 (1962):233–253.

Smith, Lillian. *Killers of the Dream.* New York: W. W. Norton and Co., 1949.

Spiller, Robert E., et al. *Literary History of the United States.* 3rd ed. rev. 2 vols. New York: Macmillan, 1963.

Stampp, Kenneth. *The Era of Reconstruction, 1865–1877.* New York: Knopf, 1965.

Starke, Catherine Juanita. *Black Portraiture in American Fiction: Stock Characters, Archetypes, and Individuals.* New York: Basic Books, 1972.

Stember, Charles H. *Sexual Racism: The Emotional Barrier to an Integrated Society.* New York: Elsevier, 1976.

Stoddard, Elizabeth. *The Morgesons and Other Writings.* Ed, with an Intro. by Lawrence Buell and Sandra A. Zagarell. Philadelphia: Univ. of Pennsylvania Press, 1984.

Stonequist, Everett V. *The Marginal Man.* New York: Scribners, 1937.

Takati, Ronald T. *Violence in the Black Imagination: Essays and Documents.* New York: G. P. Putnam's Sons, 1972.

Tandy, Jennette. "Pro-Slavery Proganda in American Fiction of the Fifties." *South Atlantic Quarterly* 21 (1922):41–50, 170–78.

Turner, Arlin. *George W. Cable: A Biography.* Durham: Duke Univ. Press, 1956.

Turner, Lorenzo D. *Anti-Slavery Sentiment in American Literature Prior to 1865.* 1929. Reprint. Port Washington: Kennikat Press, 1966.

Williamson, Joel. *New People: Miscegenation and Mulattoes in the United States.* New York: Free Press, 1980.

Wilson Edmund. *Patriotic Gore: Studies in the Literature of the American Civil War.* New York: Oxford Univ. Press 1962.

Wilson, Harriet E. *Our Nig; or, Sketches from the Life of a Free Black.* 1859. Reprint. Ed. with Intro. by Henry Louis Gates, Jr. New York: Random House, 1983.

Wyatt-Brown, Bertram. *Southern Honor: Ethics and Behavior in the Old South.* New York: Oxford Univ. Press, 1982.

Wysong, Jack P. "Samuel Clemens' Attitude Toward the Negro as Demonstrated in *Pudd'nhead Wilson* and *A Connecticut Yankee in King Arthur's Court.*" *Xavier University Studies,* 7 (1968):41–57.

Yellin, Jean Fagan. *The Intricate Knot: Black Figures in American Literature, 1776–1883.* New York: New York Univ. Press, 1972.

Zanger, Jules. "The 'Tragic Octoroon' in Pre-Civil War Fiction." *American Quarterly* 18 (1966):63–70.

Index

Cleo (*The Sins of the Fathers*), 175–78
Clotel, or, the President's Daughter (Brown), 14, 89
Clotelle (*Clotelle; A Tale of the Southern States*), 90
Clotelle; A Tale of the Southern States (Brown), 89–91
Colonel Munro (*The Last of the Mohicans*), 36–37
Concubinage, 20, 41–42, 64
The Conquest (Micheaux), 208–11
Cooper, James Fenimore, *The Last of the Mohicans*, 36–37
Cora Munro (*The Last of the Mohicans*), 36–37
Cousin Franck's Household; or, Scenes in the Old Dominion (Pearson), 86
Cox, James N., "*Pudd'nhead Wilson*: The End of Mark Twain's American Dream," 218
The Creole Orphans (Peacocke), 56–60
Creoles, 128–35
Croly, David Goodman, *Miscegenation: The Theory of the Races, Applied to the American White Man and Negro*, 113–14
Cuff (*Modern Chivalry*), 35–36
Cyrus (*Virginia*), 148

Davis, Arthur P., 93
Davis, Rebecca Harding, *Waiting for the Verdict*, 106–10
Davis, Richard Beale, "Mrs. Stowe's Characters-in-Situations and a Southern Literary Tradition," 70

Delaney, Martin, *Blake; or, the Huts of America*, 91–92
Democrats, and anti-miscegenation laws, 19
Determinism, 219, 232 n.1
Devereaux (*The Conquest*), 209–10
Dickey, Miss (*The Ebony Idol*), 61
Dickinson, Anna E., *What Answer?*, 110–13
Discrimination, 154–55, 159, 226
Disenfranchisement, 183–84, 197–98
Dissimulation, 186, 207
Divorce, miscegenation as grounds for, 16–18
Dixon, Thomas, Jr., 28–30, 164–65; *Birth of a Nation*, 180; *The Clansman*, 171–74; *Leopard's Spots*, 165–71; *The Sins of the Fathers*, 174–78
Dolores (*Subdued Southern Nobility*), 115–17
Down in Tennessee (Gilmore), 84
Dred (*Dred*), 72–73
Dred; A Tale of the Great Dismal Swamp (Stowe), 71–74
DuBois, W. E. B., *Souls of Black Folk*, 228–29
Dudley (*Maum Guinea, and Her Plantation "Children"*), 81
Duncan Heyward (*The Last of the Mohicans*), 36–37
Durham (*Leopard's Spots*), 167
Duvall, Severn, "*Uncle Tom's Cabin*: The Sinister Side of the Patriarchy," 70–71

The Ebony Idol (Flanders), 60–62

Zanger, Jules, "The 'Tragic Octoroon' in Pre-Civil War Fiction," 64–65

Zilpha (*Adela, The Octoroon*), 78–79

About the Author

JAMES KINNEY is an Associate Professor of English and Director of Composition and Rhetoric at Virginia Commonwealth University. He is the senior author of *Understanding Writing* and his articles have appeared in *The Rhetoric Society Quarterly, College English, College Composition and Communication* and *American Literary Review.*